ATROPOS PRESS
new york • dresden

All for Nothing

Rachel K. Ward

Think Media EGS Series is supported by the European Graduate School

ATROPOS PRESS
New York • Dresden

151 First Avenue # 14, New York, N.Y. 10003

cover photo: Jason Fosco
cover design: Hannes Charen

ISBN 978-0-9831734-2-7

CONTENTS

Foreword/Forward: Everything Vs. Nothing   7

I. The Establishment   11
All for You   14
On Your Honor   19
Us   24
On Behalf Of   27
Latter Day Saints   32
Diplomacy   36

II. Inheritance   47
All Previous Decadence   48
Paradise   56
Myth   69

III. Privilege   83
Birthright   84
Possibility   92
Fame   100
Noblesse Oblige   112

IV. Fortune   117
Prosperity   118
Leisure   124
Cultivation   131
Luxury   138

V. Vanitas   149
Beauty   150
Style   157
Fashion   167
Aura   177

VI. Attraction   187
Surprise   188
Flirtation   192
Hoax   201

VII. Desire   209
Lips of Blood   210
Ennui   218
Intoxication   224
Love   233

VIII. Truth   245
Grace   246
Vanishing   252
Forgetting   266
Uncondition   271

IX. Revelation   285

Foreword / Forward

Everything Vs. Nothing[1]

What is the gift of a text?
What is the surprise?
After deconstruction, we do not ask, what is the truth? We try to understand *a* truth of each text by regarding the potential in the foreword or the hope in the conclusion. We want to know how this particular text informs existence, how it could change the way humankind thinks, how it can move us forward? But where can we move if we are already here, in a reality that reveals itself and always already gives us *the* truth, each moment?

In an effort to witness truth among us, I considered what it means to be human. The desire for truth is the truth of desire.[2]
So I asked:
What is it that both a king and a peasant desire?
⟨ "What a man desires is unfailing love."[3] ⟩
The same Hebrew proverb can be read, "a man desires insatiably." We all seek not only love, but also power, beauty, wealth, pleasure, rest, without end. We live to fulfill desires, believing that we can locate an infallible treasure, or be an infallible treasure. But then I thought of how I sought, locating

---

[1] Title from the work of artist Ed Ruscha, "Everything Vs. Nothing," acrylic on paper, 1991.
[2] "The truth of desire is the desire for truth, As one is tempted to put it in a pseudo-Heideggerian way." Žižek, Slavoj "Desire: Drive = Truth: Knowledge," http://www.lacan.com/zizek-desire.htm
[3] Proverbs 19:22. *The Holy Bible.* New International Version. Grand Rapids, Michigan: Zondervan Publishing House, 1996, p. 552. In Psalms 130:7 it is written: "For with the Lord is unfailing love." Ibid. 527.

the answer of humanity by naming our "blood of desire." We honor the "power of the one who names," and naming is an effort to influence the fashion of thinking.[4] So I found that I performed, I strove to unveil *a* particular truth, and so it was desire for a king, a peasant, me.[5]

But then what of truth? The great quality of truth is that it outlasts desire. Every desire eventually reaches a vanishing point when the thing desired is consumed, it disappears from our range of choices or our desire diminishes. It is in the face of desire that we confront a moment of truth however. Desire appears and disappears but truth acts as the uncondition, the fact of the matter that is unchanged by desire or its vanishing. It is this collision of desire and truth that became the basis for this text.

In thought, we reached a moment of truth when the reign of history was defeated by deconstruction. History wanted forever. The breakdown of history and the emergence of truth compares to another Hebrew text, a prophecy. The prophecy was originally intended for Persia and Greece, but in our time the "Ram of History" was destroyed by the "Goat of Deconstruction":

> In the vision I was beside the Ulai Canal. I looked up, and there before me was a ram with two horns, standing beside the canal, and the horns were long. One of the horns was longer than the other but grew up later. I watched the ram as he charged toward the west and the north and the south. No animal could stand against him,

---

[4] Lefebvre, Henri. *Everyday Life in the Modern World*. Trans. Sacha Rabinovitch. New York: Harper & Row, 1968, p. 120.
[5] "It will be the same for priest as for people, for master as for servant, for mistress as for maid, for seller as for buyer, for borrower as for lender, for debtor as for creditor." Isaiah 24:2-3, *The Holy Bible*. New International Version. Grand Rapids, Michigan: Zondervan Publishing House, 1996, p. 701.

and none could rescue from his power. He did as he
pleased and became great.

As I was thinking about this, suddenly a goat with a
prominent horn between his eyes came from the west,
crossing the whole earth without touching the ground.
He came toward the two-horned ram I had seen
standing beside the canal and charged at him in great
rage. I saw him attack the ram furiously, striking the
ram and shattering his two horns. The ram was
powerless to stand against him; the goat knocked him to
the ground and trampled on him, and none could rescue
the ram from his power. The goat became very
great...it prospered in everything it did, and truth was
thrown to the ground.[6]

Our historical moment is a great destiny not of our choosing; our
fortune has been to arrive together at the vanishing point, when
anthropocentric meaning has been dethroned and we have the
truth, on the ground with us.

I had my own vision, a dream that I discovered the headquarters
of contemporary thought inside a Sheraton Hotel in Orlando,
Florida. There was a private room with an internet connection
and a table where all the prominent male leaders of thought were
feasting. In the dream I thought of the Ram and the Goat and
how watching male philosophers was like watching men fight
about "something versus anything," "something versus
everything," and at best "everything versus nothing." Masculine
battles aim to rule, because they do not know what women
know, that power will not satisfy desire. But in this vision, there
were no battles among these men, only celebration. Slavoj Žižek

---

[6] Daniel 8:2-12. *The Holy Bible*. New International Version. Grand Rapids,
Michigan: Zondervan Publishing House, 1996, p. 755-756.

was at the center, laughing and eating goulash. The battle that
was waged in deconstruction revealed that not all truth claims
are power plays. We have regarded the loss of ideology as a
tragedy. In what has been an era of eschatology we have also
embraced the end times with a constant second coming of the
new, rebuilding power as "other," in technology, and "harmless"
in the celebrity. And for the philosopher there is nothing left but
desire in the moment of truth, with most thinkers devoted to
desire but in fulfilling it rather than unveiling it. As Jean
Baudrillard wrote, "Yesterday they were diverted from the truth
of history–today they are diverted from the truth of their own
desires."[7]

It is desire that considers everything and truth that reveals
nothing more is needed. Here in this text I consider the ethics of
desire, the "all for nothing" that works toward its own end in the
face of "eternal return."[8] I also aim to reveal truth, though I was
told that truth is "what is not said," and that truth is "what is not
revealed." Our ontotheology is not revelation.[9] I recalled
Derrida, and his words that women are joined with "art, style
and truth."[10] Here I have written about art and style and truth.

---

[7] Baudrillard, Jean. *Seduction*. Trans. Brain Singer. New York: St. Martin's
Press, 1990, p. 175.
[8] Nietzsche's concept: "Behold, *you are the teacher of the eternal recurrence*–
that is your destiny!...Behold, we know what you teach: that all things recur
eternally, and we ourselves too; and that we have already existed an eternal
number of times, and all things with us...we ourselves are alike in every great
year, in what is greatest as in what is smallest. Nietzsche, Friedrich. *Thus Spoke
Zarathustra: A Book for All and None*. Trans. Walter Kaufman. New York: The
Modern Library. 1992, p. 220.
[9] Ingraffia, Brian. *Postmodern Theory and Biblical Theology*. Cambridge:
Cambridge University Press, 1995, p. 4.
[10] "It is impossible to dissociate the questions of art, style and truth from the
question of the woman." Derrida, Jacques. *Spurs*. Chicago: The University of
Chicago Press, 1978, p. 71.

I. The Establishment

Im Zusammensein mit dem Tode wird jeder in das Wie gebracht, das jeder gleichmäßig sein kann; in eine Möglichkeit, bezüglich der keiner ausgezeichnet ist; in das Wie, in dem alles Was zerstäubt...Was ist die Zeit? Wurde zur Frage: Wer ist die Zeit? Näher: sind wir selbst die Zeit? Oder noch näher: bin ich meine Zeit? Damit komme ich ihr am nächsten, und wenn ich die Frage recht verstehe, dann ist mit ihr alles Ernst geworden. Also ist solches Fragen die angemessenste Zugangs–und Umgangsart mit der Zeit als mit der je meinigen.

- Martin Heidegger, *Der Begriff der Zeit*[11]

---

[11] "In being together with death everyone is brought into the 'how' that each can be in equal measure; into a possibility with respect to which no one is distinguished; into the 'how' in which all 'what' dissolves into dust...What is time? Became the question: Who is time? More closely: are we ourselves time? Or closer still: am I my time? In this way I come closest to it, and if I understand the question correctly, it is then taken completely seriously. Such questioning is thus the most appropriate manner of access to and of dealing with time in each case mine." Heidegger, Martin. *Der Begriff der Zeit / The Concept of Time.* (German-English edition) Trans. William McNeill. Oxford: Blackwell, 1992, p. 22.

What is existence in "equal measure," as Heidegger proposes? Existence is the time between birth and death and that time is a resource, of various lengths, employed for various ends. How then can we best utilize thought in relation to finitude? Thought, like other media, such as literature, cinema, music, fashion, architecture, and art, is a message for an audience. The audience decides if the time invested in receiving a form of media is of greater worth than otherwise living.

You must now speculate if reading this text is more valuable than doing something else. Like most investments, you will not know until some time has passed. There is, in any moment, a risk of wasting time, that giving time to appreciate a media will be concluded worthless. Creators of media have an ethical responsibility to create information that is valuable to the human experience. But what is valuable?

We have reached with deconstruction the erasure of absolute value and confront the problem of subjectivity. Any ideological value is confirmed by individual or collective performance, such as cultural theory or political action, but that meaning is temporal and does not translate to lasting truth outside its system.[12] Yet, despite awareness of the problem of subjectivity, both individual and collective ideologies continue to thrive in democratic capitalism. Ideology still seduces because of its heroic gestures of edification. Today, there is no lack of meaning but rather a decadence of meaning combined with a lack of consideration of ontological truth. The coming together of

---

[12] In "The Task Of Destroying the History of Ontology," Heidegger explained, "Being finds its meaning in temporality," Heidegger, Martin. *Being and Time.* Trans. John Macquarrie & Edward Robinson. New York: Harper & Row Publishers, 1962, p. 41.

individual and collective desire is anthropocentrism and "anthropocentrism bears the mark of decadence."[13] Every era has its decadent dream, and in our current one we prize anthropocentric meaning by privileging our desires.

How do we contend with the self-reflexive era and retain integrity of thought? Thought is a necessary site where we can, at any moment, pose ontological questions of "what exists?" and "what is true?" Ontologically, we are reminded that survival submits to eternal return.[14] Ontological consciousness should not denigrate anthropocentric meaning but rather illuminate it as a site for learning. Like Robert Venturi and Denise Scott Brown's claim on Las Vegas, we can approach the "megatexture" of anthropocentric decadence as a landscape for understanding.[15] Along with the "nothing" of a nihilist and the "uncertainty" of an agnostic, we observe passion, joy, love, sorrow, loss and entire life spans devoted to particular perspectives. Ideology contends with the needs and aspirations of individuals and collectives and can thus satisfy a lack of ontological knowledge–it supplies answers for joy and sorrow. The false consciousness of ideology generates shared meaning that sustains civility. If ideology was completely destroyed today, the resulting disorder would return us to a primordial "state of emergency" with an equalizing

---

[13] Schirmacher, Wolfgang. "Art(ificial) Perception: Nietzsche and Culture after Nihilism," lecture, Toronto, 1999.

[14] Nietzsche, Friedrich. *Thus Spoke Zarathustra: A Book for All and None.* Trans. Walter Kaufman. New York: The Modern Library. 1992, p. 220; and "Let us think this thought in its most terrible form: existence as it is, without meaning or aim, yet recurring inevitably without any finale of nothingness: ' *the eternal recurrence.'*" Nietzsche, Friedrich. *The Will to Power.* Trans. Walter Kaufmann. New York: Random House, 1968, p. 35.

[15] Venturi, Robert, et al. *Learning from Las Vegas.* Cambridge: MIT Press, 1971, p. 13.

survival ethics of "make and take only what you need."[16] And the overproduction of ideology does not necessitate the tautology that now we should no longer produce any thought or we should only make something with ontological meaning. Past centuries have shown us that limiting or liberating anthropocentric thought, or enforcing ontological value, does not silence human desire or the question of truth. We cannot make or unmake the answer (the truth). Furthermore, the current state of ideology has become so liberal that it has allowed for deconstruction, the rebellion within the system. We have then a contemporary world that offers any number of preapproved ideological approaches for living. This is the era of the unfashionable absolute, though we can easily find that even the most mutable and subjective positions have absolute assertions.

All for You

> *INES*: Tu as rêvé trente ans que tu avais du cœur; et tu te passais mille petites faiblesses parce que tout est permis aux héros. Comme c'était commode! Et puis, à l'heure de danger, on t'a mis au pied du mur et... tu a pris le train pour Mexico.
> *GARCIN*: Je n'ai pas rêvé cet héroïsme. Je l'ai choisi. On est ce qu'on veut.
> *INES:* Prouve-le. Prouve que ce n'était pas un rêve. Seuls les actes décident de ce qu'on a voulu.

---

[16] In many ways we already operate, under democratic capitalism, in a constant state of emergency with urgency that we do not have enough, with the threat of loss ever present, and thus we take as much as we can. For Carl Schmidt and Giorgio Agamben, the "state of emergency," reinforces the power of ideology because it requires constituents to remain under its control. Agamben further addresses the "state of exception" that is applied within ideology. Schmidt, Carl. *Die Diktatur*: von den Anfängen des modernen Souverätsgedankens bis zum proletarischen Klassenkampf, Berlin: Duncker and Humblot, 1994. Agamben, Giorgio. *State of Exception*. Trans. Kevin Attell. Chicago: The University of Chicago Press, 2005.

GARCIN: Je suis mort trop tôt. On ne m'a laissé le
temps de faire *mes* actes.
INES: On meurt toujours trop tôt—ou trop tard. Et
cependant la vie est là, terminée; le trait est tiré, il
faut faire la somme. Tu n'es rien d'autre que ta
vie.
- Jean Paul Sartre, *Huis Clos* [17]

The question of life's meaning finds immediate answers in the
physical condition of finite existence.[18] An individual who
supposes a metaphysical "before" or "after" life still contends
with mortal existence, just as an individual who supposes
nothing before or after. Neither faith nor nihilism causes your
physical existence to cease. And because we lack memory of the
event of birth and have no firsthand knowledge of the event after
death, the present physical experience of a life span becomes the
locus for meaning and thus a site of total involvement.

Rising from romanticism, "existentialism" asserts the potential
value in singular existence. Paul Tillich explained, "while the
ancient world valued the individual not as an individual but as a

---

[17] Sartre, Jean Paul. *Huis Clos.* New York: Appleton-Century-Crofts, 1962, p. 87.
INEZ: For thirty years you dreamt you were a hero, and condoned a thousand
petty lapses–because a hero, of course, can do no wrong. An easy method,
obviously. Then a day came when you were up against it, the red light of real
danger–and you took the train to Mexico. / *GARCIN:* I "dreamt," you say. It was
no dream. When I chose the hardest path, I made my choice deliberately. A man
is what he wills himself to be. / *INEZ:* Prove it. Prove it was no dream. It's what
one does, and nothing else, that shows the stuff one's made of. / *GARCIN:* I died
too soon. I wasn't allowed time to–to do my deeds. / *INEZ:* One always dies too
soon–or too late. And yet one's whole life is complete at that moment, with a
line drawn neatly under it, ready for the summing up. You are your life, and
nothing else. Sartre, Jean Paul. *No Exit.* New York: Vintage, 1955, pp. 44-45.
[18] "The truth resulting from the subject's engagement in the world and history
through labor, cultural creation, and political organization, whereby the
subjectivity of the subject shows itself to be humanity, finitude, care for its being
thrown in anticipation of its end–this truth remains the truth of disclosed being."
Levinas, Emmanuel. *Basic Philosophical Writings.* Ed. Adriann Peperzak et al,
Indianapolis: Indiana University Press, 1996, p. 99.

representative of something universal, e.g. a virtue, the rebirth of antiquity saw in the individual a unique expression of the universe, incomparable, irreplaceable."[19] We are each regarded as a particular life–a unique intersection in time–and accountable to its potential glory and responsibility. Nobel Prize recipient Jean Paul Sartre explained:

> If you are born a hero, you may set your mind just as much at rest; you'll be a hero all your life; you'll drink like a hero and eat like a hero. What the Existentialist says is that the coward makes himself cowardly, that the hero makes himself heroic. There's always a possibility for the coward not to be cowardly anymore and for the hero to stop being heroic. What counts is total involvement; some one particular action or set of circumstances is not total involvement[20]

Existentialism asserts that existence takes shape by individual freedom and choice. This is your life and the choices are all for you. Søren Kierkegaard called for each of us to use freedom "to be the self that he is in truth."[21] The freedom of existence allows that the individual is truth opposed to the control of consensus. "A crowd," wrote Kierkegaard, "not this crowd or that, the crowd now living or the crowd long deceased, a crowd of humble people or of superior people, or rich or of poor, etc.—a crowd in its very concept is the untruth, by reason of the fact that it renders the individual completely impenitent and

---

[19] Tillich, Paul. *The Courage to Be*. New Haven: Yale University Press, 1952, p. 19. He continues: "Late romanticism, bohemianism, and romantic naturalism have prepared the way for present-day Existentialism, the most radical form of the courage to be as oneself," Ibid. p. 123.

[20] Sartre, Jean Paul. *Existentialism and Human Emotions*. Trans. Bernard Fretchman and Hazel E. Barnes. New York: Citadel Press, 1995, p. 35.

[21] Kierkegaard, Søren. *The Sickness Unto Death*. Trans. Howard Hong and Edna Hong. Princeton: Princeton University Press, 1980, p. 20.

irresponsible, or at least weakens his sense of responsibility."[22] Friedrich Nietzsche shared an interest in the validity of singularity, to the point that subjectivity is the source of truth[23] and he privileged the "drive of the individual far above the average and flats of the herd conscience."[24] Life then allows for each person to define life's meaning. For Kierkegaard the meaning lies in a dialogue between finitude and infinity, yet for other existentialist writers the only meaning is the present, with its continuing opportunity.[25]

In valuing the truth of the self we sacrifice the hope of external meaning, restricting ourselves to the choice at hand and its range of influence. Life is what you have in your moment. Religion, sentimentality, imaginary thought, hopes, rationalizing or concluding blame are all termed "bad faith." They deny a responsible grasp of choice in the short number of minutes you are alive. Life then only has meaning by *absolute* responsibility to the free choice at hand, your choice, to taste the fruit, feel the warmth, hear, speak, create, and choose, right now. And we always choose, even when we choose not to choose.

---

[22] Kierkegaard, Søren. "That Individual," in *The Point of View*. London: Oxford University Press, 1950, p. 114.

[23] "All credibility, all good conscience, all evidence of truth come only from the senses." Nietzsche, Friedrich. *Beyond Good and Evil*. Trans. Walter Kaufman. New York: Vintage Books Random House, 1966, p. 88.

[24] Nietzsche, Friedrich. *Beyond Good and Evil*. Trans. Walter Kaufman. New York: Vintage Books Random House, 1966, p. 113.

[25] Kierkegaard wrote against religion as a manmade structure. He emphasized the personal leap of faith to describe the individual confrontation with God. Sartre wrote against social structure, "The Marxists to whom I have spoken reply, 'You can rely on the support of others in your action, which obviously has certain limits because you're not going to live forever. That means rely on what others are doing elsewhere'....Given that man is free and that there is no human nature for me to depend on, I cannot count on men whom I do not know by relying on human goodness or man's concern for the good of society." Sartre, Jean Paul. *Existentialism and Human Emotions*. Trans. Hazel E. Barnes. New York: Carol Publishing, 1995, p. 30.

In existentialism, there is an unwritten ethics of giving meaning to a life that has none and means nothing beyond the moment. Albert Camus explained, "to work and create 'for nothing'…to know that one's creation has no future, to see one's work destroyed in a day while being aware that fundamentally this has no more importance than building for centuries," is to "give the void its colors."[26] Individuals color the void with choices that establish the quality of their existence. However, this is not a life ethics that *any* living is meaningful, rather existentialism becomes ideology because it supposes a set of values and claims a type of living that is most meaningful, and that is "authenticity" in your free choices versus bad faith in anything outside of yourself. One always has total freedom but only "authentic" choices answer truthfully to freedom. Existentialism then requires knowing the language, which means it is more of a "free use of the proper," than freedom.[27]

Existentialism also prefers to suspend *final* judgment, allowing all choices to standalone. We always act then without hope because we cannot know the exact consequences of a choice.[28] The greatest crisis of existentialism is anxiety in the face of freedom and the resulting despair from not knowing if you made

---

[26] Camus, Albert. *The Myth of Sisyphus*. Trans. Justin O'Brien. New York: Vintage International, 1955, p. 114.

[27] "Free Use of the Proper ("der freie Gebrauch des Eigenen,") Hölderlin, Friedrich. *Essays and Letters on Theory*. Trans. Thomas Pfau. New York: State University of New York Press, 1988, p. 150.

[28] Camus suggested that individuals placed hope in existentialism. "As I see once more, existential thought in this regard is steeped in a vast hope, the very hope which at the time of early Christianity and the spreading of the good news inflamed the ancient world. Camus, Albert. *The Myth of Sisyphus*. Trans. Justin O'Brien. New York: Vintage International, 1955, p. 135.

the right choice.[29] In existentialism there is no authority outside ⟵——
of the self to determine if an action is right or wrong. The lack of
authority is not a state that existentialism claims it invents, but
rather, the theory supposes, this is the true authority-less human
condition that has always existed. As Jean Baudrillard described,
good and evil "are entangled like the interwoven letters of a
monogram."[30] There is always potential for good or evil, good
being authentic and evil being bad faith and all the consequences
that go with it. But all humankind begins life equally, not
knowing if a choice is "authentic" and thus we all begin in
anxiety, which does not stop us. Life is this ambiguous, fantastic
opportunity and the choices are entirely up to you. There is
nothing but making the most of time.[31]

On Your Honor

> My grandfather used to say: "Life is
> astoundingly short. To me looking back over
> it, life seems so foreshortened that I scarcely
> understand, for instance, how a young man can
> decide to ride over to the next village–without
> being afraid that–not to mention accidents–
> even the span of a normal happy life may fall
> far short of the time needed for such a
> journey."
> - Franz Kafka, "The Next Village"[32]

---

[29] Anxiety arises out of "freedom's possibilities." Kierkegaard, Søren. *The Concept of Anxiety*. Trans. by R. Thomte and A. Anderson. Princeton: Princeton University Press, 1980, p. 155.
[30] Baudrillard, Jean. *Impossible Exchange*. Trans. Chris Turner. New York: Verso Books, 2001, p. 98.
[31] "Outside of that single fatality of death, everything, joy or happiness, is liberty." Camus, Albert. *The Myth of Sisyphus*. Trans. Justin O'Brien. New York: Vintage International, 1955, p. 117.
[32] Kafka, Franz. *The Complete Stories*. Trans. Nahum Glatzer and Willa and Edwin Muir. New York: Schocken Books, 1971, p. 404

With the theory of existentialism we are, each of us, at all times living by how much esteem we have for the finite present. What it means to be human in existentialism is how much being human means to you, during the time you have. The challenge with such a subjectively driven theory is that there is no shared basis for understanding. The only evaluation is self-evaluation. Simone de Beauvoir wrote that "any man who has known real loves, real revolts, real desires, and real will, knows quite well that he needs no outside guarantee to be sure of his goals."[33] The problem is that "real" is normally understood as that which is shared truth (the sky is blue, etc.) so if everything is internal, what is real? And more so, if all lived existence is equal with opportunity, why is there ever anything other than real love, real revolt, and real desire? Are not all choices within the same real existence? Where do we learn of the false? If false love, revolts and desires are simply those that are inauthentic by existentialist terms, then it is the person and the choice that are false not the love or other things. And if one attempts to simply divide real from the artificial, it is then natural versus manmade. We could also suppose that nothing is real anyway, "every truth is artificial," since there is no outside guarantee.[34]

The intention here is not to break the ideology of existentialism but rather to understand how it satisfies the desire for meaning. An existentialist negates the value of authority and social recognition in exchange for self-worth. Life is a limited number of minutes, a "fatal sickness" according to Kierkegaard, so why

---

[33] "It is up to each one to fulfill his existence as an absolute." De Beauvoir, Simone. *The Ethics of Ambiguity*. Trans. Bernard Frechtman. New York: Citadel Press, 1996, p. 159.
[34] Schirmacher, Wolfgang. "Art(ificial) Perception: Nietzsche and Culture after Nihilism," lecture, Toronto, 1999.

not live each moment to the fullest by our own terms?[35] It is self-generated meaning. But classic existentialism is not a personal claim on passing time with reckless living. The popular attitude of a "life is for living," is a distortion of the ideology. The existentialist phrase "total involvement" does not mean totally involved in one's own interests. The stars of such a life are the egoists. "One is free" becomes "one is free to pursue one's own happiness," typically guided by an ethics of pleasure, or quantity, or quality, supposing that the more pleasure the better, the more events the better, the more anything the better. It doesn't help that we are so sincere and enthusiastic and even painfully sentimental about our self-interest. F. Scott Fitzgerald's words in *The Beautiful and Damned* describe such a lifestyle, "in justification of his manner of living there was first, of course, The Meaninglessness of Life."[36] The main character states:

> I reached maturity under the impression that I was gathering the experience to order my life for happiness. Indeed, I accomplished the not unusual feat of solving each question in my mind long before it presented itself to me in life–and of being beaten and bewildered just the same. But after a few tastes of this latter dish I had had enough. "Here!" I said, "Experience is not worth the getting." It's not a thing that happens pleasantly to a passive you–it's a wall that an active you runs up against... Protect myself as I might by making no new ties with tragic and predestined humanity, I was lost with the rest. I had traded the fight against love for the

---

[35] Kierkegaard, Søren. *The Sickness Unto Death.* Trans. Howard Hong and Edna Hong. Princeton: Princeton University Press, 1980, p. 17.
[36] Fitzgerald, F. Scott. *The Beautiful and Damned.* New York: The Modern Library, 2002, p. 45.

fight against loneliness, the fight against life for the
fight against death.[37]

Self-directed existence is less about existential freedom and
more about satisfying desire, which never rests.

Another distortion of existentialism is that living authentically
makes one more alive, "so that I, perhaps, come out even more
'living' than you."[38] The effort is to give present existence
intensity, such a dense realness, that it dispels any doubt in its
singular meaning and thus distracts from a consideration of
imminent death and silences ontological questions. Yet
existentialist writers would consider this an exploitation of
freedom, because freedom is not something to invest in, it is
simply the ongoing, undeniable condition. Freedom is never
something one has to obtain or defend by intense living, just as it
is not about *freedom to* accumulate your own self-service desires
or *freedom from* consequences. You are always already free and
each circumstance has authentic conditions that deny any
consistent strategy.

The resolution of meaning via singular existence is in fact prior
to and after any historical ideology such as "existentialism,"
though it somehow continues to give people a framework for
accessing the moment they already possess. We always occupy a
free choice, but that choice resulted from something before it.
This means we are all in relation to an original event of human
existence. The relationship can be one of gratitude: "life is
experienced as a gift," writes Judith Butler, but then "life

[37] Ibid, p. 214.
[38] Dostoevsky, Fyodor. *Notes from Underground*. New York: Vintage Books
Random House, 1993, p. 130.

becomes understood as a kind of endless debt."[39] Avital Ronell writes, "You find yourself incontrovertibly obligated: something occurs prior to owing, and more fundamental still than that of which any trace of empirical guilt can give an account. This relation–to whom? to what? Is no more and no less than your liability–what you owe before you think, understand, or give; that is, what you owe from the very fact that you exist…You do not have to *do* anything about your liability, and most finitudes don't. Still it copilots your every move, planning your every flight."[40] This attitude of endless debt is a type of bad faith however, as even Ronell discusses, because one feels one is always receiving and reacting and thus not acting.[41]

We simply cannot deny the actions of "the other,"[42] or the influence of our actions. As de Beauvoir notes, "no project can be defined except for its interference with other projects."[43] De Beauvoir explains that we are always accountable, in that any choice can be utilized to "serve the universal cause of freedom."[44] The best choice then for existentialism is maximizing freedom. But, de Beauvoir continues,

---

[39] Butler, Judith. *The Psychic Life of Power*. Stanford: Stanford University Press, 1997, 49.

[40] Ronell, Avital. *Crack Wars: Literature, Addiction, Mania*. Lincoln: Univ. of Nebraska Press, 1992, p. 57.

[41] It "does not signify a free floating potentiality-for-Being … Dasein, as essentially having a state-of-mind, has already got itself into definite possibilities." Heidegger, Martin. *Being and Time*. Trans. John Macquarrie & Edward Robinson. New York: Harper & Row Publishers, 1962, p. 183.

[42] For Karl Marx, it was "to see other men, not as the realization, but rather the limitation of his own liberty." Marx, Karl, "On the Jewish Question," *Early Writings*. Trans. T. B. Bottomore, *The Marx-Engels Reader*. New York, 1963, pp. 28-29.

[43] De Beauvoir, Simone. *The Ethics of Ambiguity*. Trans. Bernard Frechtman. New York: Citadel Press, 1996, p. 71.

[44] Ibid. p. 90 and p. 129.

> As soon as one considers a system abstractly and theoretically, one puts himself, in effect, on the plane of the universal, thus, of the infinite. That is why reading the Hegelian system is so comforting...existentialism does not offer to the reader the consolations of an abstract evasion: existentialism proposes no evasion... If it came to be that each man did what he must, existence would be saved in each one without there being any need of dreaming of a paradise where we would all be reconciled in death.[45]

In existentialism, we are reconciled in life. Your particular life and particular choices are the basis for total meaning because it is precisely the inability to be anyone else *and* the inability to die that makes each choice significant. The extension of freedom is the only existential hope and regardless of the action of any other, each man must do "what he must." This survival ethic directly opposes the shared values, even in shared human experience.

Us

> What we have is usually neck and neck with what we want, though what we want usually ends up ahead...and in our quiet moments, we realize that we want our lives to have weight and substance and grow toward some kind of fullness that lies beyond ourselves. Our own selves, and especially the pleasures of our own selves, are insufficient to give meaning to our lives.
> - Miroslav Volf [46]

> Being singular plural means the essence of Being is *co*-essence.

---

[45] Ibid. p. 159.
[46] Volf, Miroslav. "God at Work," Yale Center for Faith and Culture, http://www.yale.edu/faith/downloads/x_volf_godwork.pdf, p. 14.

- Jean-Luc Nancy [47]

Heidegger attempted to address individual existence as always "together with" others. The broadest view of being is also as Jean-Luc Nancy described, "being singular plural." Being is with the other in community such as society, subculture or relationships and thus the basis of existence is co-existence. Unlike existentialism, with collective meaning we actually consider other people's feelings, but more than just being considerate, it is actually feeling *for* them. As Heidegger explained, "fearing for" someone is a subjective feeling of fear "precisely when the Other is not afraid." [48] The fear is *not* experienced by the other, thus one fears *for* them. This is empathy, expressed through compassion and mercy that then permeate the highest collective aims, such as those set forth by the United Nations or other global bodies that aim to protect humanity.

Collective associations however do not mean that individuals immediately feel for everyone. [49] Hannah Arendt describes that we consider our singularity as part of a collective because of "the condition for remembrance that is for history." [50] Thus we take pleasure in the collective as long as it also serves ourselves, to be validated and carry on our memory. Wilhelm Hegel suggested, however, that because existence continues in the collective, we then each have a responsibility to be in service to

---

[47] Italics mine. Nancy, Jean-Luc. *Being Singular Plural.* Trans. Robert D. Richardson and Anne E. O'Byrne. Stanford: Stanford Univ. Press, 2000, p. 30.
[48] Heidegger, Martin. *Being and Time.* Trans. John Macquarrie & Edward Robinson. New York: Harper & Row Publishers, 1962, p. 142.
[49] "What we have by nature is an impulse to preserve our own children and grandchildren," Lewis, C.S. *The Essential C.S. Lewis.* Ed. Lyle W. Dorsett. New York: Simon & Schuster, 1988, p. 444.
[50] Arendt, Hannah. *The Human Condition.* Chicago: The University of Chicago Press, 1958, p. 9.

greater collective being. Hegel illuminated the freedom to establish great history is just for the benefit of guiding others. Each life then is meaningful by a shared existence in one's lifespan and influencing several subsequent generations, or at the very longest, the destiny of humankind.

What then are we to make of ahistorical events, such as unrequited love? Or of actions considered but then left undone? Nothing, because they did not serve a greater collective purpose and thus, they disappear in death along with the body. What we have according to Hegel is "intuited becoming" so that no personal event has any lasting priority.[51] Individual emotion is simply part of a shared experience of existence, meaning that birth, love, marriage, success, loss, and death, are simply rites of passage for all. The true ethics of the collective then cannot be about a particular hero or specific event. The emphasis is on the anonymous and ongoing "we." "We share understanding between us: between us all, simultaneously–all the dead and the living, and all beings," wrote Nancy.[52]

Humankind becomes the total value by which all is judged. Rather than the existentialist threat of confronting despair by a poor choice, with collective thinking one faces the possible annihilation of all life.[53] We are accountable to the total measure of all life.[54] The approach then gives us an authority that is

---

[51] Appears as a quote in Heidegger's text and does not indicate the original source. Heidegger suggests this is just an abstraction the passage of time. Heidegger, Martin. *Being and Time*. Trans. John Macquarrie & Edward Robinson. New York: Harper & Row Publishers, 1962, p. 483.

[52] Nancy, Jean-Luc. *Being Singular Plural*. Trans. Robert D. Richardson and Anne E. O'Byrne. Stanford: Stanford Univ. Press, 2000, p. 99.

[53] An "'excessive' measure or measured excess, also provides the scale of total responsibility." Ibid. p. 179.

[54] "Hence, there is nothing more illusory," wrote Jacques Maritain, "than to pose the problem of the person and the common good in terms of opposition. In

lacking in existentialism. "Justice" describes Nancy, "is returning to each existence what returns to it according to its unique, singular creation in its *coexistence* with all other creations."[55] For example, we are born as a new being and given love and thus are subsequently evaluated by returning that love to the collective. The measure is all of us. In the words of Thomas Merton, "Love is our true destiny. We do not find the meaning of life by ourselves alone–we find it with another."

On Behalf Of

> In the fall of the Empire, our leaving behind all but each other became the revolution.
> - Yoko Devereaux[56]

The aim then is not my aim alone, but our aim in what we find to be the best of all possible worlds. This is the thinking in collective ideology, to think as a group whether that group is two lovers or the entire society. Collectives provide companionship and emotional support. Collectives, such as political entities, claim to protect and give safety. People allow a collective authority to make up for individual lack of strength or courage so that the collective serves as guardian.[57] It is groupthink, "the herd" as Nietzsche termed, it that substitutes for individual will.[58]

---

reality, it is posed in terms of reciprocal subordination." Maritain, Jacques. *The Person and the Common Good.* Trans. John Fitzgerald. Baltimore: University of Notre Dame Press, 1966, p. 65.
[55] Nancy, Jean-Luc. *Being Singular Plural.* Trans. Robert D. Richardson and Anne E. O'Byrne. Stanford: Stanford Univ. Press, 2000, p. 187.
[56] Printed on invitation for Yoko Devereaux, Fall 2005 collection.
[57] Habermas, Jürgen. *The Structural Transformation of the Public Sphere.* Cambridge, Massachusetts: The MIT Press, 1989, p. 104.
[58] "One still follows the old habit and seeks another authority that can speak unconditionally and command goals and tasks. The authority of conscience now

A collective may stand in the place of individual consciousness with "a quantity of readymade opinions and so relieves him of the necessity of forming his own," wrote Alexis de Tocqueville in *Democracy in America*.[59] The result is shared belief and shared hope. Much like the first line of the Roman Catholic Catechism, "I believe–We believe," a collective is united by the belief that "I exist–We exist" and because it is certain that "We" will continue to exist that "I" continue in relation to it.[60] Therefore "I" can feel good because of "We" and I can also influence how "We" continue.

Most collectives are based on values that position them against other collectives, while total being seems to continue in eternal return, indifferent to special interests. Faith denominations, fashion, music, art movements, and interest groups unite individuals into a being-in-common with a set of Chatham House Rules. Subcultures and interest groups like to make "private vices into public aims," by publicly expressing whatever particular value they privilege in the form of clothing, events or promotional communication.[61] The shared meaning is a pleasure gained through publicizing a certain value.

---

steps up front... or the authority of reason. Or the social instinct (the herd). Or history with an immanent spirit and a goal within, so one can entrust oneself to it. One wants to get around the will, the willing of a goal, the risk of positing a goal for oneself, one wants to ride oneself of the responsibility." Nietzsche, Friedrich. *The Will to Power*. Trans. Walter Kaufmann. New York: Random House, 1968, p. 16-17.

[59] De Tocqueville, Alexis. *Democracy in America*. Trans. G. Lawrence. New York: Penguin Classics, 1969, p. 399-400.

[60] Liberia Editrice Vaticana. *Catechism of the Catholic Church* for the United States of America. New York: Doubleday, 1995.

[61] Habermas, Jürgen. *The Structural Transformation of the Public Sphere*. Cambridge, Massachusetts: The MIT Press, 1989, p. 117.

Even if a collective claims to be about "human rights" or "universal" aims it does not necessarily mean that it is of benefit to total being. Some groups claim that they are undeniably all inclusive of being suggesting that being human is the only being-in-common. Agencies like Human Rights Watch or the United Nations claim to have the best interest of all in mind, as do churches and many American nonprofits. Fighting for humanity however often becomes fighting for a particular ideal of living such as equality, happiness, or eternal life. Democratic capitalism is founded on the *pursuit* of happiness.[62] Thus collective meaning is based on pleasure. Collectives may also claim to eliminate humanity's problems. Even Jean-François Lyotard claimed it was the unique call of technoscience that would rescue everyone from "the death of the sun."[63] The investment into physiological progress in terms of life extension is rooted in denial that being will continue to thrive regardless of science. The call is to step outside of being today, in order to save being tomorrow because "possibility is the only salvation."[64]

The efforts to "save us all," apparently begin with an informed "we" and move "towards world citizenry."[65] Adam Smith, Sam

---

[62] Habermas, Jürgen. *The Structural Transformation of the Public Sphere.* Cambridge, Massachusetts: The MIT Press, 1989, p. 85.

[63] Lyotard claimed we must be in "service to complexification," in order to "solve the problem of evacuating humanity to another place before the death of the sun." Lyotard, Jean-François. *The Postmodern Explained to Children: Correspondence 1982-1985.* Trans. Thomas Pefanis. London: Turnaround, 1992, p. 100.

[64] Kierkegaard, Søren. *The Sickness Unto Death.* Trans. Howard Hong and Edna Hong. Princeton: Princeton University Press, 1980, p. 39.

[65] "The thought and action of the 19th and 20th centuries are ruled by the Idea of the emancipation of humanity," explained Jean-François Lyotard, "the promise of freedom is for everyone the horizon of progress and its legitimization." Lyotard, Jean-François. *The Postmodern Explained to Children:*

Weber and Karl Marx consider the individual a tangible asset
that must work for collective survival. Utopian Charles Fourier
emphasized the need for an aristocracy who would step out of
the collective, not needing its financial resources and thus
guiding all to ultimate being.[66] Ecumenism, the United Nations,
and the American civil rights movement are collectives claiming
to lead all with a torch of truth. The call of particular collectives
is like an "Oath of Horatii:"[67]

> "We are one...alone...and only...we look ahead, we
> beg our heart for guidance in answering this call no
> voice has spoken, yet we have heard."[68]

Just as "freedom from" consequence is an abuse of freedom in
existentialism, the proposition that "we hear a separate call" is a
limited view of being. The problem we face is in-group/out-
group morality, loyalties, and hostilities.[69] Rather than uniting
humankind, particular collective aims have resulted in

Correspondence 1982-1985. Trans. Thomas Pefanis. London: Turnaround, 1992,
p. 97.
[66] Fourier, Charles. *The Theory of Four Movements.* Gareth Jones, et al. Ed.
Cambridge: Cambridge University Press, 1996.
[67] David, Jacques-Louis. "Oath of Horatii," oil on canvas, 1784, The Louvre,
Paris.
[68] "The word 'we' is a lime poured over men, which sets and hardens to stone,
and crushes all beneath it, and that which is white and that which is black are lost
equally in the grey of it." Rand, Ayn. *Anthem.* Caldwell, Ohio: Caxton Press.
1999. pp. 87 & 93.
[69] "Religion is a *label* of in-group/out-group enmity and vendetta, not necessarily
worse than other labels such as skin colour, language or preferred football team."
and "Even if religion did no other harm in itself, its wanton and carefully
nurtured divisiveness-its deliberate and cultivated pandering to humanity's
natural tendency to favour in-groups and shun out-groups-would be enough to
make it a significant force for evil in the world." Dawkins, Richard. *The God
Delusion.* New York: Houghton Mifflin Company, 2006, pp: 259 & 262.
Dawkins interpretation reads religion as ideology. The Christian gospel calls to
"everyone according to what he has done," and not by measure of an in-group of
any type. Revelation 22:12, *The Holy Bible.* New International Version. Grand
Rapids, Michigan: Zondervan Publishing House, 1996, p. 1048.

decadence and division. The dismantling of ideology has exposed how all collectives endorse some form of illusion. Authors Moshe Halbertal and Avishai Margalit explain:

> The secular Enlightenment is associated with the shift from the criticism of religion to the criticism of ideology as a type of collective illusion…Ideologies as interest-dependent social beliefs manipulate the masses by making use of the power of the imagination …these ideological illusions are so blatant, according to the critics, that there is no reason to investigate their truth value.[70]

Ideology stood in the place of truth and then "what ideology already was, society has now become."[71] By and large, "we are witnessing the ruin of great collective enterprises that we once imagined carried within themselves the seeds of emancipation and truth."[72] Those collective aspirations have come to pass and the same individual and collective problems remain. With deconstruction, we recognized the subjective status of privileged concepts. We made evident "the deconstruction of accepted facts of our modernity…the idea of the historical subject, the idea of progress, the idea of revolution, the idea of humanity, and the ideal of science. Its aim is to show these great constructions are outdated."[73] But amazingly, people continue to form alliances based on subjective values. Collectives continue to revisit old approaches. Julia Kristeva described how deconstruction

---

[70] Halbertal, Moshe and Avishai Margalit. *Idolatry*. Trans. Naomi Goldblum. Cambridge, Massachusetts: Harvard University Press. 1992, pp. 114-115.
[71] Debord, Guy. *The Society of the Spectacle*. Trans. Donald Nicholson-Smith. New York: Zone Books, 1994, p. 153 and 152.
[72] Badiou, Alain. *Infinite Thought*. Trans. Justin Clemens. New York: Continuum, 2003, p. 54
[73] Ibid. p. 44.

"doesn't prevent prospective ideologies from appearing to satisfy the psychological need for ideals and seduction."[74]

Whenever any collective acts "on behalf of" all humans, it is never the same as all being acting together.[75] A united collective consciousness is emerging in social networking and the expansion of global communications, even though more people are disconnected than connected at the moment. But even a world totally connected is still a world of differing subjective, individual and collective values.

Latter Day Saints

> But now we have reached the opposite point; indeed, we wanted to reach it: the most extreme consciousness, man's ability to see through himself and history. With this we are practically as far as possible from perfection in being, doing, and willing: our desire, even our will for knowledge is a symptom of a tremendous decadence. We strive for the opposite of that which strong races, strong natures want–understanding as ending.
> - Friedrich Nietzsche, *Will to Power*[76]

Now, we "see through ourselves and history." With deconstruction, we should have completed this aim, debunking absolute rationale. But we find that we occupy a moment of excess of meaning, singular and collective aims coming together

---

[74] Kristeva, Julia. *Revolt, She Said*. Trans. Brian O'Keefe. New York: Semiotext(e), 2002, p. 54.

[75] "What is more enigmatic: that beings are, or that Being is? Or does even this reflection fail to bring us close to that enigma which has occurred with the Being of beings?" Heidegger, Martin. *Existentialism*, 1946 appears at www.thecry.com: http://www.thecry.com/existentialism/heidegger/existence.html

[76] Nietzsche, Friedrich. *The Will to Power*. Trans. Walter Kaufmann. New York: Random House, 1968, p. 44.

but none of them having authority. In his text, *Impossible Exchange*, Jean Baudrillard describes how we are "free electrons," and "the modern individual" is "a victim of his own will."[77] He asks, "who cares about bad faith today,"[78] especially when the ability to "disobey oneself marks the highest freedom"[79] and that "leaving intelligence to machines is relinquishing responsibility?"[80] He also critiques post-modernism as "expressing what has no desire to be expressed, forcibly exhuming the only things which ensure the continuity of the Nothing."[81] Thought at the close of the 20th century was "indulging more in the spectacle of thought than thought itself"[82] thus "maintaining the radical uselessness of thought."[83]

The existentialist project has been reabsorbed by collective capitalism; philosophy has declined into theory. "We might say in a schematic, but not inexact way," Badiou writes, "that contemporary philosophy institutes the passage from a truth-oriented philosophy to a meaning-orientated philosophy."[84] In what is a phase of eschatology, contemporary thought is concerned with our "aspiration to accident,"[85] with scandal, trauma, shame, anxiety, dismemberment and atrocity of meaning.[86] There is an arbitration of vices and virtues.[87]

---

[77] Baudrillard, Jean. *Impossible Exchange*. Trans. Chris Turner. New York: Verso Books, 2001, p. 48.
[78] Ibid. p. 73.
[79] Ibid. p. 60.
[80] Ibid. p. 114.
[81] Ibid. p. 13.
[82] Ibid. p. 115.
[83] Ibid. p. 119.
[84] Badiou, Alain. *Infinite Thought*. Trans. Justin Clemens. New York: Continuum, 2003, p. 46.
[85] Lecture with Jean Baudrillard, European Graduate School, Saas-Fee Switzerland, June 12, 2004.
[86] Topics from lectures and dissertations of the European Graduate School.

Yet globally, the only valid position is a collective concern for all humanity, thus an ethics of mortality dominates world leadership like the United Nations. As Michel Houellebecq writes, "A society governed by pure principles of universal mortality could last until the end of the world."[88] That is the contemporary hope, that humanity is the great meaning.

Bertrand Russell explained, "What the world needs is not dogma but an attitude of scientific inquiry combined with a belief that the torture of millions is not desirable."[89] The value of mortality is anthropocentric, returning us to the basis of many other sources for meaning. With post-deconstruction thinking we invalidate ideology but ultimately allow the discipline of science so to preserve life for anthropocentric value. In many ways, the advocates of an ethics of mortality are regarded as our latter day saints. Since we can no longer institutionalize meaning, we can only recognize those who support the only agreed upon global meaning of life itself, thus the adoption of children from impoverished regions and supporters of human rights make the news, as do those scientists who discover the pill to cure disease or wrinkles and extend life.

We gain understanding of one another with an ethics of mortality and we gain improved technique with science, but understanding and technique are not absolute truth. They are mutable and subject to change. Lacan sought "to investigate the

---

[87] "This time is ours and we cannot live hating ourselves. It has fallen so low only through the excess of virtues as well as through the extent of its vices." Camus, Albert. *The Myth of Sisyphus.* Trans. Justin O'Brien. New York: Vintage International, 1955, p. 192.
[88] Houellebecq, Michel. *Atomized.* Vintage: New York, 2001, p. 37.
[89] Russell, Bertrand. *Why I am Not a Christian.* New York: Simon & Schuster, 1957, p. 206.

status of truth as knowledge"[90] implying truth was only one facet of human reason. But knowledge does not have a direct correlation to what endures. There is the capacity for misunderstanding and the subjectivity of knowledge that oppose the very basis of what is understood as truth, as constant and objective.[91]

Alain Badiou writes: "contemporary philosophy puts the category of truth on trial, and with it the classical figure of philosophy."[92] We call for the end of philosophy and the beginning of thought,[93] releasing us from "thinking about something" to "thinking something." [94] Badiou continues:

> ...the theme of the end, of a drawing close, of an accomplishment. This theme can be articulated in another way: the ideal of truth as it was put forth by classical philosophy has come to its end. For the idea of truth we must substitute the idea of the plurality of meanings. This opposition between the classical ideal

---

[90] Lacan, Jacques. *The Seminar of Jacques Lacan: On Feminine Sexuality, The Limits of Love and Knowledge* (Book XX, Encore 1972-1973), Ed. Jacques-Alain Miller, Trans. Bruce Fink, New York: W. W. Norton & Company, 1998, pp. 107-8.

[91] "It is not so much a question of scientific knowledge. Nor certainly can it be a question of confidence. There are certain things that force your hand." Ronell, Avital. *Crack Wars: Literature, Addiction, Mania.* Lincoln: Univ. of Nebraska Press, 1992, p. 57.

[92] Badiou, Alain. *Infinite Thought.* Trans. Justin Clemens. New York: Continuum, 2003, p. 46.

[93] Arendt describes "Heidegger's contribution to the collapse of metaphysics." Arendt, Hannah and Martin Heidegger. *Letters: 1925-1975.* Ed. Ursula Ludz. Trans. Andrew Shields. New York: Harcourt, Inc., 2004: p. 153.

[94] Arendt explained that "For it is not Heidegger's philosophy but, rather, Heidegger's thinking that has had such a decisive influence on the century of intellectual physiognomy. This thinking has a singularly probing quality that, if one wanted to grasp and trace it in words, lies in the transitive use of the verb 'to think.' Heidegger never thinks 'about' something; he thinks something." Ibid. p. 152.

of truth and the modern theme of polyvalence of meaning is, in my opinion, an essential opposition.[95]

"Decadence wants to do without truth," to depend on relative subjectivity at the vanishing point of meaning. [96] With so many people filling existence with desires, the larger world agencies fixate on death, and the prevention of it. Paul Tillich writes: "We have become a generation of the End...the End is more than all this; it is in us, it has become our every being...it is the end for all finitude which always becomes a lie when it forgets that it is finite and seeks to veil the picture of death."[97] We cannot hide our mortality and while we sanctify the efforts to preserve and extend life, the truth is death for all. Mortality is our only shared truth. What then for thought? Without an ideology, there is simply theory. The abundance of theory from the 1980s through the turn of the century has not advanced the question of truth. Nancy suggests, "Behind us theory, and before us practice."[98]

Diplomacy

There is no doubt that philosophy is ill...Truth is suffering from two illnesses. In my opinion, it is suffering from linguistic relativism, that is, its entanglement in the problematic of the disparity of

[95] Badiou, Alain. *Infinite Thought*. Trans. Justin Clemens. New York: Continuum, 2003, p. 46.
[96] "Unknowing Decadence," by Charles Bernheimer in Constable, Liz and Dennis Denisoff and Matthew Potolosky. *Perennial Decay: On the aesthetics of politics and decadence*. Philadelphia: University of Pennsylvania Press, 1998, p. 62.
[97] Tillich, Paul. *The Essential Tillich*. Ed. F. Forrester Church. New York: Macmillan Publishing Company, 1987, pp. 159-160.
[98] Nancy, Jean-Luc, and Philippe Lacoue-Labarthe. *Retreating the Political*. Ed. Simon Sparks. London: Routledge, 1997, p. 157.

meanings; and it is also suffering from historical pessimism, including about itself.[99]
- Alain Badiou, *Infinite Thought*

Mortality provides shared experience by which to gauge meaning yet mortality is a condition, not the philosophical explanation. Unfortunately the contemporary celebration of the human condition leaves truth as residual. This is where we are today, no longer able to deeply consider truth because we have invalidated absolutes. When asked about the outcome of deconstruction, Jacques Derrida replied, "Unfortunately, I do not feel inspired by any sort of hope which would permit me to presume that my work of deconstruction has a prophetic function...The fact that I declare it 'unfortunate' that I do not personally feel inspired may be a signal that deep down I still hope. It means that I am in fact still looking for something."[100]

If we know that mortality is the only individually experienced and globally shared meaning, then why would we pursue anything more, why would the leader of contemporary thought be "still looking for something." The persistence of desire is the dominant feeling of decadence. We find that "we are surrounded by emptiness but it is an emptiness filled with signs."[101] We occupy a universe of many things that assert meaning. Desire remains unresolved, even after tasting every pleasure. The "what next?" anxiety arrives because one does not know what could possibly be a solution since everything already appears to be

---

[99] Badiou, Alain. *Infinite Thought*. Trans. Justin Clemens. New York: Continuum, 2003, p. 53.
[100] Kearney, Richard. *Dialogues with Contemporary Continental Thinkers: The Phenomenological Heritage*. Manchester: Manchester University Press, 1984, p. 119.
[101] Lefebvre, Henri, *Everyday Life in the Modern World*. Trans. Sacha Rabinovitch. New York: Harper & Row, 1968, p. 135. Reading everything as meaningful is also common to eschatology.

exhausted. Yet if thought is total territory then the lack of or need for "something" that Derrida observes must be something within human thought.

How then do we contend with what Badiou calls our "point of excess" in academia and thought?[102] The struggle we face with the abundance of anthropocentric meaning and lack of truth is however nothing new. Ernest Renan wrote in 1891:

> For us the die is cast: and even should superstition and frivolity, henceforth inseparable auxiliaries, succeed in deadening human conscience for a time, it will be said in the nineteenth century, the century of fear, that there were still men, who, in spite of common contempt, liked to be called men of the other world; men who believed in the truth, who were ardent in its search, in the midst of an age, frivolous because it was without faith and superstitious because it was frivolous.[103]

Over a century has passed since Renan and we find the same marginalization of truth. In our contemporary diplomacy we allow every point of view so that our problem is not *an* absolute but an abundance of absolutes.[104] Richard Dawkins explains: "it has to be admitted that absolutism is far from dead. Indeed, it rules the minds of a great number of people in the world."[105]

---

[102] "It is literally impossible to assign a 'measure' to this superiority in size... We must begin at the beginning, and show that the multiple of the subsets of a set necessarily contains at least one multiple which does not belong to the initial set. We will term this *the theorem of the point of excess*." Badiou, Alain. *Being & Event*. Trans. Oliver Feltham. London: Continuum International Publishing Group, 2005, p. 84.

[103] Renan, Ernest. *The Future of Science*. Boston: Roberts Brothers, 1891, p. 459.

[104] "Evil is the desire for 'Everything-to-be-said." Badiou, Alain. *Infinite Thought*. Trans. Justin Clemens. New York: Continuum, 2003, p. 67.

[105] "Such absolutism nearly always results from strong religious faith, and it constitutes a more reason for suggesting that religion can be a force for evil in

Many hold to the claim of absolute truth, which is not easily reversed once it has been asserted.[106] Dawkins suggests that the absolute is a grave problem and the source of evil. We assert that an absolute undermines freedom and oppresses people, yet we answer to all types of desires and pleasures that limit freedom and oppress. Moshe Halbertal and Avishai Margalit describe the situation of absolute truth and idolatry:

> Granting ultimate value does not necessarily mean attributing a set of metaphysical divine attributes; the act of granting ultimate value involves a life of full devotion and ultimate commitment to something or someone. Absolute value can be conferred upon many things–institutions such as the state, persons, goals, ideologies, and even a football team…What makes something into an absolute is that it is both overriding and demanding. It claims to stand superior to any competing claim, and unlike merely an overriding rule it is also something that provides a program and a cause, thereby demanding dedication and devotion. The falseness of idolatry is that the object of this devotion is not worthy of it. Idolatry in this extension means leading a false life, a life dedicated to an unworthy cause. The opposition between idolatry and proper worship is not between the false and the true god but between the unworthy and the worthy god. It is not easy to draw the exact line between attributing value and

---

the world." Dawkins, Richard. *The God Delusion*. New York: Houghton Mifflin Company, 2006, p. 286.

[106] "That it is the true religion, as it claims, is not an excessive claim, all the more so in that, when the true is examined closely, it's the worst thing that can be said about it. Once one enters into the register of the true, one can no longer exit it." Lacan, Jacques. *The Seminar of Jacques Lacan: On Feminine Sexuality, The Limits of Love and Knowledge* (Book XX, Encore 1972-1973). Ed. Jacques-Alain Miller, Trans. Bruce Fink, New York: W. W. Norton & Company, 1998, pp. 107-8.

conferring absolute value, between being indifferent
and leading a life of total devotion.[107]

Value formation and expression is an undeniable aspect of
existence. We are unable to avoid encounters with value systems
and it is not easy to draw the line between a value and total or
absolute value. At times, subjective values can assert dominance
over entire lifestyles. A 1992 Supreme Court ruling ordained:
"the heart of liberty is to define one's own concept of the
meaning of the universe and of the mystery of human life."[108]
We have personal absolutes to which we answer, and many
minor values, all based upon our own preferences. The result is a
bricolage of meaning and a decadence of values.[109]

In this introduction, I have tried to explain how contemporary
thought is dominated by subjective meaning. Meaning is what
you choose; meaning is your group; meaning is mortality. These
are dominant explanations. But in our postmodern diplomacy
none of them claim to be right, none of them dare suggest they

---

[107] "Idolatry can thus be formulated in a kind of general rule: 'any nonabsolute
value that is made absolute and demands to be the center of dedicated life is
idolatry.' ... Stronger formulations can be extended to include any value: 'any
human value should not be made absolute.' ... If the knowledge of the worthy
God is ultimately channeled through humans, then it cannot itself be made
absolute...What will stand in opposition to idolatry will not be any sense of
absolute but the freedom from absolutes and the denial of ultimates; extension
reaches its extreme limit." Halbertal, Moshe and Avishai Margalit. *Idolatry*.
Trans. Naomi Goldblum. Cambridge, Massachusetts: Harvard University Press.
1992, pp. 245-6.

[108] "At the heart of liberty is the right to define one's own concept of existence,
of meaning, of the universe, and of the mystery of human life." United States
Supreme Court, *Planned Parenthood of Southeastern Pa.* v. *Casey*, 505 U.S. 833
(1992).

[109] "The desire to create new meanings which enables bricolage." Derrida also
wrote that "if one calls *bricolage* the necessity of borrowing one's concepts from
the text of a heritage which is more or less coherent or ruined, it must be said that
every discourse is *bricoleur*." Derrida, Jacques. *Writing and Difference*,
Chicago: University of Chicago Press, p. 285.

are *the* truth. This phenomenon of an avoidance of truth resembles prior eras of decadence. Importantly, this text is not the historical account of decadence from beginning to end. The research presented here attempts to address the early 21st century as dense with subjective values and lacking in the assertion of truth. The text also analyzes media as an extension of values. Media serves as the arena for the arbitration of our anthropocentric desires. A work of media is a performance of thought in which particular values are privileged. The ongoing appearance and disappearance of media represents collective decadence.

We have just witnessed a fantastic prime of development in the last century.[110] We are however still functioning among the ruins of ideologies.[111] For Nietzsche, this means there is a corruption of morals and weakness of will.[112] Decadent values are always overrun by desire and laid bare with nonchalance. They are easy to find, as a decadent is led by desire to the sources of pleasure identified here in chapters on influence, privilege, fortune, leisure, vanity, attraction and others. But there is always in decadence a moment of truth, when excess reaches an end. This is perhaps why the frivolity of decadence hinges upon unveiling death, because it is always an exhaustion of resources to reach an end, in death or truth.

---

[110] "Where centuries come apart, there too gathers the strength." Nancy, Jean-Luc, and Philippe Lacoue-Labarthe. *Retreating the Political*. Ed. Simon Sparks. London: Routledge, 1997, p. 158.
[111] "This time is ours and we cannot live hating ourselves. It has fallen so low only through the excess of virtues as well as through the extent of its vices." Camus, Albert. *The Myth of Sisyphus*. Trans. Justin O'Brien. New York: Vintage International, 1955, p. 192.
[112] Nietzsche, Friedrich. *The Will to Power*. Trans. Walter Kaufmann. New York: Random House, 1968, p. 26.

Approaching the realm of thought includes the ontological and involves a capacity to ask the radical question, "What is *the* truth?"[113] Can we answer to truth without power claims?[114] Do we allow for truth in which we share? We want truth to be something of our own efforts because then we could control it. With the eradication of credible truth, accompanied by the presence of desire, we approach the vanishing point. It means we can see only the immediate present, and we accept it as destiny. This cannot be a relative point, one that allows for a promiscuity of meaning like our current decadence. The vanishing point implies an absolute. It was rejected in painting as dogmatic but it is also a natural phenomenon of visual convergence. It is a crux of the eternal return and the point of our ultimate fascination with being.[115] Yet the aim of thought is not now, or ever, edification. And we may also put aside expectation of discovery. I ask you to look at the existing conditions–to witness decadence, desire and truth. Decadence does not harbor a secret to be taught or remembered–it is the human condition of subjective meaning in finitude and on its own communicates the want for uncondition.

---

[113] Academic dissertation titles include: *Negotiation and Truth* (Harvard Law, 2004), *Knowing What We Can't Believe* (Rhodes University, 2004), *Contingency, Truth, and Tradition* (Princeton University, 2006), *Truth and Moral Discourse* (CUNY, 2006).

[114] "Ontological primacy then amounts, in the final analysis, to truth." Nancy, Jean-Luc. *The Experience of Freedom.* Trans. Bridget McDonald. Stanford: Stanford University Press, 1993, p. 41.

[115] Derrida describes "a dying man reaching the turning moment," and it is this turn that is the vanishing point. Derrida, Jacques. *Dissemination.* Chicago: The University of Chicago Press, 1981, p. 366.

התנוונות

إنْحطاط، إنْحلال

衰微堕落
退廃
퇴폐 소퇴
декадентство
παρακμή
allakäik
çöküş
kemerosotan
hanyatlás
hnignun,
pagrimums
rappio
smukimas
úpadek
úrkynjun
decadentie
decadenza
dekadanse
dekadencja
decadência
decadenţă
décadence
die Dekadenz
decadencia
dekadans
dec·a·dence:
1) the act or process of falling into an inferior condition or state;
deterioration; decay
2) moral degeneration or decay; turpitude
3) unrestrained or excessive self-indulgence
4) the decadent movement in literature

The following text contains aphorisms that can be read in any order. The intention is to formally present the concept of decadence as the "impulse that fragments."[116]

---

[116] There is a "decadent impulse that fragments," Bernheimer, Charles. "Unknowing Decadence," in Constable, Liz and Dennis Denisoff and Matthew Potolosky. *Perennial Decay: On the aesthetics of politics and decadence.* Philadelphia: University of Pennsylvania Press, 1998, p. 62. Jean-Luc Nancy wrote that "philosophical discourse today is a fragmentation of itself." Nancy, Jean-Luc. *The Experience of Freedom.* Trans. Bridget McDonald. Stanford: Stanford University Press, 1993, p. 148.

II. Inheritance

The task and potential greatness of mortals lie in their ability to produce things–works and deeds and words– which would deserve to be and, at least to a degree, are at home in everlastingness, so that through them mortals could find their place in a cosmos where everything is immortal except themselves...by their ability to leave nonperishable traces behind, men, their individual mortality notwithstanding, attain an immortality of their own and prove themselves to be of a "divine" nature. The distinction between man and animal runs right through the human species itself: only the best, who constantly prove themselves to be the best and who "prefer immortal fame to mortal things," are really human; the others, content with whatever pleasures nature will yield them, live and die like animals.
- Hannah Arendt, *The Human Condition.*[117]

[117] Quotations in reference to Heraclitus. Arendt, Hannah. *The Human Condition.* Chicago: The University of Chicago Press, 1958, p. 19.

All Previous Decadence

> To be comprehended: That every kind of decay and
> sickness has continually helped to form overall value
> judgments; that decadence has actually gained
> predominance in the value judgments that have become
> accepted; that we not only have to fight against the
> consequences of all present misery of degeneration, but
> that all *previous* decadence is still residual, i.e.,
> survives. Such a total aberration of mankind from its
> basic instincts, such a total decadence of value
> judgments–that is the question mark par excellence, the
> real riddle that the animal "man" poses for the
> philosopher.
> - Friedrich Nietzsche, *The Will to Power*[118]

1.

From where does decadence first arrive? The term comes from
Latin to describe a loss of vigor.[119] Decadence is normally ⟵
understood as an inverse of beginning, as indulgence to decline
and eventual disappearance. Something loses vitality, strength,
or simply decreases in value. Whenever we are able to locate
decadence, in individuals or collectives, it is often progressed
and seemingly destined to be "a thousand pities all the same."[120]

We recognize decadence afterward, by what is "still residual."
Decadence appears to have been glorious and also self-

---

[118] Nietzsche, Friedrich. *The Will to Power*. Trans. Walter Kaufmann. New York:
Random House, 1968, p. 25.
[119] Gilman, Richard. *Decadence: The strange life of an epithet*. New York:
Farrar, Straus and Giroux, 1979, p. 14.
[120] Huysmans, J.K. *A Rebours*. Trans. Havelock Ellis. New York: Dover, 1969,
p. 70 "Ce serait tout de même dommage, se dit-il, car, an agissant de la sotre." *A
Rebours*. French Edition. France: Fasquelle Éditeurs, 1972, p. 106.

destructive. We can still hear the ringing in the ears or see the after-effects from the great excess. Crab Nebula is 6,000 light years away. We have observed this supernova disaster in the sky for over 200 years. Is the event over? The star has already died, but the light from its explosion is still visible. Even when we can no longer see it from Earth, it will continue past us to a vanishing point in the universe. Decadence is this type of event, a brilliant force of reality and illusion.[121]

2.

Nietzsche chose to address the condition with the French word "décadence," instead of the German "Dekadenz." His word choice, not represented by Walter Kaufman's translation, implies Nietzsche's awareness of the French literary movement that valued superficial artifice and excess.[122] In everyday language, the word "decadence" can imply both excess and decline, that is, something to a great extreme and/or at its last extreme. Decadence then involves a question of the relationship between extravagance and depravity. It is not necessarily a causal relation that all excess necessitates the end but excess depletes resources thus accelerating the end.

3.

A problem in decadence appears to be that one "confuses cause and effect" because "one fails to understand decadence as a

---

[121] "There is a fantastic excess, which comes from the sun or from love, and that energy must be expanded." Baudrillard, Jean. *Paroxysm*. Trans. Chris Turner. New York: Verso Books, 1998, p. 26.

[122] For a complete analysis on Nietzsche's use of the term "decadence" see Bernheimer, Charles. *Decadent Subjects*. Baltimore: The Johns Hopkins University Press, 2002. Bernheimer suggests that Nietzsche looks at the world as spiritually fallen.

physiological condition."[123] Decadence precedes the addictions, precedes the end. According to Nietzsche, it is decadence that causes "vice—the addiction to vice; sickness—sickliness; crime—criminality; celibacy—sterility; hystericism—weakness of the will; alcoholism; pessimism; anarchism; libertinism. The slanderers, underminers, doubters, destroyers."[124] "The 'good' and 'bad' man are merely two types of decadence," explains Nietzsche.[125] Decadence is always sure of itself, whether legalistic or liberated, making particulars into absolutes.

4.

Decadence is evident in society, in every era, lifestyle, media, politics, academia; in every area and strata of wealth or morality there is decadence, rising from human desire. The human condition is an ongoing negotiation of desire.[126] Desire can never be completely resolved because like hunger, it is recurrent. But desire can be satiated by immediate resources, in which we are often far too easily pleased.

5.

The decadent individual can exist on a small budget simply by investing it in expendable waste. The attitude is one of consuming any resources for unchecked self-interest and vanity, for pleasure. The resource of decadence is really immaterial; decadence is in the behavior. So then it is not elaborate quality

---

[123] Nietzsche, Friedrich. *The Will to Power*. Trans. Walter Kaufmann. New York: Random House, 1968, p. 27.

[124] In decadence, explains Nietzsche, "its supposed causes are its consequences." Nietzsche, Friedrich. *The Will to Power*. Trans. Walter Kaufmann. New York: Random House, 1968, p. 25.

[125] Ibid. p. 27.

[126] "The nihilistic movement," explains Nietzsche, "is merely the expression of physiological decadence." Nietzsche terms pessimism as "not a problem but a symptom." Ibid. p. 24.

or quantity of resources, but the gesture of squandering that affirms decadence. Squandering is related to the subjective devaluation of resources. Resources are futile by being out of fashion, outdated, obsolete, or simply not the desired solution. Motivated by a particular whim, one then enjoys a resource as inessential and it is then left without reserves. Decadence is like being stranded on a desert island and pouring out the only drinking water available; this is how we have regarded ontological truth.

6.

Nietzsche wrote: "I understand depravity...in the sense of décadence: my assertion is that values in which mankind at present summarizes its highest desideratum are décadence values."[127] Today, much of the Western world is exempt from survival needs and enacts an augmented survival.[128] The situation is intensified in that democratic capitalism permits and even encourages excess. Augmented survival is emphasis on quantity and quality in styles of living; put another way, our decadence is "decay with style."[129] The decadent values today can be observed in the prized extremes of our lifestyles–*our* pursuits of happiness, *our* privileges, *our* leisure, *our* appearances, *our* luxury, *our* desires; we claim we have a right to them, that we are entitled. We validate them openly, visibly among us, on the surface like cultural decoration, where we last expect to find the crime (though it is on the surface that decadence is most apparent in any other time or place).

---

[127] Nietzsche, Friedrich. *Twilight of the Idols / The Anti Christ*. New York: Penguin Books, 1990, p. 129.
[128] Important concept for Debord who believed that such an idea of augmented survival occurs when the "consumer becomes a consumer of illusion." Debord, Guy. *The Society of the Spectacle*. Trans. Donald Nicholson-Smith. New York: Zone Books, 1994.
[129] Schirmacher, Wolfgang. Private meeting, Fall 2003.

7.

> Don't all these beautiful things run the risk of being
> reduced to a strange mise-en-scène, destined to make
> sacrilege more impure?
> - Georges Bataille, *Visions of Excess*[130]

We can imagine one occupying a state of great excess, of life beyond survival. This is perhaps the result of a gift of a prior generation, as is the state of global abundance today. Comfortably living with augmented survival does not necessitate the decadent gesture of taking those resources in frivolity but it is an opening for it. Decadent frivolity is a force that rests on some knowledge of ultimate futility. The decadent over estimates resources, as if they are infinite, yes, but also he is somehow aware that the resources are ripe in the moment and will expire. Consider a natural state of abundance in an entire field of flowers. In a decadent gesture, one picks all the flowers, and in a few days, the flowers die. Yet if no one picked the flowers, they die anyway. Decadence acts in concert with inevitable decay. When fueled by desire's accelerator, we are inclined to reach the vanishing point, often prematurely, by our own command.[131]

8.

It is not that decadence is without hope but rather that most decadence results from disregarding the next step all together, from sabotaging hope. If we consider thought, we can observe a decadent practice of investing time into avenues of

---

[130] Bataille, Georges. *Visions of Excess: Selected Writings, 1927-1939*. Ed. and Trans. Allan Stoekl. Minneapolis: University of Minnesota Press, 1985, p. 14.
[131] Nancy, Jean-Luc. *The Experience of Freedom*. Trans. Bridget McDonald. Stanford: Stanford University Press, 1993, p. 168.

anthropocentrism. In the 15th century, the Copernican revolution established a platform for doubt of the human awareness of truth. The limit of human reason was reinforced with Cartesian doubt during the 16th century.[132] By the 18th century, the Enlightenment ushered in plurality, leading us into the reign of ideology in the 19th and 20th centuries, until we concluded "truth profane."[133] Humankind gives us the means and end, without a next step. Decadence is a decline that warrants a turnover of values.[134] Anything can mean something but only temporarily in terms of finitude.[135] The exception is truth, because we still allow it some type of infinite potential. Decadence hinges on mortality and must so separate itself from eternal truth.[136]

---

[132] "Cartesian doubt did not simply doubt that human understanding may not be open to every truth or that human vision may not be able to see everything, but that intelligibility to human understanding does not at all constitute a demonstration of truth, just as visibility did not at all constitute proof of reality." Arendt, Hannah. *The Human Condition*. Chicago: The University of Chicago Press, 1958, p. 275.

[133] Feuerbach, Ludwig. *The Essence of Christianity*. Trans. George Eliot. New York: Harper & Brothers Publishers, 1957.

[134] "The ideas of progress and decadence are really two sides of an illusion, then their persistence is an illustration of the power of language and thought to keep the nonexistent in imaginary existence." I disagree that progress is opposed to decadence but rather an ideological form of decadence. Gilman, Richard. *Decadence: The strange life of an epithet*. New York: Farrar, Straus and Giroux, 1979, p. 160.

[135] "Lead as I do, the flown-away virtue back to earth-yes, back to body and life; that it may give the earth its meaning, a human meaning! May your spirit and your virtue serve the meaning of the earth..." Nietzsche, Friedrich. *Thus Spoke Zarathustra: A Book for All and None*. Trans. Walter Kaufman. New York: The Modern Library. 1992, p. 102.

[136] "Decadence wants to do without truth," "Unknowing Decadence," by Charles Bernheimer in Constable, Liz and Dennis Denisoff and Matthew Potolosky, Eds.. *Perennial Decay: On the aesthetics of politics and decadence*. Philadelphia: University of Pennsylvania Press, 1998, p. 62.

9.

Our days on earth are like a shadow, without hope.
- 1 Chronicles 29: 15[137]

In the novel *A Rebours* by J.K. Huysmans, Des Esseintes, a great baron of decadence, "had organized a funeral feast in celebration of the most unmentionable of minor personal calamities," to willfully be the end of the family line.[138] He recites Charles Baudelaire's "L'Ennemi":

Ma jeunesse ne fut qu'un ténébreux orage,
Traversé çà et là par de brillants soleils;
Le tonnerre et la pluie ont fait un tel ravage,
Qu'il reste en mon jardin bien peu de fruits vermeils.

Voilà que j'ai touché l'automne des idées,
Et qu'il faut employer la pelle et les râteaux
Pour rassembler à neuf les terres inondées,
Où l'eau creuse des trous grands comme des tombeaux.[139]

Decadence is being marked for death and thus desiring only all that appears, often precluding whatever is unseen. In this sense, the spectacle is the great contemporary decadence. The spectacle not only affirms all the decadent values but also is the funeral

---

[137] *The Holy Bible*. New International Version. Grand Rapids, Michigan: Zondervan Publishing House, 1996, p. 366.
[138] Huysmans, J.K. *A Rebours*. Trans. Havelock Ellis. New York: Dover, 1969, p. 11.
[139] "My youth has been nothing but a tenebrous storm, Pierced now and then by rays of brilliant sunshine; Thunder and rain have wrought so much havoc, That very few ripe fruits remain in my garden. I have already reached the autumn of the mind, And I must set to work with the spade and the rake, To gather back the inundated soil, In which the rain digs holes as big as graves." Baudelaire, Charles. Trans. William Aggeler, *The Flowers of Evil*. Fresno, CA: Academy Library Guild, 1954, p. 34.

feast of appearances in an elaborate culmination of vanity and pleasure. It offers us elaboration of perceptions, but not escape.[140]

10.

Imagine a world without decadence or decline, a world with a guarantee of absolute infinity. Without condemnation to death, humankind would possess choices with infinite influence. Would this world have infinite honor? Would this world have infinite shame? Or would the world rely upon the eternal return, or constant erasure?[141] We now speak of the eternal return in contemporary thought, so the end is always coming in order for the new beginning. This is our defense of decadence, as essential to rebirth.[142] Yet has our acceptance of decadence and our embrace of novelty replaced the unconditional truth?

Francois Lyotard suggested that humanity was finally free of decadence because we have reached a great moment of technoscience that will protect excellence beyond decay.[143] Lyotard's assumption was founded on a spectacularization of today, a privileging of technoscience above mortality. The production of contemporary technology has revealed considerable obsolescence and includes a grand production of

---

[140] Informed by the counsel of Raymond Zahradnik, Ph.D.
[141] Eternal return or recurrence is a hypothesis that "all things recur eternally." Nietzsche, Friedrich. *Thus Spoke Zarathustra: A Book for All and None*. Trans. Walter Kaufman. New York: The Modern Library. 1992, p. 220.
[142] "The phenomenon of decadence is as necessary as the increase and advance of life: one is in no position to abolish it." Nietzsche, Friedrich. *The Will to Power*. Trans. Walter Kaufmann. New York: Random House, 1968, p. 25.
[143] "But this decline of the 'project of modernity' is not decadence. It is accompanied by the quasi-exponential development of technoscience. Now there is not, and never again will there be a loss or diminution of knowledge and expertise, even if it means destroying humanity." Lyotard, Jean François. *Post-Modern Explained for Children: Correspondence, 1982-85*. Trans. Thomas Pefanis. London: Turnaround, 1992, p. 98.

artifice, as in any other time. Science (not even to mention science fiction entertainment or lifestyle inventions) rises from desire for answers and preserving life. Science involves efforts to give meaning to what we see, to explain what is already often, self-evident. Science does not claim to be truth but rather a means of gathering information, which often stands in for truth until the information is reformed by the next generation. It is never a claim to truth that makes something decadent but rather it is fueling the desire to know, in place of accepting evident truth. This is why gossip is pure decadence, along with history.

Paradise

> Here you stand, close to the first–undecipherable–stone, which is not one, or which–of all those stones, whether petrified by the Medusa, precious or not, that have marked your path–*was*, numerous.
> - Derrida, *Dissemination*[144]

11.

Decadence abides in a paradise of pleasures and the precise location is not specific. Decadence can take place anywhere because it is simply a human condition. But the great, most notable demonstrations of decadence have been associated with places where desire is easily satisfied. Places of intense decadence are places of abundance and expendable resources. There is often collective familiarity with a site of abundance, as in gathering at an oasis. The same practice is evident today in the attraction to economic and cultural centers that suggest an immaterial oasis. To attribute ultimate value to a locale, or to a

---

[144] Derrida, Jacques. *Dissemination*. Chicago: The University of Chicago Press, 1981, p. 358.

moment, for all time, is to "find paradise." As soon as we aspire to another world, a fantasy for the next paradise, we envision utopia.

12.

> On the pedestal these words appear:
> "My name is OZYMANDIAS, King of Kings.
> Look on my works ye Mighty, and despair!"
> Nothing beside remains. Round the decay
> Of that Colossal Wreck, boundless and bare,
> The lone and level sands stretch far away.
> - Percy Bysshe Shelley, "Ozymandias"[145]

If we consider the historic sites of prior decadence, we find what looks like a scene of a crime–vacant locations where so-called decadence may have taken place and now stands in ruins. We only know what it may have looked like because architecture, especially in the territory of luxury and extravagance remains for centuries as lasting evidence. Decadence, in its early state is perceived to be a great pinnacle for humanity and warrants new construction. The famed sites of decadence were achievements in their original moments–Solomon's temple, Louis XIV's Versailles, Franz Joseph's Vienna, Gaudi's Barcelona and others. "Sites of congratulations" describes these expansive sites of honor and celebration. Such excessive style is one of squander that also involves an eventual dissemination of power. The sites of congratulations have a limited life span, because one day the significance will not confer with the new reigning power. Ultimately, there are no witnesses of the end of a decadent era, of the grand sites in their decay, because people disappear at the

---

[145] Bernbaum, Ernest, Ed. *Anthology of Romanticism.* New York, The Ronald Press Company, 1933, p. 869.

vanishing point, in order to dissociate from decline, e.g. Detroit. The sites in late decadence are also distanced from the sovereign authority that does not wish to align with death. Eventually large ruins are given a very public restoration in order that the sovereign power may be aligned with renewal.

13.

A constructed site is valued for sustaining survival but in doing so creates a false sense of permanency. What is the expiration date for architecture? When a site becomes a ruin it is reused by passersby. The skateboarder takes on vacant social space, and shifts the use for leisure. The most decadent gesture of the skater is using empty swimming pools, which are even in their original form *enjoyment without essence*. The extravagant but awkward private vacation homes of decadent modernism–Casa Mila by Antoni Gaudi (1910), Villa Noailles by Robert Mallet-Stevens (1925), Villa Savoye by Le Corbusier (1929), Falling Water by Frank Lloyd Wright (1937), and Casa Malaparte by Adalberto Libera (1937)–became vacant cultural sites within 50 years and are now enjoyed by anonymous visitors. By contrast the extreme "Case Study" houses of Los Angeles are prized for their theatricality, especially John Lautner's Chemosphere house (1960). The uncompromising designs work in a city of stage sets and false fronts.

14.

The transformation of social space during the 20th century was a transformation of structure and values. Henri Lefebvre describes how the overproduction of commercial social space resulted in an abstract space of sprawl:

> Manors, monasteries, cathedrals–these were the strong points anchoring the network of lanes and main roads to

> a landscape transformed by peasant communities.
> ...Capitalism and neo-capitalism have produced
> abstract space, which includes the world of
> commodities, its logic, and its worldwide strategies...
> founded on the vast network of banks, business centers
> and major productive entities, as also on motorways,
> airports and information lattices.[146]

Lefebvre suggests that capitalist ideology generated an abstract network for social space, much like we find in Los Angeles. There are, for example, still cathedrals in the greater Los Angeles area. In Orange County, there is the Crystal Cathedral designed by Philip Johnson. It is not a Catholic cathedral in the formal sense but a large postmodern protestant church, also called a megachurch. The structure is entirely made of one-way glass, creating a large amphitheater complete with dense media systems for broadcasting sermons. The enormous scale accommodates nearly 3,000 people. Yet rather than anchor the community, the Crystal Cathedral is but another site off the Santa Ana freeway, a neighbor to Disneyland, which hosts 39,000 people daily, in an area of 3 million residents. The cathedral then no longer dictates the community but participates, as Lefebvre described, in an abstract territory of mobility that facilitates the fulfillment of various types of desires.

The vast sprawl of social space created in Los Angeles throughout the 20th century indicates a great anticipation for growth that can now also be read as a great decadence. Shopping malls, strip malls, enormous parking lots and sports arenas now stand vacant for their obsolescence or lack of use, some of which are being re-purposed. Echo Park, California for example, was

---

[146] Lefebvre, Henri. *The Production of Space*. Trans. Donald Nicholson Smith. Cambridge: Blackwell Publishers, 1991, p. 53.

founded at the start of the 20th century. The name was originally
a reference to the site's vacancy. It was quickly popularized and
developed by incoming residents from the film industry. By the
middle of the 20th century, Echo Park was dense with mass
produced housing. Los Angeles artist Ed Ruscha, photographed
the area for several of his books, *Some Los Angeles Apartments*
(1965), *Every Building on the Sunset Strip* (1966), and
Thirtyfour Parking Lots (1967). His black and white
photographs captured the modernist social space at the cusp of
its decline. "2206 Echo Park Ave" from *Some Los Angeles
Apartments* shows an apartment building suspended on a
mountainside, to maximize space for overpopulation.[147] The
names of Echo Park apartment complexes seen in Ruscha's
photos are like product labels, selling a California paradise that
was not delivered. Some apartments suggest a high standard of
living as in "Elite," "Rampart Manor." Others refer to foreign
places as in "Algiers," "Fountain Blu," and "Il Pompeii."
"Garden Terrace" at 5947 Carlton Way, has neither gardens nor
terraces. There are also those that suggest the California beach,
over 20 miles away, like "Dolphin," "Lee Tiki," and "Bronson
Tropics." The consistent appearance of the "vacancy" and "now
renting" signs in Ruscha's photos foreshadow the decline of
Echo Park, portrayed thirty years later in *Mi Vida Loca* (1993).
More recently Echo Park has undergone gentrification. The
territory is one example of the resurgence of capitalist demand
for material progress within the abstract space.

---

[147] In 1960, California's density was the greatest in the states and could only be
compared statistically to the populations of Northwestern Europe, the
Mediterranean or Asia. According to Jean Gottman, in 1960 Los Angeles had a
density of 200 inhabitants per square mile. Gottman, *Megalopolis*. Nowood, MA:
The Plimpton Press, 1961, p. 27.

15.

> Empty space is never wasted space. Wasted space is
> any space that has art in it.
> - Andy Warhol, *The Philosophy of Andy Warhol* [148]

The work *The Lightning Field*, (1977) by Walter De Maria
reveals a tension between natural and constructed space. The
natural plot of land measured 1 mile by 1 kilometer has been
strategically installed with a grid of 400 lightning poles. The
project negates the natural vacancy of the land as well as
anthropocentric need for agriculture or constructed shelter, in
favor of attracting a lighting show.

Despite a pre-existing natural order, it is constructed space that
usually lays down the law of contemporary living. It is
"supercode." [149] "Space thus acquires symbolic value... space
indeed 'speaks.'" [150] Constructed space determines where we
gather resources, where we sleep, eat, experience pleasure or
pain, power or submission; these are divisions otherwise "poorly
distinguished in nature." [151] When we construct space for art, we
assign a space for decoration, a space for expression and
pleasure, a space authorized for decadence. But when the space
of art is also natural, as in *The Lightning Field*, the work
becomes a dialogue with truth. The abundant lighting asserts that
nature overdetermines human efforts, not only by commanding
space but also in performing.

---

[148] Warhol, Andy. *The Philosophy of Andy Warhol*. New York: Harcourt Brace &
Company, 1975, p. 143.
[149] Lefebvre, Henri. *The Production of Space*. Trans. Donald Nicholson Smith.
Cambridge: Blackwell Publishers, 1991, p. 17.
[150] Ibid. p. 141-142.
[151] Ibid. p. 137.

16.

Is the commodification of architecture on a monumental scale a doomed ruin?[152] Eero Saarinen's monumental airport terminal at New York City's John F. Kennedy Airport was constructed in 1962 for the corporation Trans World Airlines. The site was abandoned in 2001 when TWA went out of business. The structure stood as a vacant temple to modernism. In 2004, I curated an art exhibition, including 19 artists from 10 countries, installed throughout the vacant airport terminal.[153] The exhibition opened to the public but because of a security incident involving a public guest, the exhibition and terminal were immediately closed. The intervention with the modern landmark confronts the legacy of modernism and addressed the question of re-use as to the relevance of modernity. Art and architecture also contend with a sovereign power. Does an airport, a highly guarded access point, always control constructed space with the demand of function over form? How are art and architecture relevant to the points of entry? Art and architecture often elaborate socially constructed boundaries but they do not determine or control them. The artist and architect take part in an arbitration of power–not only with a site, but also with ideas, aesthetics and importantly, the systems that sanction liberty itself.

17.

Men of Athens! I see that in every way you are very religious. For as I walked around and looked carefully at your objects of worship, I even found an altar with

---

[152] "Monumentality, for instance, always embodies and imposes a clearly intelligible message…monumental buildings mask the will to power and arbitrariness of power beneath signs and surfaces which claim to express collective will and collective thought." Ibid. p. 143.
[153] www.terminalfive.com

this inscription: TO AN UNKNOWN GOD. Now what
you worship as something unknown I am going to
proclaim to you.
- Acts 17: 22-23[154]

What is the ethical role for architecture in relation to ideology
and false consciousness? The decadent sites of congratulations
evidence the "truth" of performance based ideologies. Yet isn't
the construction of any territory an altar to some value? This is
why a book or film is also an ideological site of congratulations.
But any site of congratulations is temporal as it is only ever
worth anything within the moment of achievement, within the
ideology, and its closed value set. The construction of
monumental spaces in support of a collective with "universal"
constituents can serve to reinforce the community, making
"truth" visible.[155]

18.
The overproduction of theory has been an effort to extend
ideological territories such as Marxism. What began as an effort
to dispel the opium, is the opium. The same kind of territorial
expansion is seen in branding. A business uses a logo to claim
both physical and ideological territory. We also see personal
brand expansion with celebrity products. In the past, a celebrity
would endorse a product, thus expanding the territory of a brand
and gaining valued association. Now products can endorse
celebrities and expand celebrity brand. Yet, in the gesture of
expansion there is inevitable loss of singularity and an inability
to withhold from varied external influences, e.g. Colonialism.

---

[154] *The Holy Bible*. New International Version. Grand Rapids, Michigan:
Zondervan Publishing House, 1996, p. 937.
[155] Lefebvre, Henri. *The Production of Space*. Trans. Donald Nicholson-Smith.
Cambridge: Blackwell Publishers, 1991, p. 143.

19.

Walter Benjamin's *Arcades Project* has been called a "monumental ruin."[156] His analysis of shopping corridors in France was never completed. The corridors were both throughways and blind alleys. Dead ends are the great symptom of architectural and theoretical decadence. They are evidence of giving up, or continuing hopes that meet real world limitation.

20.

> Far from the marketplace and from fame, happens all
> that is great.
> - Friedrich Nietzsche[157]

There is no requirement that decadence be a grand public show. The black market is a site of decadence because it offers abundance and services desires. But it seeks to be invisible. The life of decadent person has a fictional gaze upon every place, creating one scene of decadence after another.[158] Travel can be used strategically, to always be in motion and avoid ultimate decay. It is the sites of travel that have no status, and are rarely prized as decadent. Yet streets and sidewalks are continually vacated and they have the capacity to appear like a post-apocalyptic wasteland, as in Eugene Atget's photos, and *Bladerunner* (1972). This similarity in the post-decadent ruin and the end times that is evident in media, suggests a greater consciousness and enactment of working toward a dystopic end.

---

[156] Phrase used by the publisher Harvard University Press in various promotional materials.
[157] Nietzsche, Friedrich. *Thus Spoke Zarathustra: A Book for All and None.* Trans. Walter Kaufman. New York: The Modern Library. 1992, p. 53.
[158] Marc Augé describes that "travel constructs a fictional relationship between gaze and landscape." Auge, Marc. *Non-Spaces.* New York: Verso, 1995, p. 86.

This is contrasted by media images of renewal and sustainability.

21.

> We move amongst the ruins of desires, false problems, status symbols, caricatures and monsters, in the purpose of the merchandizing of reality…thus, instead of culture, taste is favored.
> - Superstudio[159]

If we were to invent the most decadent rebellion, it would be a rebellion of style that is never produced. The architects of Superstudio rejected the language and practices of modern commercial architecture and design. They complained that the world is encumbered by excess and in need of more thought and inaction. "What we want to do," explained Superstudio, "is lay the foundations for an existence that is one long protest."[160] The protest involved renouncing the overdetermined wasteland of modernity:

> I did NOT want to find a monumental architecture.
> I did NOT want to find a fashionable architecture.
> I did NOT want to find a *beautiful* architecture.[161]

The original desire was not to find and not to build. But the architects became obsessed with building legacy. They invested their decadent work in an ideology of progress: ideal cities and continuous monuments. They created an atmosphere of the future by making only models of things to come that never were.

---

[159] Lang, Peter and William Menking. *Superstudio: Life Without Objects*. New York: Rizzoli, 2003, p. 168.
[160] Ibid. p. 117.
[161] Ibid. p. 83.

And in the present, they posed, we should live not among old ruins but among our models, or anything else that is a little vessel for hope from the future. "Our problem is to go on producing objects, big brightly colored cumbersome useful and full of surprises... They will exorcise our indifference. Things that can modify time and space and serve as signposts for a life that is going ahead."[162]

The architect, like the poet, artist, filmmaker or fashion designer shines the light onto tomorrow.[163] Like any decadent situation, Superstudio invested in a particular fantasy, a paradise.[164] They wrote for *Vogue* in 1969, "in a period of redundancy and false problems (and furnishing is one of these), every act with a tendency to clarity, and every object made with the instruments of reason, appears as a black stone fallen from the sky into the desert. The only thing to do is search for black stones and polish them for a long time giving them a definite form."[165] This desire is like an apex of decadence–when the truth is a sincere endorsement of surfaces.[166]

22.

In the story of Moses and the burning bush, Moses moved forward without knowledge of the "holy" ground until God

---

[162] "We shall no longer do anything unless for love and in hope and we shall surely die of ingenuity, happy." Ibid. p. 117.
[163] André Breton described they "will surmount the depressing idea of the irreparable divorce between action and dream and hold out the magnificent fruit of the tree." Breton, André. *Communicating Vessels.* Trans. Mary Ann Caws et al. Lincoln: University of Nebraska Press, 1990, p. 146.
[164] "The problem is not to furnish rooms...the problem is to furnish deserts, to awake consciousness from long, dogmatic sleep." Lang, Peter and William Menking. *Superstudio: Life Without Objects.* New York: Rizzoli, 2003, p. 75.
[165] Ibid. p. 77.
[166] Ibid. p. 168.

announced it, and required the removal of shoes.[167] The "sacred" refers back to the original, inaccessible moment. There is an anthropocentric effort to access original truth, as if truth were at a particular location requiring pilgrimage.[168] The effort to get at truth by getting to a place rises from the desire for the moment of truth. The memory of an important event also becomes the memory of the site, consequently making an anonymous location personally meaningful, especially if inhabited regularly.[169]

Más allá del azar y de la muerte
Duran, y cada cual tiene su historia,
Pero todo esto ocurre en esa suerte
De cuarta dimensión, que es la memoria

En ella y sólo en ella están ahora
Los patios y jardines. El pasado
Los guarda en ese circulo vedado
Que a un tiempo abarca el véspero y la aurora.
¿Cómo puede perder aquel preciso
Orden de humildes y queridas cosas,
Inaccesibles hoy como las rosas
Que dio al primer Adán el Paraíso?

El antiguo estupor de la elegía
Me abruma cuando pienso en casa
Y no compendo cómo el tiempo pasa,

---

[167] Exodus 3:5. *The Holy Bible*. New International Version. Grand Rapids, Michigan: Zondervan Publishing House, 1996, p. 49.

[168] "The refusal to meet God at the place where God has come to meet us," is typically human (quoting D. T. Niles) Rutenborn, Guenter. *The Sign of Jonah*. Trans. Bernhard Ohse and Gerhard Elston. Chicago: The Lutheran Student Association of America, 1954, p. 7.

[169] There is potential, described Sigmund Freud, that we "forget rather easily things that have happened only once, and remember more readily things which occur repeatedly." Freud, Sigmund. *The Interpretation of Dreams*. New York: Gramercy Books, p. 1996, p. 31.

Yo, que soy tiempo y sangre y agoniá.
- Jorge Luis Borges, from "Adrogué"[170]

Memorials are designated spaces for memory. The World Trade Center memorial in New York City is a great mark of decadence because even amid the most expensive and profitable commercial real estate we do not need to develop it. We are so successful, so beyond survival, that we do not even need the business. Instead we create a site for memory and honor of fellow humans. The memorial denies the living and tries to keep the dead alive based on the fallacy that the past doesn't go away because you occupy one of its consequences.

23.

I took her hand in mine, and we went out of the ruined place.
- Charles Dickens, *Great Expectations*[171]

Architecture is built to last but determined to decay. We maintain ruins as collective memento mori. But we are a humankind continually fascinated by making new sites amid existing ruins. We continually manufacture more sites all of the time with overarching expectation to be more majestic and then

---

[170] "Far beyond accident and death itself / they endure, each one with its particular story / but all this happens in the strangeness of / that fourth dimension which is memory. / In it and it alone do they exist / the gardens and the patios. The past / retains them in that circular preserve / which at one time embraces dawn and dusk. / How could I have forgotten that precise / order of things both humble and beloved, / today as inaccessible as the roses / revealed to the first Adam in Paradise? / The ancient aura of an elegy / still haunts me when I think about that house– / I do not understand how time can pass, / I who am time and blood and agony." Excerpt from "Adrogué," Borges, Jorge Luis. *Selected Poems*. Ed. Alexander Coleman. New York: Viking Penguin Group, 1999, pp. 134-135.
[171] Dickens, Charles. *Great Expectations*. Oxford: Oxford University Press, 1998, p. 479.

only more tragic. So then, where in the end *is* paradise? Every place is east of Eden, even though every generation asserts itself as the finality, as if the only thing that could follow is the same thing forever, or nothing.

Myth

> When tradition thus becomes master, it does so in such a way that what it "transmits" is made so inaccessible, proximally and for the most part, that it rather becomes concealed. Tradition takes what has come down to us and delivers it over to self-evidence; it blocks our access to those primordial "sources"...and makes us suppose that the necessity of going back to these sources is something which we need not even understand.
> - Heidegger, *Being and Time* [172]

24.

The old proclaims meaning. The old determines what is valuable. The old bestows inheritance. At its most essential form, our inheritance is myth and that myth is transferred by tradition and history. Tradition and history are co-dependent; they refer backward and they aim to continue forward. They are memory and traces of memories, with efforts to continue remembering what has already decayed.

25.

Being taught tradition is like being given a set of weapons and medals from former triumphs. The gift is bestowed like an honor but the elements are now rusted and useless. The protecting and

---

[172] Heidegger, Martin. *Being and Time*. Trans. John Macquarrie & Edward Robinson. New York: Harper & Row Publishers, 1962, p. 43.

passing on material of no survival function is decadent tradition
(e.g. La Chevalière ring). Yet in order for tradition to continue it
requires tangible heirlooms and ritual practice. Tradition also
asks for obedience to form through discipline, consistency and
collective participation. Ritual reinforces a collective in its own
right, and serves as a kind of edification even if the actual
meaning of a tradition is not understood or truly lived. That is
why tradition is so attractive: It can mean absolutely nothing,
which is often the case, and still organize the barbarians.[173]

26.

Ritual obedience to form is often without understanding.[174]
Takashi Homma writes:

> Outward appearance is the mere cloth for an ideal that
> is invisible to the eye but palpable in its
> underpinnings…Thus kings wear celestial garments,
> thunderbolts are hurled by gods, winged words fill the
> air, and promised lands await on other sides of
> mountains. Scriptures, epics, folk tales, games, and
> religion carry on this tradition. No one needs to know
> that hopscotch, jack climbing the bean stalk, going to
> the head of the class, being "kinged" in checkers,
> receiving communion, earning a diploma, and scoring a

---

[173] By contrast it has been argued that tradition or ritual is the complete meaning, specifically in terms of religion. Halbertal and Margalit write "According to such a view (the influence of tradition) the reference to the 'right God' is guaranteed by the tradition, by the shared form of worship, and by the worshipper's intent to worship the God of his father's. The reference to God is fixed and independent of the worshipper's own description; what matters is the proper worship and his participation in a common tradition. According to this view, the problem of idolatry is not the wrong concept of god in the worshipper's mind but the wrong form of worship." and "it is not the object of worship that constitutes the central problem, but the method and nature of worship." Halbertal, Moshe and Avishai Margalit. *Idolatry*. Trans. Naomi Goldblum. Cambridge, Massachusetts: Harvard University Press. 1992, p. 162 & p. 188.

[174] "Only rituals abolish meaning," Baudrillard, Jean. *Seduction*. Trans. Brain Singer. New York: St. Martin's Press, 1990.

goal are all rite of renewal. It is continuity and achievement that are important.[175]

Education often begins with formal obedience emphasized over appreciation of value. Etiquette, for example, is obedience to form often without either understanding of value or permission to act freely. Thought, especially academic thought, has engaged in etiquette of form, rather than a free us of the proper. And like knowing which knife is appropriate for which dish, there is now an accepted truth for one instance and a different truth for another. But just as dining etiquette does not translate to knowing how to use a knife to kill in the wild, postmodern theory and comparative reasoning does not answer to the always already presence of ontology.

27.

The aim of tradition is to establish its ongoing position in this world.[176] In this way we can consider that tradition and history want to occupy the place of truth, of that which was, is and will be. Halbertal and Margalit write "The religious Enlightenment's presumption is that a claim supported by tradition should continue to be held as true as long as there is no proof it is false."[177] Tradition desperately needs collective effort to be maintained because it is not truth.[178] Tradition is a valuable

---

[175] Homma, Takashi, "Tradition," in *Purple*, Issue 2, Winter 1998-1999, p. 207.

[176] "The mortal individual and societies, work to produce the condition for remembrance, that is for history." Arendt, Hannah. *The Human Condition.* Chicago: The University of Chicago Press, 1958, p. 9. Like history, tradition also establishes the law. The law is not the same as the truth but the law is that which we use surrogate truth. Rule is surrogate law.

[177] Halbertal, Moshe and Avishai Margalit. *Idolatry.* Trans. Naomi Goldblum. Cambridge, Massachusetts: Harvard University Press. 1992, p. 118.

[178] "Convention for the Safeguarding of the Intangible Cultural Heritage" An UNESCO initiative, www.unesco.org.

reminder that truth exists, but it limits a free use of the present. Gadamer writes:

> There is one form of authority particularly defended by romanticism, namely tradition. That which has been sanctioned by tradition and custom has an authority that is nameless, and our finite historical being is marked by the fact that the authority of what has been handed down to us-and not just what is clearly grounded-always has a power over our attitudes and behavior...the real force of morals, for example, is based on tradition. They are freely taken over but by no means created by a free insight or grounded on reasons.[179]

Extreme preservation of tradition and history may disable the potentiality or responsiveness of a collective.[180] Halbertal and Margalit write that "people have a tendency to adopt whatever is customary; this is the reason that nomads prefer their difficult life of wandering to living in magnificent palaces. People become blind to the truth and slaves to habit."[181]

---

[179] Gadamer, Hans-Georg. *Truth and Method*. Translation revised by Joel Weinsheimer and Donald G. Marshall New York: Continuum, 1999, p. 280.

[180] Veblen, Thorstein. *The Theory of the Leisure Class*. New York: Dover Publications, 1994, p. 119.

[181] The authors describe tradition as a source of error in thinking about truth, specifically in terms of Alexander of Aphrodisias and Maimonides. "Alexander's three causes (of error) are: the love of power, which distances a person from the truth because he is preoccupied with power struggles and had no time for quiet and truly disinterested contemplation; the difficulty of the achievement, that is, the complexity of the object to be known; and the lack of ability, or the limitations of the knower. In positing a fourth cause, Maimonides considers the fact that people are educated according to the tradition prevailing in their social environment to be an important cause of error. According to Maimonides, people have a tendency to adopt whatever is customary; this is the reason that nomads prefer their difficult life of wandering to living in magnificent palaces. People become blind to the truth and slaves to habit." Halbertal, Moshe and Avishai Margalit. *Idolatry*. Trans. Naomi Goldblum. Cambridge, Massachusetts: Harvard University Press. 1992. 116-117.

Decadence is always a blindness, an inability, willing or not, to see the self in relation to truth, with a limit of free use. The traditionalist or historian is willingly blind to today. For Nietzsche, it was the libertine and the skeptic that were blind. The libertine is free to act but not to think and the skeptic, free to think but not to act. A traditionalist is not free to think or to act.

28.

Tradition is not class or culture specific. It is continued by collectives everywhere with an indebtedness to the ancestors who created it.[182] It is considered an honor and a privilege to participate in tradition, because at its best understanding, it is considered to be a gift of the truth.[183] We uphold traditions, initially in believing their historic accuracy but then they are regarded as truth in itself. There is however, a fallacy that any history, or more so, any collective, constitutes truth. Authors Halbertal and Margalit describe the condition of "double truth" that arises when we submit to dogma:

> The religious Enlightenment's view of the relation between ancient beliefs and superstitions is a complex one that incorporates the idea of "double truth." The meaning we give to the concept of double truth is different from the meaning traditionally associated with it. The doctrine of double truth traditionally refers to the idea that there are two sorts of truth, one philosophical and one religious. The religious intellectual compartmentalizes the two types of truth so that there is

---

[182] "Wealth acquired passively by transmission from ancestors or other antecedents presently becomes even more honorific than wealth acquired by the possessor's own effort." Veblen, Thorstein. *The Theory of the Leisure Class.* New York: Dover Publications, 1994, p. 19.

[183] Honor is that which we take care of not only because it is something outwardly valuable, but, because we believe to know its worth intimately, as *even more* than others speculate and is thus deserving of respect and service.

no relation between them and they cannot engender a contradiction: each truth is correct within its own framework (relativism)...The question is which claim has priority in both practical matters and issues of belief until the apparent contradictions are reconciled...The concept of double truth thus refers to two sorts of truth, but it also refers to two sorts of believers: the intellectuals and the masses. Holding a double truth (as a temporary standpoint) is a privilege of the intellectuals. The masses may only be presented with the truth of the religious tradition, in order to preserve order and social stability. Only the intellectual elite is capable of dealing with the specious contradiction between two sorts of truth.[184]

People may be subject to two virtually opposing truths, one religious and one political, or one traditional and another philosophical. The plurality and relativism arises whenever we allow the tradition and its historical evidence to mean truth, rather than ongoing ontological revelation. Gadamer writes, "The text that is understood historically is forced to abandon its claim to be saying something true."[185] The same idea is addressed by Sam Harris in *The End of Faith*. In passing along tradition, we force the past forward and lose presence.[186]

---

[184] Halbertal, Moshe and Avishai Margalit. *Idolatry*. Trans. Naomi Goldblum. Cambridge, Massachusetts: Harvard University Press. 1992, pp. 119-120.

[185] Gadamer, Hans-Georg. *Truth and Method*. Translation revised by Joel Weinsheimer and Donald G. Marshall. New York: Continuum, 1999, p. 303.

[186] "The idea, therefore, that religious faith is somehow a sacred human convention—distinguished, as it is, both by the extravagance of its claims and by the paucity of it evidence—is really too great a monstrosity to he appreciated in all its glory. Religious faith represents so uncompromising a misuse of the power of our minds that it forms a kind of perverse, cultural singularity—a vanishing point beyond which rational discourse proves impossible. When foisted upon each generation anew, it renders us incapable of realizing just how much of our world has been unnecessarily ceded to a dark and barbarous past." Harris, Sam. *The End of Faith: Religion, Terror, and the Future of Reason*. New York: Norton & Co., 2005, p. 25.

29.

An heirloom is a continuation of value within a family or community.[187] It communicates that a certain standard of life or symbolic meaning is worthwhile. Because there is no monetary value equal to the intangible value of one's family or community, an heirloom is an "impossible exchange."[188] An heirloom also brings with it an expectation of continued stewardship. Our greatest heirloom is history. We have inherited the grand canon and yet our prodigal century has already discounted its value, without agreeing on an alternate reality. We still have history lying around, but we do not want it. That is also how decadence looks, with reminders of old practices, none of which are still used or understood, and yet kept around in their decay.[189]

30.

> History and fashion are both made up of cycles...they
> remain permanent in their dialectical configuration of
> modernity and antiquity–l'esprit moderne in intimate
> contact with l'esprit antique...'Behold,' the young
> guide advised his visitor, 'the attire you are wearing
> does not sufficiently link the past and the present for it
> to conform to tradition.
> - *Un Autre Monde*, 1844

Tradition needs history to stay alive. History is kept alive by re-enacting tradition. But both tradition and history collide with the

---

[187] Veblen, Thorstein. *The Theory of the Leisure Class*. New York: Dover Publications, 1994, p. 79.

[188] Baudrillard, Jean. *Impossible Exchange*. Trans. Chris Turner. New York: Verso Books, 2001.

[189] So it is "rather by excess than rarefaction that we have gradually lost the concept and meaning of history," Baudrillard, Jean. *Paroxysm*. Trans. Chris Turner. New York: Verso Books, 1998, p. 8.

present. The collision does not require giving into the past or giving up to the present, but rather a constant mediation, also inclusive of the unseen next moment. That mediation in thinking is understanding. "Understanding is to be thought of less as a subjective act," writes Gadamer, "than as participating in an event of tradition, a process of transmission in which past and present are constantly mediated."[190]

31.

In a German text from 1879 there was an observation that "the present novelty of facts and the need for diversions has become so decisive that the people's opinion is deprived of the support of a firm historical tradition...the complacent and intellectually lazy mass I supplied with pretext for avoiding the labour of thinking for themselves."[191] This statement, not only still relevant today, assumes that "historical tradition" actually allows thinking for ourselves. People often avoid tradition and history in order to think for themselves but then they acquire the view of the day. A value of tradition and history is to make evident dominant thinking so to recognize thinking for oneself.

32.

Baudrillard wrote, now, "only the false is certain," but rather, after deconstruction, only the false is discussed. We now regard history as both past events and a farce.[192] Yet somehow this does not stop us from letting history keep its throne. We willingly live in history's shadow. The result of knowing the former great

---

[190] Gadamer, Hans-Georg. *Truth and Method.* Translation revised by Joel Weinsheimer and Donald G. Marshall New York: Continuum, 1999, p. 290.

[191] F. von Holtzendorff, *Wesen und Wert der öffentlichen Meinung.* München, 1879, 91f see Habermas, Jürgen. *The Structural Transformation of the Public Sphere.* Cambridge, Massachusetts: The MIT Press, 1989, p. 240.

[192] "History ends in parody" Lecture with Jean Baudrillard, European Graduate School, Saas-Fee Switzerland, June 12, 2004.

valor of history, and living in contemporary civilizations that were established by past action, is that we have nothing to do. This is the second, third, fourth, fifth, sixth, seventh generation of leisure, in which survival has already been won for us. Thus, in passively inheriting augmented survival we have a nonchalance and effortlessness to life. We have lost the ability to fight for ourselves and only know the empty battle cries such as "Just say no," or "Just do it," without knowing truly why or why not.[193]

For those who want to be part of history, this is unfortunate. Kristeva described, "it is going to be very difficult to remain one of the last members of an elite. We are in a period that resembles somewhat the end of the Roman Empire, where the utopia according to which the whole world would be capable of self-interrogation, of self-questioning and of a free life, is in the process of disappearing... There will be few people left who keep a memory of the past and who question this past."[194] To send our times into oblivion is a very popular reading. We are just as human as the Romans, and just as prone to failure, and also writing our own history.[195] Yet we now have instant history,

---

[193] The motivation for the "Just say no" campaign was attractive in that it evoked a spirit of rebellion though blatant tautology similar to religious fanaticism observed in Martin Luther who wrote, "I urge all men to submit!" Luther, Martin. *The Bondage of Will*. Trans. James L. Packer. Grand Rapids, Michigan: Baker Book House Company, 1957, p. 320.

[194] Kristeva, Julia. *Revolt, She Said*. Trans. Brian O'Keefe. New York: Semiotext(e), 2002, p. 114.

[195] "Do we misunderstand what's really going on, is our perception biased, unable to free itself from the ills of authority, anthropocentrism, and logocentrism? This traditional view of the world functions as a useless filter, darkened by truism as well as by scientific knowledge." Schirmacher, Wolfgang. Homo Generator: Media and Postmodern Technology. Ed. G. Bender, T. Duckrey. *Culture on the Brink: Ideologies of Technology*. The New Press. New York, 1994/1999. Quote appears from lecture at http://www.egs.edu/faculty/schirmacher/schirmacher-homo-generator.html.

online news always creating the "latest sacred." If a magazine declares "what's hot" or "what's in" we take the dogma as equal weight to all the old efforts of a revolution. So in contrast to Kristeva, it is easier to be an elite. We are all now self-entitled. Finally, we accept the present as worthy of our utmost attention. Our decadence is utter focus on what appears before us–our performance, our places, our beauty and desires. With media we constantly elaborate the present. In this way our contemporary decadence is like a constant vanishing point of desire because we are always already erasing yesterday with the abundance of information and events of today. But it also means that we have created for ourselves a tradition of the new.

33.

When we grow tired of history, we call for progress.[196]

"The great argument against decadence is that it knows no tomorrow,"[197] yet modern decadence was obsessed with tomorrow, it wanted to be the second coming. If revolution is "I revolt so we are still to come," progress is "I dream and therefore we are still to come." Progress is imagining future inheritance.[198] The fantasy of progress does not break the spell of history but maintains it, because progress wants future history. Oscar Niemeyer explained the spirit, "It's so easy for us Brazilians to take over the world of imagination and fantasy! Our past is a humble one and every option is open to us…It must

[196] "History reproducing itself becomes farce; Farce reproducing itself becomes history," Baudrillard, Jean. *Screened Out*. Trans. Chris Turner. New York: Verso Books, 2002, opening page of book unnumbered.
[197] Bourget, Paul. "Baudelaire and the Decadent Movement." http://www.studiocleo.com/librarie/baudelaire/essaymain.html.
[198] Kristeva, Julia. *Revolt, She Said*. Trans. Brian O'Keefe. New York: Semiotext(e), 2002, p. 42.

be so difficult for you people to innovate, after spending your whole life around monuments! ... We have a different task: to create today the past of tomorrow."[199] We may rebel against the "intellectual furniture"[200] of the old guard but do not reject their desire.

34.

The new element which, in the shape of bravery, prowess, magnanimity, occupies the place of the previous despotic pomp goes through the same cycle of decline and subsidence. And this subsidence, therefore, is not really such; for through all this restless change no advance has been made.
- Hegel, The Philosophy of History[201]

The newest code, the latest fashion negates tradition, usurps it. But we make "no advance," writes Hegel. The twentieth century was a believed paradigm shift from history. "The revelation is a turning point and perhaps even a break with the past," write Halbertal and Margalit, "but at the same time the revelation itself must be transmitted and preserved by tradition."[202] Modernism was a break but also a re-establishment. James Howard Kunstler explains:

In their effort to promote a liberated and classless society, the Modernists and their successors tried to

[199] Niemeyer, Oscar. *The Curves of Time: The Memoirs of Oscar Niemeyer.* London: Phaidon, 2000, p. 128. 129.
[200] Veblen, Thorstein. *The Theory of the Leisure Class.* New York: Dover Publications, 1994, p. 233.
[201] Hegel, Georg Wilhelm Friedrich Hegel. *The Philosophy of History,* in *Half Hours with the Best Thinkers,* Ed. Frank J. Finamore. New York: Gramercy Books, 1999, p. 146.
[202] Halbertal, Moshe and Avishai Margalit. *Idolatry.* Trans. Naomi Goldblum. Cambridge, Massachusetts: Harvard University Press. 1992, p. 117.

stamp out history and tradition, and the meanings associated with them, as embodied in the places where we live and work. They failed to create a social utopia, but they did tremendous damage to the physical setting for civilization. Worshipping the machine and industrial methods as ends in themselves, they became the servants of an economy that plundered the future in order to power the engines of production and consumption for the present. This is the essence of the hubris that tries to destroy history: Yesterday's tomorrow turns out to be no future at all. And this destructive, futureless economy is precisely the predicament in which America finds itself today.[203]

This dark perspective does not consider that we can now speak of outdated fear, of what is no longer a threat in disease or the elements. But in each generation, we appear to replace more than advance. We update values, repositioning truth in terms of the contemporary self.

35.

We commonly believe that history is what came first, though Baudrillard expressed, "people first have a destiny, then a history."[204] Baudrillard explains:

The world, if we take it as we find it, has no history. It has, at best, a destiny, but how are we to know what that is? ... History is a kind of luxury Western societies have afforded themselves. It's their history. The fact that it seems to be disappearing is unfortunate for us,

---

[203] Kunstler, James Howard. *The Geography of Nowhere*. New York: Simon & Schuster, 1993, p. 84.
[204] Baudrillard, Jean. *Paroxysm*. Trans. Chris Turner. New York: Verso Books, 1998, p. 21

but it allows destiny, which has always been the lot of other cultures, to take over...[205]

We are a product of and party to the destiny of humankind. We know that the past was "theirs" and we have made the future exclusively ours.[206] Like Des Esseintes self-proclaimed funeral of impotency, we can do whatever we want with our inheritance. This is the most dominant American decadence, not that we occupy too many abandoned shopping plazas of modernity, but that we do nothing with it, we take the resources and service desires of the most ordinary type. If we reject our inheritance in total, our traditions and history, we have decadently squandered them before considering what they contain. James Howard Kunstler spoke about how to contend with a history of America. He wrote that "Finally, we arrive at the recognition that civilization needs an honorable dwelling place, and that the conditions of making that place ought to depend on what is most honorable in our nature: on love, hope, generosity, and aspiration."[207] Through values of the condition we come to understand what survives history and thus where to invest our best interests.

36.
The aristocratic eras prize influence above all things; the bourgeois eras mediate influence. What is influence but residual power? What is residual power but lingering decay that is eventually nothing but hollow charcoal, burning out and collapsing at a touch. But to know of previous power is to be

---

[205] Ibid. p. 21.
[206] The State of South Dakota has the motto "Own Your Future." The company John Hancock has the motto "The future is yours." There are many businesses that "sell" your future from education and career planning, to fitness, to finances.
[207] Kunstler, James Howard. *Home from Nowhere.* New York: Simon & Schuster, 1996, p. 20.

influenced. Are we ever free from influence, from the shadow of
"before"? The turnover of power, throughout time, has been a
struggle to occupy one throne, the seat of eternal influence.
Rather than desiring eternity, we desire our own influence *as*
eternal end. Like every prior generation, we continue to cast our
shadow outward, forward, extending our reign as far as Byron's
description of the night: "the rivers, lakes and oceans all stood
still ...and the clouds perish'd...—She was the universe;" even
darkness wanted to be queen of the world forever.[208]

37.

In *Russian Ark* (2002) by Aleksandr Sokurov, Russia's history is
told from the eyes of an ordinary "unknown" man. The man tells
the story of Russia via generalized events from history. The film
is characteristic of the current democratic post-deconstruction
era in which history is suspect unless it uses a powerless eye on
power.

---

[208] Byron, Lord. *Selected Poems*. New York: Gramercy Books, 1994: 64.

III. Privilege

After their dance as Homecoming King and Queen, Trip had ushered Lux though the knot of applauding subjects...Lux was still wearing the Miss America tiara Mr. Durid had placed on her head. They both bore royal ribbons across their chests.

"What do we do now?" Lux had asked.

"Whatever we want."

"I mean as King and Queen. Do we have to do something?"

"This is it. We danced. We got ribbons. It only lasts for tonight."
- Jeffery Eugenides, *The Virgin Suicides* [209]

---

[209] Eugenides, Jeffery. *The Virgin Suicides*. New York: Warner Books, 1993, pp. 137-138.

Birthright

> *KOFMAN*: What philosopher could or would be your mother?
> *DERRIDA*: I could never have a philosopher for a mother.
> *KOFMAN*: Who could then be the heir to deconstruction, the impossible mother?
> *DERRIDA*: It's 'me,' Derrida himself, but no... It must be 'my son,' the inheritor of deconstruction who continues to interrogate texts and textuality, then in the final slippage the philosopher-mother 'will be,' when she arrives, Derrida's 'grand-daughter,' 'a woman who thinks.'
> - *Derrida*, 2002[210]

38.

Birth is the most respected event.[211] It is the beginning of the assignment of life–to receive a gift of life in a particular moment in time. We commemorate the original event of birth each year with a birthday celebration, yet our actual birth is an event that we cannot consciously recall, an event of which we know nothing.

Artist Sophie Calle organized a series of birthday parties for herself, each year inviting a number of guests to correspond to her age plus one to signify the coming year.[212] The party

---

[210] *Derrida*, 2002, film, http://www.derridathemovie.com/comment-1.html

[211] Lyotard advocated that we maintain fascination and "bear witness to what really matters: the childhood of an encounter, the welcome extended to the marvel that something is happening, the respect of the event. Don't forget you were and are this yourself: the welcome marvel, the respected event." Lyotard, Jean-François. *The Postmodern Explained to Children: Correspondence 1982-1985*. Trans. Thomas Pefanis. London: Turnaround, 1992, p. 112.

[212] Sophie Calle, *The Birthday Ceremony* created between 1980-1993 and presented in 1998 at the Tate Modern.

memorabilia was then later displayed as art objects. The birthday project signifies that the only guarantee of birth is like the only guarantee of a delusion–we need others to verify our claim. Being told "happy birthday" is a reminder that we exist, because others acknowledge it. Then, we desire some type of souvenir each year, in order to remember our most significant life event, of which we have no memory. Our own births then are *remembered for us* by others and in objects. This is one of the first understandings we have of truth, the very singularity of truth. Truth then is what is conferred by others and by things.

The birthday may also be the introduction to decadence because a birthday is a site of both decoration and decline. The decadence of the birthday party is an excessive covering over finitude all while finitude is the centerpiece. In the phenomenon of a birthday celebration, it is not actually the singular individual that alone warrants collective celebration but rather *all life* is the essence of birthday parties. They align with renewal and the eternal return more than the specific individual or particular date.

39.

Birth is to begin powerless, dependent upon pre-existing elements. To be born is to immediately yearn for physiological needs, as well as emotional security and identity expression.[213] "Birthright" however is to be born into pre-existing advantages, to be instantly entitled to benefits and recognized by others. To be born an heir, for example, is to begin with rights to power or

---

[213] These needs are a small number of those identified by Abraham Maslow as part of a healthy becoming to increasing appreciation of "truth, goodness and beauty." Maslow, Abraham. *Toward a Psychology of Being.* New York: Van Nostrand Reinhold, 1968, p. 172.

estate; it is to have pre-ordained status, parlayed for a lifetime of privileges.[214]

The United Nations has identified the core "Human Rights" that begin at birth, and thus are birthrights.[215] The rights include not only security and equality before the law, but the right to education and leisure, all given with freedom.[216] The contemporary birthright par excellence is freedom and with it comes the grave measure of how to use unlimited liberty. The great danger is that we consider ourselves born free thus we know nothing of creating freedom and are the only ones who have the right to take it away from ourselves.[217]

40.
A birthright, like any resource in decadence, can be squandered and thus today we squander our freedom. Writers may acknowledge that "the free use of what is one's own is the most difficult," but most individuals express a "born free" attitude that uses freedom to fulfill desire.[218] And "pushed to the end of its

---

[214] In the public obituary of Nathan Mayer Rothschild, founding father of the British Rothschild family, it was written, "His resources always enabled him to make requisite advances, while it was his influence and perseverance afterwards that uniformly enabled him to recover the money which had been advanced." Rothschild, Lord. *The Shadow of a Great Man*. London: Hand Press Limited, 1991, p. 14.

[215] "One has no right to existence or to work, to say nothing of a right to 'happiness': the individual human being is in precisely the same case as the lowest worm." Nietzsche, Friedrich. *The Will to Power*. Trans. Walter Kaufmann. New York: Random House, 1968, p. 399.

[216] Universal Declaration of Human Rights, 1948.

[217] It gives the "right for man to think of himself as cause of his exalted state." Nietzsche, Friedrich. *The Will to Power*. Trans. Walter Kaufmann. New York: Random House, 1968, p. 162.

[218] Hölderlin, Friedrich. *Essays and Letters on Theory*. Trans. Thomas Pfau. New York: State University of New York Press, 1988, p. 150.

experience freedom would only result in death."[219] Yet the ultimate squander of freedom is a promiscuous use of time, failing to acknowledge potential in the undemanding time of youth.

41.

> The lands bestowed on the veterans, of free reward of their valor, were henceforth granted under a condition which contains the first rudiments of the feudal tenures; that their sons who succeeded to the inheritance should devote themselves to the profession of arms as soon as they attained the age of manhood; and their cowardly refusal was punished by the loss of honor, fortune, or even life.
> - Edward Gibbon, *The Decline and Fall of the Roman Empire*[220]

Birthright is a gift and obligation. Unfortunately our freedom often becomes irresponsibly misunderstood as "free from consequence," or "free from harm," and most often "free from losing freedom." Birthright is however not given for one's own end but only for the continuation of the right to the following generation. Birthright is bestowed passively, but with expectation on the recipient. Today, all are passive heirs to freedom, but the expectation is what the recipient expects to get with the right to freedom, namely wealth and fame.

---

[219] Nancy, Jean-Luc. *The Experience of Freedom*. Trans. Bridget McDonald. Stanford: Stanford University Press, 1993, p. 168.
[220] Gibbon, Edward. *The Decline and Fall of the Roman Empire*. New York: Random House, 2003, p. 337.

42.

Freedom has no need to be named. By naming "freedom" we then create something that we feel *must* be used and sustained: "Nur der vierdient sich Freiheit wie das Leben, der täglich sie erobern muss."[221] We feel, perhaps because of its intangibility, and lack of existence in fact, that freedom could escape us. So we proclaim and reclaim freedom, though we are conquering what we already possess. This is the dilemma of postmodern democracy, everything is free, everything is available. Contemporary man has no mêlée, but yet we take the stance of a voracious revolutionary with a long list of demands.

43.

If there were such a thing as an economy of liberty, then a birthright of freedom would be a rare honor. By contrast, we assume freedom is endless, and thus available to anyone, ready for the taking. Yet if the concept of freedom is based upon freedom as endless, then perhaps we underestimate the potential of freedom; perhaps in fact we are not yet free. Alain Badiou writes: "this world already decrees itself free... our world, standardizes and commercializes the stakes of such freedom....it does not guarantee us free use of this freedom, since such use is in reality already coded, orientated and channeled by the infinite glitter of merchandise."[222] We are free to buy but not free to live without buying. We know freedom for wants, but not from wants.[223] What we employ is a limited freedom, with only a limited number of uses. Nietzsche wrote:

---

[221] "He only earns his freedom and existence who daily conquers them anew." Von Goethe, Johann Wolfgang. *Faust.* New York: Anchor, 1962, p. 241.
[222] Badiou, Alain. *Infinite Thought.* Trans. Justin Clemens. New York: Continuum, 2003, p. 40.
[223] "This freedom from wants is only a metaphysical idea...the need for worship is supposed to exist only on one side, the subjective side." Feuerbach, Ludwig.

You are not free. You still *search* for freedom. You are
worn from your search and over-awake. You aspire to
the free heights, your soul thirsts for the stars. But your
wicked instincts, too, thirst for freedom. Your wild
dogs want freedom; they bark with joy in their cellar
when your spirit plans to open all prisons. To me you
are still a prisoner who is plotting his freedom: alas, in
such prisoners the soul becomes clever, but also
deceitful and bad...[224]

Desire pushes to employ freedom for the fulfillment of pleasure,
rather than the fulfillment of other things. We consistently use
our freedom as entitlement to pleasure–this is not freedom but
being bound to pleasure, the vices of pleasure.

44.

History is the sphere in which man *determines himself*
in freedom. And history, at the same time, is the sphere
in which man *is determined* by fate against his freedom.
Very often the creation of his freedom are the tools
used by fate against him.
- Paul Tillich[225]

It is no longer fashionable to privilege the concept of human
freedom because it was the top of the global agenda during the
20th century. As a result, we don't witness many struggles for
physical freedom anymore, as much as demand for particular

The Essence of Christianity. Trans. George Eliot. New York: Harper & Brothers
Publishers, 1957, p. 273.
[224] Nietzsche, Friedrich. *Thus Spoke Zarathustra*: A Book for All and None.
Trans. Walter Kaufman. New York: The Modern Library. 1992, p. 43.
[225] Tillich, Paul. *The Essential Tillich*. Ed. F. Forrester Church. New York:
Macmillan Publishing Company, 1987, p. 114.

"freedoms."[226] We also tolerate the abuse of freedom, especially in freedom from consequence. We commonly consider ourselves free, explains Nancy, to the limit only of "destiny and sovereignty."[227] This is an essential thrust for decadence, a charge to interrupt the world until it stops us. It is not a "state of exception," but rather "state of exemption" that applies at all times.[228] Free to destroy, free to abuse, free to waste freedom–all only minor offenses. It is when humankind is forced to answer to the law or a serious consequence that we have grievance, and occasionally evoke ancient chants from the cult of the Eagle: "live free or die," and "give me liberty or give me death." This is the great American ultimatum, opposing the typical cry heard on other colonies: "make us your slaves but just don't kill us."

45.

What of our capacity to use freedom for "greatness?"[229] It is when we are not bound to serving freedom that we are free? The authority of freedom is over choice. This is how we move away from appreciation of freedom in itself to our value of performance. Freedom is anyone's, thus "greatness" is in the individual who uses freedom for the best choices. This is why we love celebrities because they signify good use of freedom in the open call of entertainment. But evaluation of a good use of

---

[226] "All those who are struggling for freedom today are ultimately fighting for beauty." Camus, Albert. *The Myth of Sisyphus*. Trans. Justin O'Brien. New York: Vintage International, 1955, p. 192.

[227] "The sites where freedom obstinately renounces itself." Nancy, Jean-Luc. *The Experience of Freedom*. Trans. Bridget McDonald. Stanford: Stanford University Press, 1993, p. 166.

[228] The challenge to Agamben's 'state is exception' is that we are already operating *exempt* from restrictions. Agamben, Giorgio. *State of Exception*. Trans. Kevin Attell. Chicago: The University of Chicago Press, 2005.

[229] "Freedom of the will is supposed to be essential to moral agency, virtue and vice, reward and punishment, praise and blame." Opening title assertion. Edwards, The Rev. Jonathan. *Freedom of the Will*. Morgan, Pennsylvania: Soli Deo Gloria Publications, 1996.

freedom is always a backwards analysis of time. If we do not look backward, we will look forward to use freedom for anything but death.[230]

46.

> Now there was a man of the Pharisees named Nicodemas, a member of the Jewish ruling council. He came to Jesus at night and said, "Rabbi, we know you are a teacher who has come from God. For no one could perform the miraculous signs you are doing if God were not with him." In reply, Jesus declared, "I tell you the truth, no one can see the kingdom of God unless he is born again." "How can a man be born when he is old," Nicodemas asked..." Jesus answered, "I tell you the truth, no one can enter the kingdom of God unless he is born of water and the Spirit. Flesh gives birth to flesh, but the Spirit gives birth to spirit. You should not be surprised at my saying, 'You must be born again.'"
> - John 3:1-7[231]

In Christianity, birthright is in second coming of the self. A legal birthright is only as good as the government or legal entity that acknowledges it. And despite all contemporary global rights to freedom, the body dies. The promise of Christianity is a second birthright into eternity, above and beyond temporal law. The eternal birthright is through the water and spirit, interpreted as baptism. Any renewal, and especially one that claims eternity, is the opposing force to decadence. Renewal suggests that something is stronger than the will to depravity.

---

[230] Heidegger, Martin. *Being and Time.* Trans. John Macquarrie & Edward Robinson. New York: Harper & Row Publishers, 1962, p. 302.
[231] *The Holy Bible.* New International Version. Grand Rapids, Michigan: Zondervan Publishing House, 1996, p. 780.

Possibility

> He was young now as he would never be again, and
> more triumphant than death.
> - F. Scott Fitzgerald, *The Beautiful and Damned*[232]

47.

Youth is synonymous with possibility. In old age we assume that possibility has been foreclosed, but that denies that possibility is an always-present agency. Possibility arises through circumstance, with recognition and action, and it is a resource with great responsibility. Possibility is perhaps the greatest asset at risk in decadence.[233] Decadence is normally blind to the "necessary connection of all events," meaning possibility is simply expendable without much consideration.[234]

But one can become entangled in possibility. In essence, possibility allows that anything is possible, or "everything is possible," writes Kierkegaard, but

> for this reason, it is possible to become lost in
> possibility in all sorts of ways...Legends and fairy tales
> tell of the knight who suddenly sees a rare bird and
> chases after it, because it seems at first to be very close;

---

[232] Fitzgerald, F. Scott. *The Beautiful and Damned*. New York: The Modern Library, 2002, p. 107.

[233] Jacques Barzun describes socio-economic decadence as "a very active time, full of deep concerns but peculiarly restless, for it sees no clear lines of advance. The loss it faces is that of possibility. The forms of art as of life seem exhausted, the stages of development have been run through. Institutions function painfully. Repetition and frustration are the intolerable result. Boredom and fatigue are great historical forces." Barzun, Jacques. *From Dawn to Decadence*. New York: Harper Collins, 2000, p. xvi.

[234] Edwards, The Rev. Jonathan. *Freedom of the Will*. Morgan, Pennsylvania: Soli Deo Gloria Publications, 1996, p. 311.

but it flies again, and when night comes, he finds
himself separated from his companions and lost in the
wilderness where he now is. So it is also with desire's
possibility. Instead of taking the possibility back to
necessity, he chases after possibility.[235]

Possibility could then become a decadent end itself, as in the
decadent opportunist. Opportunism is the obsession with
possibility for personal advancement and is a core force of
decadence. So, while the basis of decadence is desire, we can see
a co-dependency in desire and possibility because together they
result in relentlessly exchanging the present for the next best
thing.

48.

> It is thought that there is a certain age that is especially
> rich in hope, or we say that a certain time, at a
> particular moment of life one is or was so rich in hope
> and possibility. All this, however, is merely a human
> manner of speaking that does not get at the truth.
> - Søren Kierkegaard, *The Sickness Unto Death*[236]

Existence is an ongoing relation to need, to resolve need
definitively, yet never. But if need alone were the basis of
decadence it would not look so majestic.[237] We associate
necessity with nature and possibility with choice and also

---

[235] Kierkegaard, Søren. *The Sickness Unto Death*. Trans. Howard Hong and Edna
Hong. Princeton: Princeton University Press, 1980, p. 37.
[236] Ibid. p. 38.
[237] Heidegger explained that "the whole world seems to agree that only what is
necessary can be meaningful. I consider such a position pathetic." Arendt,
Hannah and Martin Heidegger. *Letters: 1925-1975*. Ed. Ursula Ludz. Trans.
Andrew Shields. New York: Harcourt, Inc., 2004: p. 136.

improvement.[238] A defining moment is when necessity and possibility meet, especially when possibility is read as opportunity. For Kierkegaard there is a continual meeting of necessity and possibility in being.[239] The individual can expect that necessity will always re-appear and that there is always possibility in being.[240]

Kierkegaard tells a story of possibility to a poor old man and woman.[241] One day a woman was going to the hearth and found a valuable gemstone. She showed it to her husband and they realized they were rich for the remainder of their lives. They decided to wait a day to sell it. That night the woman dreamt that she was in the after-life and was given a tour. She saw her very own throne but on top of the throne there was a missing gemstone. She asked the tour guide who said, "that was the precious stone you found on the hearth. You received it in advance, and so it cannot be inserted again." The next day, the woman returned the stone to the hearth and left it there. Is the only way to prosperity to remain poor today, to have less than

---

[238] This is in part because if we say we are "naturally unable to do a thing," it is because "we cannot do it if we will." Edwards, The Rev. Jonathan. *Freedom of the Will*. Morgan, Pennsylvania: Soli Deo Gloria Publications, 1996, p. 26 and p. 28.

[239] "Possibility and necessity are equally essential to becoming…just as finitude is the limiting constraint in relation to infinitude, so also necessity is the constraint in relation to possibility." Kierkegaard, Søren. *The Sickness Unto Death*. Trans. Howard Hong and Edna Hong. Princeton: Princeton University Press, 1980, p. 35.

[240] Heidegger explains that "Possibility, as an existentiale, does not signify a free floating potentiality-for-Being in the sense of the 'liberty of indifference.' In every case Dasein, as essentially having a state-of-mind, has already got itself into definite possibilities…Dasein is the possibility of Being-free *for* its own most potentiality-for-Being. Its Being possible is transparent to itself in different possible ways and degrees." Heidegger, Martin. *Being and Time*. Trans. John Macquarrie & Edward Robinson. New York: Harper & Row Publishers, 1962, p. 183.

[241] Kierkegaard, Søren. *Attack Upon "Christendom."* Trans. Walter Lowrie. Princeton: Princeton University press, 1944, p. 246-247.

we will tomorrow? Perhaps it is the desire for increased prosperity that denies present worth? The future, on earth or heaven, is always the hope of the poor who often sacrifice their present conditions for some future potential. Life cannot be looked forward to or else it is looked forward to as an indefinite vanishing point.

49.

Kant explained that "All desire contains (doubtful or certain) anticipation of what is possible."[242] We desire what seems possible, just beyond our reach. But when something is prevented from us we find that it "frustrates endeavor or desire."[243] Any sense of "impossibility" will fuel desire into need. We now say something is necessary, not to mean it is naturally needed to survive but just to mean it "must" happen out of our own will and want.[244] As Richard Wagner described, "I must have brilliance and beauty and light. The world owes me what I need."[245] The self-entitled attitude occurs when "taste throws a veil over physical necessity."[246] The French *necessaire*, a box for traveling with fine liquor, is the example par excellence. The entire basis of capitalist democracy is making privileges into necessities while negating essential needs. Kierkegaard describes the risk of one for which "everything has

---

[242] Kant, Immanuel. *Anthropology from a Pragmatic Point of View*. Trans. by Victor Lyle Dowdell, *Carbondale, IL:* Southern Illinois University Press, 1978, p. 77.

[243] Edwards, The Rev. Jonathan. *Freedom of the Will*. Morgan, Pennsylvania: Soli Deo Gloria Publications, 1996, p. 16.

[244] Ibid. pp. 15 - 16.

[245] Offit, C. "Patriotic music." *Concord Review*, Spring 2005, p 95.

[246] Von Schiller, J. C. Friedrich. "Letters Upon the Aesthetic Education of Man," in *Literary and Philosophical Essays*. Ed. Charles Eliot. New York: Collier and Son, 1910, p. 312.

become necessity. He is like the king who starved to death because all his food was changed to gold."[247]

50.

> What, then in a word is the "height of our times"? it is not the fullness of time, and yet it feels itself superior to all times past, and beyond all known fullness. It is not easy to formulate the impression that our epoch has of itself; it believes itself more than the rest, and at the same times feels that it is a beginning. What expression shall we find for it? Perhaps this one: superior to other times, inferior to itself. Strong, indeed, and at this same time uncertain of its destiny; proud of its strength and at the same time fearing it.
> - Jose Ortega Y Gasset, *The Revolt of the Masses* [248]

The will to progress thrives on particular strategies that aim to advance humanity beyond historical context.[249] Progress is working to satisfy "higher" needs. Are not higher needs just increasing demands for more power, knowledge, beauty, comfort, pleasure–more? The movements of previous centuries were born out of real potential in technology and illusions in ideology. Today in democratic capitalism, when essential needs are being better met, we not only privilege possibility but "we

---

[247] Kierkegaard, Søren. *The Sickness Unto Death*. Trans. Howard Hong and Edna Hong. Princeton: Princeton University Press, 1980, p. 40.

[248] Ortega Y Gasset, Jose. *The Revolt of the Masses*. Trans. Anonymous. New York: Norton, 1957, p. 36-37. Also: "There has been so much talk of decadence of Europe, that many have come to take it for a fact. Not that they believe in it seriously and on proof, but that they have grown used to take it as true, though they cannot honestly recall having convinced themselves decidedly in the matter at any fixed time." Ibid. p. 132.

[249] Jonathan Edwards writes that it is "in determining itself to a certain choice or preference that the act of the will wherein it is free, and uses its own sovereignty, consists in its causing or determining the change or transition from a state of indifference to a certain preference." Edwards, The Rev. Jonathan. *Freedom of the Will*. Morgan, Pennsylvania: Soli Deo Gloria Publications, 1996, p. 78.

have made the claim to infinite happiness possible."[250] A motto of the French movement in 1968 was "'We're realists, we want the impossible,'... The impossible and more, happiness for all," added Julia Kristeva."[251] The American ideology has made common the freedom we once called a unique privilege. We have subsequently made other privileges into basic rights. Thus we now tolerate rebellion as if it were ordinary behavior, especially in France, because we know there is no satisfaction for the demand for pleasure.[252]

51.

To know of freedom and responsibility causes anxiety in the face of possibility.[253] Yet even if individuals act conservatively in the face of possibility, we socially celebrate those that maximize possibilities to increase wealth, territory and all aspects of life. We also continually want evidence from media that anything is possible to the greatest degree. But "the new" which is constantly churned out by media is not possibility. The new is a surprise, something we either have not seen before or have not seen in a particular context. We appear to have no limit to new combinations. But the new is only ever relevant for us when it fulfills both necessity and possibility–it must meet both terms. The new that does not meet needs is immediately forgotten and the new that has no possibility turns obsolescent.

---

[250] Kristeva, Julia. *Revolt, She Said.* Trans. Brian O'Keefe. New York: Semiotext(e), 2002, p. 35. The mass claim for happiness comes after the mass production which gave everyone some right to ownership and self-satisfaction. The right transformed privilege to need and made taste democratic.
[251] Ibid. p. 13.
[252] Possibility is not the same as desire. Privileging desire for pleasure may limit possibility. Present action "may be will and endeavor against future acts of will," Edwards, The Rev. Jonathan. *Freedom of the Will.* Trans. Brian O'Keefe. Morgan, Pennsylvania: Soli Deo Gloria Publications, 1996, p. 30.
[253] Based loosely on ideas of Kierkegaard, http://www.quodlibet.net/pound-repetition.shtml.

52.

> I don't believe any longer in wonderful things
> happening.
> - Henrik Ibsen, *A Doll's House*.[254]

Possibility contains the option of negation and a "criticism of
the world in the name of its own promises."[255] We may demand
the impossible and find the world unsatisfactory. Such a closure
of possibility is resignation. In *The Beautiful and Damned*,
Gloria explains:

> She became conscious that she was miserable and that
> the tears were rolling down her cheeks. She wondered if
> they were tears of self-pity, and tried resolutely not to
> cry, but this existence without hope, without happiness,
> oppressed her, and she kept shaking her head from side
> to side, her mouth drawn down tremulously in the
> corners, as though she were denying an assertion made
> by someone, somewhere. She did not know that this
> gesture of hers was years older than history, that, for a
> hundred generations of men, intolerable and persistent
> grief has offered that gesture, of denial, of protest, of
> bewilderment, to something more profound, more
> powerful than the God made in the image of man, and
> before which that God, did he exist, would be equally
> impotent. It is a truth set at the heart of tragedy that this
> force never explains, never answers—this force
> intangible as air, more definite than death.[256]

---

[254] Ibsen, Henrik. *A Doll's House*. New York: Dover Publications, 1992, p. 72.
[255] Wording in a question from Philippe Petit. Baudrillard, Jean. *Paroxysm*.
Trans. Chris Turner. New York: Verso Books, 1998, p. 21.
[256] Fitzgerald, F. Scott. *The Beautiful and Damned*. New York: The Modern
Library, 2002, pp. 348-349.

In a state of security, one can read through circumstances and rest in possibility. In despair, one denies hope and overdetermines possibility through a pre-decided failure to act. But to close oneself from aspiration cannot remove possibility. It is possibility that always already overdetermines negation by arriving again.

53.

> But even if I find my way out of the forest
> I shall be left with inconsolable memory
>
> Of the treasure I went into the forest to find
> And never found, and which was not there
> And perhaps is not anywhere? But if not anywhere,
> Why do I feel guilty at not having found it?
> - T.S. Eliot, *The Cocktail Party*[257]

Walter Benjamin wrote of a man who, on his deathbed, told his sons that there was a treasure in the vineyard. After he dies, the sons dig through the vineyard "without finding a trace of the treasure," but according to Benjamin's reading, the lesson was that "blessings are to be sought not in gold but in diligence."[258] By contrast, we could consider that blessings are self-evident. In truth, the father did leave them a treasure in the vineyard; he just did not hide it. He left them land, a treasure for all generations to come. The seeking of something more, particularly of secrets hidden below, or relief of work, is a decadent exaggeration of possibility and desire for more than enough. We already have the

---

[257] Eliot, T.S. *The Cocktail Party*. New York: Harcourt, Brace and Company, 1950, p. 138.
[258] Benjamin, Walter. "Experience and Poverty," *Walter Benjamin: Selected Writings, Vol. 2 1927-1934*. Cambridge: Harvard University Press, 1999, p. 731.

reward we seek, but have grown to love the feeling of possibility and the sound of increasing applause for constant improvements.

Fame

> The tightrope walker, believing that the world concerned him, began his performance.
> - Friedrich Nietzsche, *Thus Spoke Zarathustra*[259]

54.

The self-interest known to every era is made more visible through contemporary media. We make ourselves known online through social networking and websites. But more than a global village it has become a global entitlement to the spotlight. And media is always already ready for the star. This is the time of pre-recorded applause, when everything is pre-approved to try to keep our interest. But given the competition in capitalism we compete for it. We perform for the applause and then bask in fame, however brief. Our grand "era of performance" reveals our decadence.[260] This is not a theater performance, but one that resembles the authentic and strives for the genuine. It aims to look real.

55.

Arbiet Macht Frei
- Auschwitz, Poland[261]

---

[259] Nietzsche, Friedrich. *Thus Spoke Zarathustra: A Book for All and None.* Trans. Walter Kaufman. New York: The Modern Library. 1992, p. 14.
[260] This is specifically in reference to Formula One, Baudrillard, Jean. *Screened Out.* Trans. Chris Turner. New York: Verso Books, 2002, p. 166.
[261] "Work will set you free," the deception on the gates of Auschwitz.

In an increasingly global capitalist democracy, what distinguishes us from one another is how well we use our freedom. This is a widespread misconception that work determines fate, that a great deal of effort will lead to success. This dominant mentality can be summarized in "performance is the signature of truth."[262] So while we assume a human is different from other species because every other animal has been tamed to work for us, we work for one other. We are however given the freedom to choose to become anything. "Our roles are not pre-assigned," writes Miroslav Volf, in terms of bakers and butchers or families of craftsman, which became increasingly rare after industrialization. But "the transmission of excellence" was "one advantage of having a course charted from the start. The other advantage may be freedom from the paralyzing effect of having been faced with multiple choices, unable to discern clearly neither what we are suited for nor what the future holds if we embark on a given path."[263] We start out believing that in an era of competitive performance we can apply ourselves to achieve success and consequently we are later disenchanted if we become entrenched in unpleasant work or an anonymous position. But if "performance is the signature of truth," the consequence of unpleasant work is not only disappointment but a shattering of the self. This is the flaw of work ethic, that your effort determines you, all while your effort is not actually bound to all ensuing consequences. The collective consciousness of success without effort (as in reality TV fame, lotto winners or YouTube) has resulted in mass entitlement. Now it is no longer

---

[262] Schirmacher, Wolfgang. "Homo Generator: Media and Postmodern Technology." Ed. G. Bender, T. Duckrey. *Culture on the Brink: Ideologies of Technology.* The New Press. New York, 1994/1999. Quote appears from lecture at http://www.egs.edu/faculty/schirmacher/schirmacher-homo-generator.html.
[263] Volf, Miroslav. "God at Work," Yale Center for Faith and Culture, http://www.yale.edu/faith/downloads/x_volf_godwork.pdf, p. 9 & p. 10.

possible to argue one must work to be successful. Instant success
is a myth perpetuated by capitalist media.

56.

When society hinges on performance as truth, and we cannot
recognize the worth in our own performance, we look to the
performance of others, which results in glorification and/or
criticism of those in power, such as celebrities. C.S. Lewis
writes:

> I believe in democracy because I believe in the Fall...
> We are so fallen that no person can be trusted with
> unchecked power over others. Aristotle said that some
> people were fit to be slaves but I reject slavery because
> I see none fit to be masters... But still democracy is
> medicine, not food... The mind that hates all superiority
> is stunted... The one who cannot conceive of a joyful
> and loyal obedience on the one hand nor an
> unembarrassed and noble acceptance of that obedience
> on the other, who has never even wanted to kneel or
> bow is a prosaic barbarian. It would be wicked folly to
> restore the old inequalities on the legal or external
> plane. Their proper place is elsewhere... Where we are
> forbidden to honor a king, we honor billionaires,
> athletes or film stars instead. For spiritual nature, like
> bodily nature, will be served. Deny it food and it will
> gobble poison.[264]

The over-valuation of performance not only creates the hunger
for earning our own accolades but also an obsession with
evaluating the performance of others. We judge others and
actually desire to be judged. This is evident in the contemporary
emphasis of reality television competitions and the role of media
in general as an arena for collective performance evaluation.

---

[264] Lewis, C.S. *The Business of Heaven*. New York: Harvest Books, 1984, p. 23.

57.
Reality television consists mostly of competitions in which the total freedom of reality is suspended for a confinement.[265] The limited situation of games demonstrate "the difference between man and man," offering a prize, which at its best is just honor.[266] Performance then substantiates meaning by attempting to showcase values that cannot normally be fixed. We perform for the best beauty or strength for example, but these sources of meaning are always subjectively in flux in the individual. Beauty is an interesting area of performance because it is assumed to have a magical effortlessness to it. Despite all efforts, there is always that which is simply born beautiful. This is also evident in athletics and music where talent is assumed to be not effort but divine "gifts" entitled to fame. But the idea of fame as a reward, that is of designating something worthy of collective attention is not the same as the state of *being famous*.

"Many will say to me on that day, 'Lord, Lord, did we not prophesy in your name, and in your name drive out demons and perform many miracles?' Then I will tell them plainly, 'I never knew you.'"[267] *Being famous* is the ongoing condition of being known by strangers. There is fame in a village and fame in a global village. There is fame from victory and fame from shame. But *being famous* with contemporary media is the result of fame as a fixture in social fabric, sanctioned by governments and the entertainment industry that control image dominance. Those

---

[265] "Everyone is equal before the law...there is no equality before the rule." Baudrillard, Jean. *Seduction*. Trans. Brain Singer. New York: St. Martin's Press, 1990, p. 136.
[266] Kierkegaard, Søren. *The Sickness Unto Death*. Trans. Howard Hong and Edna Hong. Princeton: Princeton University Press, 1980, p. 37.
[267] Matthew 7:22-23, *The Holy Bible*. New International Version. Grand Rapids, Michigan: Zondervan Publishing House, 1996, p. 842.

same entities employ strategic "publicity" [268] that manage fame like an asset.[269]

58.

> He felt that to succeed here the idea of success must grasp and limit his mind. It seemed to him that the essential element in these men at the top was their faith that their affairs were the very core of life.
> - F. Scott Fitzgerald, *The Beautiful and Damned*[270]

Many people pursue personal advancement as edification. The question is if it is possible to be entirely dedicated to work and one's performance and honor essential values of living. What we find is that "we are good as workers but we are bad as people. We are maybe a bit like Albert Speer, Hitler's architect- a great architect involved in a corrupt project and turned out to be an extraordinarily bad person. He worked for Hitler because he was an exceptionally good architect who wanted to succeed. The goals of his profession took precedence over his integrity as a human being."[271]

---

[268] Jürgen Habermas described how Versailles was like a theater performance outside of Paris. "'With Versailles, the royal bedroom develops into the palace's second center... one finds here the bed set up like a stage, placed on a platform, a throne for lying down... where what is most intimate is raised to public importance.' In the etiquette of Louis XIV concentration of the publicity representation at the court attained the high point of refinement." Habermas, Jürgen. *The Structural Transformation of the Public Sphere*. Cambridge, Massachusetts: The MIT Press, 1989, p. 10.

[269] "Publicity loses it critical function in favor of staged display." Ibid. p. 206.

[270] Fitzgerald, F. Scott. *The Beautiful and Damned*, New York: The Modern Library, 2002, p 194.

[271] Volf, Miroslav. "God at Work," Yale Center for Faith & Culture, http://www.yale.edu/faith/downloads/x_volf_godwork.pdf, p. 6.

59.

Alarum. Enter KING RICHARD.
K. RICH. A horse! A horse! My kingdom for a horse!
Cate. Withdraw, my lord; I'll help you to a horse.
K. RICH. Slave! I have set my life upon a cast,
And I will stand the hazard of the die.
I think there be six Richmonds in the field;
Five have I slain to-day, instead of him.—
A horse! A horse! My kingdom for a horse!
- William Shakespeare, *The Tragedy of King Richard
III*, Act V, Scene IV[272]

"My kingdom for a horse" signifies an urgent demand for the
King's survival, willing to sacrifice his whole kingdom to ride
upon a horse. In the 20th century, the American television show
Knots Landing produced an episode called "My Kingdom for a
Horse," in which a valuable racehorse was stolen to extort a
ransom. The plan failed because the horse's owner had insurance
in an amount greater than the required ransom.[273] Victory is now
in the advance strategy.[274] There is also an increasing shift away
from the natural heir (the king does not exist!), to the ordinary
man who simply knows how to perform like one.

Authors Halbertal and Margalit write:

> Augustine analyzed the Roman character as composed
> of two desires, the desire for glory and the desire for
> freedom. The pagan Roman citizen longed for earthly

---

[272] Shakespeare, William. *The Complete Works.* Ed. G. B. Harrison. New York:
Harcourt Brace, 1952, p. 269.
[273] *Knots Landing.* Episode Number: 341, Season Num: 14, First Aired:
Thursday March 4, 1993, Central Broadcasting System (CBS).
[274] And power is now "possessing means of observation and action, having a
choice of response, being less predictable." Virilio, Paul. *Strategy of Deception.*
Trans. Chris Turner. New York: Verso Books, 2000, p. 12.

glory; he aspired to victory and raised military bravery
to the status of supreme virtue. The Christian is
indifferent to such victories; he interprets everything
that occurs to him as an expression of supreme
providence, so it makes no difference to him if he wins
or loses. 'What is the difference, asks Augustine,
between the winners and the loses except for the empty
glory of victory?'... (but then after Nietzsche) The
nobleman who once achieved vitality through the use of
power against his environment, achieves it now by his
war against his own will to power.[275]

We strive for glory and fame via our own effort and ultimately
find our own will is the greatest competition. Our performance is
an expenditure of will and resources into our own finite
existence. The consequence, as with any decadence: exhaustion
and decline. And thus we have become a culture dependent on
performance enhancing, to keep the show going.[276] There is also
the opposite force in contemporary culture, to resist the popular
performance. This is another type of effort, the effort to "be
Zen," to "let go."

60.

Showmen offer a performance of appearances known as
showmanship. It is not a "charlatan" as Derrida described, the
"imitators and masters of illusion,"[277] but one with such a love of
presentation that he is thus mastered *by* illusion. A showman

---

[275] Halbertal, Moshe and Avishai Margalit. *Idolatry.* Trans. Naomi Goldblum.
Cambridge, Massachusetts: Harvard University Press. 1992, p. 248.
[276] "To evoke God's help in critical situations seems to reduce God to a
performance-enhancing drug...so prayer becomes a way of avoiding
responsibility or making up for a lack of it." Volf, Miroslav. "God at Work,"
Yale Center for Faith & Culture,
http://www.yale.edu/faith/downloads/x_volf_godwork.pdf, p. 3.
[277] Derrida, Jacques. *Dissemination.* Chicago: The University of Chicago Press,
1981, p. 138.

finds utmost pleasure in "the space of appearance."[278] Barry Lyndon is a showman who is seduced by the space of aristocracy and the appearance of power.[279] A magician, a musician, and a professional athlete are showmen, seduced by the event.[280] A parade of soldiers who have never been to war is an army of showmen seduced by pageantry. What the showman does is irrelevant, be it good or evil, because it is not the act but the futility of the show that matters.[281]

The showman is always memorable. It is the act of showing, the costume, the vitality, his ongoing engagement in culture that makes his performance so fascinating. Like a hero, he is of value to the individual because he affirms the potential of absurd singularity. He is also of value to the collective because he provides the performance that hypnotizes and thus unifies. The showman can appear at any time in the development of decadence, though he most often appears in prosperity. The showman prefers to arrive after the hero has already saved the day. Thus after Christ we find Paul, after Hegel we have Heidegger.

---

[278] "That precedes all formal constitution of the public realm and the various forms of government." Arendt, Hannah. *The Human Condition*. Chicago: The University of Chicago Press, 1958, p. 199.

[279] *Barry Lyndon*, 1975.

[280] Gadamer writes of athletic performance that, "The player experiences the game as a reality that surpasses him. This is all the more the case where the game is itself 'intended' as such a reality-for instance, the play which appears as *presentation for an audience*." Gadamer, Hans-Georg. *Truth and Method*. Translation revised by Joel Weinsheimer and Donald G. Marshall New York: Continuum, 1999, p. 109.

[281] "The 'good' and 'bad' man are merely two types of decadence." Nietzsche, Friedrich. *The Will to Power*. Trans. Walter Kaufmann. New York: Random House, 1968, p. 26.

61.

> We'll do newness, like airport construction, but we'll
> also do decay, sex and drugs like in a real city.
> - Rem Koolhaas[282]

Contemporary showmanship is evident in Julian Schnabel or Jeff
Koons, David Bowie or Kurt Cobain, Vivienne Westwood or
Jean-Charles de Castelbajac. Auteurs of their own pleasures such
as Vincent Gallo or Larry Clark are also showmen because they
are nothing more than egotistical voyeurism. Showman Rem
Koolhaas is egotistical monumentalism. There is however never
in any time period shortage of the ego because as Arthur
Schopenhauer wrote, all "seek the favorable opinion of others,"
We want to obtain the "official honor."[283] People like to throw
ego around anytime, anyplace as if it is an acceptable currency
but a showman asserts ego and the ongoing establishment of its
worth. This means not only recognition is sought but recognition
of the highest value for the longest time. He aims at being
"essential" to life itself, and creating an immortality, thus then
the ultimate showman is not the one we assume greatness but the
writer on whom all performances are dependent to be
remembered.[284]

---

[282] Obrist, Hans Ulrich. *Interviews, Volume 1*. Milan: Charta, 2003, p. 527.
[283] Schopenhauer, Arthur. *Philosophical Writings*. Ed. Wolfgang Schirmacher.
New York: The Continuum Publishing Company, 2002, p. 278 and p. 281.
[284] Arendt, Hannah. *The Human Condition*. Chicago: The University of Chicago
Press, 1958, p.193-194.

62.

You great star, what would your happiness be had you
not those for whom you shine.
- Friedrich Nietzsche, *Thus Spoke Zarathustra*[285]

Not all performance is self-serving but in our contemporary
decadence we have forgotten that some perform for reasons
other than fame. The architect Le Corbusier described when
meeting clients that they did not want him, his ideas, or even his
buildings, as much as they wanted a famous showman for the
spirit of modernity.[286] In *Die Große Ekstase des Bildschnitzers
Steiner* (1974) we meet a skier who loves the sport and is given
an unwanted fame.[287] Talented individuals are celebrated by the
cult of personality who see everyone as a showman. Showmen
however normally evade deep meaning. They do not seek
positions of grave responsibility or essential problem solving,
even though because of their likeability they may be appointed.
Like an artist, a showman will always give a sensational type of
answer to the people.[288] And this is how we distinguish the
showman from the philosopher because the philosopher has no
answers.

---

[285] Nietzsche, Friedrich. *Thus Spoke Zarathustra: A Book for All and None.*
Trans. Walter Kaufman. New York: The Modern Library, 1992, p. 9.

[286] "They don't want me anymore, because in the end my utter scrupulousness
disgusts the people. One has to be conceited, sanctimonious, sure of oneself,
swaggering, and never doubting-or at least not let it show. One has to be like a
show salesman." Jencks, Charles. *Le Corbusier and the Continual Revolution in
Architecture.* New York: The Montacelli Press, 2000, p. 104.

[287] *The Great Ecstasy of Woodcarver Steiner* by Werner Herzog, 1974.

[288] Among the American classes, the performance of showing is normally lower
to middle class. Showing is considered inauthentic, fake and thus rejected by the
establishment. "What constitutes a good party varies from class to class. At the
upper-class level the cliques tend to prefer a good deal of relaxed informality,
with the emphasis on scalability laced with whiskey, rather than show." Packard,
Vance. *The Status Seekers.* New York: Simon and Schuster, 1959, p. 158.

63.

The one who is entitled is always affirming his or herself as the center of attention, which involves denigrating others (as in Perez Hilton). In *The Aspern Papers*, Henry James writes, "with the force of a soul was a new conception–to smile at me in her abjection."[289] A showman is not only celebrating humanity but at all moment also capable of humiliating the other. That is the showman's act, the magic act of supporting and attacking, of revealing and concealing. That is why the showman is more dangerous than any other aspect of decadence. What can generate interest can also destroy it because the showman does not need to be rich or powerful or even in control but only a master of the audience.

64.

Media supplies paparazzi shots of celebrities in ordinary life, known as a "celebrity sighting." Celebrities are watched because they fulfill the role of aristocracy, in which all ways and manners are observed and imitated. Yet unlike the aristocracy who are appointed at birth and raised to continually provide an example for others, the celebrity is discovered then suddenly rich and famous, often incapable of leading by example. We observe their private lives to see if they can live up to our great expectations. In the celebrity sighting however, we have the precise sight of a celebrity not showing, not performing a role. The celebrity sighting is seeing the ordinary person while the celebrity is *not* seen.

It is rumored that Elizabeth Taylor, who is publicly understood to be cloistered in guarded comfort and obscurity, holds regular

---

[289] James, Henry. *The Aspern Papers*. New York: The Book of a Month Club, 1996, p. 155.

screenings of her films. Such a speculation is only reinforced by her charade in *Boom!* (1968), in which she portrays a drug-addicted, memoir-telling version of herself, across from her real life lover the rugged soul-seeking Richard Burton. The film is utter decadence, not only because of the defeatist narrative, based on a nothing happening play by Tennessee Williams, but because the film was created on a Mediterranean island with an extravagant budget.[290] Despite the crowns of seashells, Taylor wears what seem like no more than embellished bathrobes, a sort of "pre-notification of death uniform" that reveals self-pity.[291] The choices of film roles communicate more of a celebrity's character than a snapshot at the airport.

65.

> Calling together his friends and Zeresh, his wife,
> Haman boasted to them about his vast wealth, his many
> sons, and all the ways the king had honored him and
> how he had elevated him above the other nobles and
> officials. "And that's not all," Haman added. "I'm the
> only person Queen Esther invited to accompany the
> king to the banquet she gave. And she has invited me
> along with the king tomorrow. But all this gives me no
> satisfaction as long as I see that Jew Mordecai sitting at
> the king's gate."
> - Esther 5:10-13[292]

The showman is different from the scenester. The showman loves the show but the scenester loves association with fame.[293]

---

[290] Waters, John. "Filth 101," www.egs.edu,
http://www.egs.edu/faculty/waters/waters-filth-101-2001.html
[291] Salinger, J.D. *Franny and Zooey.* New York: Little, Brown and Company, 1955, p. 73.
[292] *The Holy Bible.* New International Version. Grand Rapids, Michigan: Zondervan Publishing House, 1996, p. 424.

The scenesters, also named status seekers or the entourage, usually hover around the showmen and sites of decadence like bees to a hive of honey.[294] They are *always* the sign that decadence is already taking place and they usually imitate the behavior of showmen, such as bold assertions of self-worth. However the scenester does not act boldly on his own and he is not famous; he is only an imitator and uncertain of self-worth. Thus he fears the loss of value because he does not have the capacity to maintain his own status. A scenester constantly fears the motives of the others because they could take away from some believed greater economy of social status.

Noblesse Oblige

> They were to travel from summer land to summer land, returning to a gorgeous estate and possibly idyllic children, then entering diplomacy or politics, to accomplish, for a while, beautiful and important things, until finally as a white-haired (beautifully, silkily, white-haired) couple they were to loll about in serene glory, worshipped by the bourgeoisie of the land.
> -F. Scott Fitzgerald, *The Beautiful and Damned*[295]

66.

The greatest privilege of aristocracy is giving back. Noblesse oblige is the obligation of nobility, to do good with privilege by extending to others the grace that you have received. This is the code of aristocracy: lead by example and preserve virtue for all

---

[293] Arthur Schopenhauer described honor as "indirect," "other people's opinion of our worth and subjectively our fear of that opinion." Schopenhauer, Arthur. *Philosophical Writings.* Ed. Wolfgang Schirmacher. New York: The Continuum Publishing Company, 2002, p. 227.

[294] Packard, Vance. *The Status Seekers.* New York: Simon and Schuster, 1959.

[295] Fitzgerald, F. Scott. *The Beautiful and Damned.* New York: The Modern Library, 2002, p. 233.

time. In contemporary life, we have retained only the appearance of an aristocracy in power and fame that allows privilege. With decadence, privileges are used instead to further desire. We have politicians and celebrities who use their fame to advocate human rights or the climate. But by in large, the most notable media figures are recognized for their pleasurable performances, not their social responsibility.

In the United States, with a birthright of unlimited freedom in a land of unlimited possibility, you could argue that regardless of status, we each inherit a noblesse oblige. Yet we serve ourselves first. We use our privileges to advance ourselves, through education, class and land ownership. And only then, after the basic pleasures of materiality and increased status have been accomplished, do we consider giving back. Noblesse oblige appears to start only when we have finished with selfish obligations to our own desires.

67.

> *ANDREA laut*: Unglücklich das land, das keine Helden hat!
> *GALILEI*: Nein. Unglücklich das land, das Helden nötig hat!
> - Bertol Brecht, *Leben Des Galilei* [296]

The hero, a secular term for a saint, is someone who acts with a gesture that affirms being. "Do not throw away the hero in your

---

[296] "Andrea [_loudly_]: Unhappy the land that has no heroes! Galileo: No. Unhappy the land where heroes are needed." Brecht, Bertol. *Leben Des Galilei.* Ed. H. F. Brookes and C. E. Fraenkel. London: Heinemann Educational Books, 1955, p. 118.

soul! Hold holy your highest hope," wrote Nietzsche.[297] The hero rescues or dies in the act of rescuing being. The hero represents the value of singularity that ultimately reinforces the value of a collective. The hero may at first be an outsider of a collective, but in time his good deeds are recognized and the hero is welcomed into the group, to increase the status of the collective by becoming a hero-among-them. The hero can also quiet the desire for action among the collective because the hero satisfies desire for glory and event. A child is born and is a hero because he is the singular mark of continuation of the group, just like the solider surviving a battle and so on. But the hero is always circumstantial and despite the fact it is an illusion of greater possibility, his heroism is of no use to outside of the pleasure of fame and accolades. As soon as his tries to make use of fame, the hero stops being heroic.

68.

In 1954 when Guenter Ruttenborn wrote the introduction of his play *The Sign of Jonah*, he emphasized anonymity: "The players should not regard themselves as actors, therefore they should remain anonymous: the names of the performers, directors, and stage helpers should not appear on the program."[298] Name recognition is not only a standard part of the entertainment industry but all aspects of our anthropocentric culture. The contemporary aristocratic code is making the news only at birth, marriage and death. But by in large most donations are public donations. Organizations publish long lists of names of everyone who has given support. Thus the contemporary noblesse oblige is a very public one.

---

[297] Nietzsche, Friedrich. *Thus Spoke Zarathustra: A Book for All and None.* Trans. Walter Kaufman. New York: The Modern Library. 1992, p. 44.
[298] Rutenborn, Guenter. *The Sign of Jonah.* Trans. Bernhard Ohse and Gerhard Elston. Chicago: The Lutheran Student Association of America, 1954, p. 5.

69.

With a birthright of freedom and a life of possibility and recognition, we may believe that we make our world. But can we help ourselves? The most widespread human condition of late capitalist anthropocentric decadence is helping oneself. Home remedies from natural medicine to alcoholism rise from a sense of one believing that one knows what is best. But it is "believing one chooses the remedies" that is the risk of decadence because there is no remedy for finitude.[299] Baudrillard explains: "The singularity plays it out itself, in control of the rules of the game. The singularity is made for a very rapid disappearance. But that isn't a catastrophic fatality. Appearance and disappearance are destiny."[300] Despite all of our efforts, for self-development, we are individually unable to transcend mortality. In faiths that claim eternity, it is through a connection to one another that we could continue. The collective also calls us to engage in the here and now. Why help the beggar if he is destined to die? Help the beggar because you are going to die.

---

[299] Nietzsche, Friedrich. *The Will to Power*. Trans. Walter Kaufmann. New York: Random House, 1968, p. 27
[300] Baudrillard, Jean. *Paroxysm*. Trans. Chris Turner. New York: Verso Books, 1998, p. 51.

IV. Fortune

The world lies ahead of me brighter than usual and more serious. Yes! It pleases me how it works, pleases me as when, in the summer, "the old holy father pours down lighting with calm hand out of red clouds." For among everything that I can see of God this sign has become the chosen one. At other times, I could jubilate about a new truth, an improved outlook on what is above us; now I fear that I might end like the old Tantalus who received more from the gods than he could take.

-Friedrich Hölderlin, Letter to Casmir Ulrich Böhlendorff[301]

---

[301] Quote in quote is from Goethe's poem, "Die Grenzen der Menschheir." Hölderlin, Friedrich. *Essays and Letters on Theory*. Trans. Thomas Pfau. New York: State University of New York Press, 1988, p. 151.

Prosperity

Maior sum quam cui possit Fortuna nocere,
Multaque ut eripiat, multo mihi plura relinquet.
Excessere metum mea iam bona.
- Ovid, *Metamorphoses*[302]

70.

The term "prosperity" involves an ongoing process of meeting needs, continually re-investing resources into survival and avoiding loss.[303] Prosperity is not the same as abundance, but rather it is a good use of resources in any quantity. Prosperity is often associated with aristocracy, who seek to consistently maintain wealth and augmented survival for many generations. While one may be born into privilege, prosperity is the wisest use of fortune in the ongoing establishment of wealth throughout life and coming generations.

As Fitzgerald expressed, "Aristocracy's only an admission that certain traits which we call fine—courage and honor and beauty

---

[302] "I am above being injured by fortune; though she takes much, more will remain with me. My blessings transcend fear." Ovid, *Metamorphoses*. Trans. Frank Justus Miller. New York: Putnam, 1916, pp. 300-301.

[303] Prosperity can also be associated with satisfaction, from the Latin *satisfacere* meaning "to make enough." Earthly prosperity has been taken as proof of favor from the heavenly gods, and also used to justify the basis of Christianity, in terms fruits of good works and grace. Lessing writes that "For although unequal distribution of the goods of this life, Virtue and Vice seem to be taken too little into consideration, although this unequal distribution does not exactly afford a strong proof of the immortality of the soul and of a life to come, in which this difficulty will be reserved hereafter, it is certain that without this difficulty, the human understanding would not for a long time, perhaps never arrived at better or firmer proofs." Lessing, Gotthold. "The Education of the Human Race," in *Literary and Philosophical Essays*. Ed. Charles Eliot. New York: Collier and Son, 1910, p. 201. By contrast, Arendt discusses "eudaimonia," as a unchangeable identity of well-being, Arendt, Hannah. *The Human Condition*. Chicago: The University of Chicago Press, 1958, p. 193.

and all the sort of thing—can best be developed in a favorable environment, where you don't have the warpings of ignorance and necessity."[304] Prosperity is a meeting of needs that results in what is considered "healthy." According to Abraham Maslow, prosperity forms individuals with "a high level of maturation, health, and self-fulfillment," almost a "different breed of human beings," who represent "the highest reaches of human nature and of its possibilities and aspirations."[305] In contemporary thought, we are most prosperous to reach the highest ideals such as truth, when we wisely use existing resources, that is what we already know by truth, with responsibility to continuation, thus ultimately responding to the eternal needs of being.[306]

71.

The prosperity of "pastoral life" refers to shepherds in seasonal motion, going from one grassland to the next, balancing work with repose. Their life is a form of non-permanence, but unlike the wanderer who is lost, or the contemporary scenester who follows the show, the pastoral shepherd knows a particular territory well and its natural timing. He uses just enough because he knows that he will be back again.

The 18th century birth of factory production and the labor class transformed the pastoral relation to the earth to one of demand and drudgery. By the early to mid-20th century, the pastoral spirit was replaced by the efficiency of mechanical invention. *Det Perfekte Menneske* (1967) is a film that presents instructions for

---

[304] Fitzgerald, F. Scott. *The Beautiful and Damned*. New York: The Modern Library, 2002, p. 343.
[305] Maslow, Abraham. *Toward a Psychology of Being*. New York: Van Nostrand Reinhold, 1968, p. 72.
[306] Some of these comments are based upon lectures with Wolfgang Schirmacher.

how to use and enjoy mechanical devices for optimal survival. But unlike the shepherd, using land and moving on, we have become dependent on machines. Rather than using tools as we need; we use a tool for every need. We do not move about to them, but instead, we make them portable so they move with us, but weigh us down.

72.

> Florin ladled out the punch, seeing that the younger ones did not get the glasses intended for their elders, but that each, according to his capacity, got a little more, but not much more, than was good for him. The Colonel tasted the punch and pronounced it excellent.
> - Evelyn Waugh, *Vile Bodies*[307]

Joie de vivre is often visible in a child because for the child everything has already been decided and there is a constant meeting of needs, not unlike advanced capitalism. In order to prevent decadence, a parent or more so a civilization, should guide an individual to know what is good for survival so to meet needs independently. Tradition teaches how much to take (not too much) and what is deemed excellent (whatever we already have). Contemporary society in the ethics of late capitalism says "too much is never enough," and nothing is good enough that we should not improve it in the next model.[308]

73.

With the exportation of factory production from the United States, there is an increase in service, administration and

---

[307] Waugh, Evelyn. *Vile Bodies*. New York: Little, Brown and Company, 1958, p. 310.
[308] Billy Idol for MTV, 1983.

intellectual work. Labor is only ever urgent when things demand attention, as in breakdown, disaster or death. But with less emphasis on physical labor, we now face primarily the task of refinement that emphasizes intangible skills like virtues.[309] We must be increasingly "civilized." Prosperity allows "independence of economic circumstances, which at the same time appeals with such convincing force to our sense of what is right and gracious."[310] But the idea of living "right" or "gracious" is far removed from the survival skills we needed in the first place and thus one consequence of continued prosperity is a lack of connection to original truth.

74.

Is the most prosperous civilization the one that has lasted the longest time? Is it the most primitive culture that has never needed to change, or the one that is most new? "The 'better' culture," writes Maslow, "gratifies all basic human needs and permits self-actualization," yet "the 'poorer' cultures do not." [311] Maslow continues that even if we achieve a state of health and have "transcended the problems of Becoming," there remain the problems of Being," such as conflict or enemies. And "to be untroubled when one should be troubled can also be a sign of sickness."[312] Thus even in a state of prosperity we cannot avoid the frailty of the human condition. This is why, suggests Maslow, that prosperity is not built on effort but on an effortless relationship, not only with "truth, goodness and beauty but also

---

[309] These traits include "truthfulness, peaceableness, good-will, and a non-emulative, non-invidious interest in men and things." Veblen, Thorstein. *The Theory of the Leisure Class.* New York: Dover Publications, 1994, p. 138.
[310] Ibid. p. 33.
[311] Maslow, Abraham. *Toward a Psychology of Being.* New York: Van Nostrand Reinhold, 1968, p. 211. In the better cultures it is then possible "that higher values are chosen and preferred consistently more often." Ibid. p. 173.
[312] Ibid. p. 210.

regressive, survival and/or homeostatic values of peace and quiet, of sleep and rest, of surrender, of dependency and safety, or protection from reality and relief from it...of retiring into fantasy, even wishing for death."[313] So in this sense, prosperity is similar to the Puritan ethic of moderation, much like Hegel's principle of aristocracy.[314] It is also a result of discretion. Nathan M. Rothschild advised his children: "I wish them to give mind, and soul, and heart, and body, and everything to business; that is the way to be happy. It requires a great deal of boldness and a great deal of caution, to make a great fortune; and when you have got it, it requires ten times as much wit to keep it."[315] The sensibility for keeping prosperity is to be *on guard for ruin*, especially of our own making.

75.

> In a sense, life suffocates within limits that are too close; it aspires in manifold ways to an impossible growth; it releases a steady flow of excess resources, possibly involving large squanderings of energy.
> - Georges Bataille, *The Accursed Share*[316]

The subjective terminology "First," "Second," "Third" and "Fourth World" are used to describe civilizations in various socio-economic conditions. The categories are based primarily

---

[313] Ibid. p. 172.

[314] Hegel writes, "the fact that 'moderation' is cited as the principle of aristocracy implies the beginning at this point of a divorce between public authority and private interest. And yet at the same time these touch each other so directly that this constitution by its very nature stands on the verge of lapsing forth with into tyranny or anarchy–the harshest of political conditions." Hegel, G. W. F., *Philosophy of the Right*, www.marxists.org,
http://www.marxists.org/reference/archive/hegel/works/pr/prstate1.htm

[315] Rothschild, Lord. *The Shadow of a Great Man*. London: Hand Press Limited, 1991, p. 3.

[316] Bataille, Georges. *The Accursed Share*. Trans. Robert Hurley. New York: Zone Books, 1988, p. 30.

upon their stability as well as the "United Nations Human Development Index." The "First World" status goes to those places with the best economy and the longest life span. Thus a great nation is one of financial merit and long life, not unlike the assessment given to great individuals. We evaluate worthiness by long performance. The size of a country or territory does not appear to correlate directly with prosperity, yet for individuals, property and equity are connected.[317] The prime resources at risk for decadence then are expenditure of health, wealth and territory.

The G8 includes the First World countries that represent 65% of the world's economy, roughly 40 trillion USD in equity.[318] The group consists of Canada, France, Germany, Italy, Japan, Russia, the United Kingdom, and the United States, expanding with emerging countries as the G20. The existence of such a group prompts the ethical question of global prosperity. We have reached a point of production with so much, so far from essential needs, that we find that "there is nothing left to take," and thus we give, or rather loan.[319] When First World countries do give, it is really like the "strategic giving" of major corporations. We use rational and transparent strategies that aim to reduce risk and "not so much destroy the enemy as neutralize him."[320] The group gives to Third and Fourth World countries, for an outward movement of excess resources. This appears to alleviate the excess accumulation of wealth, an "accursed share." The

---

[317] Property is "evidence of a reputable degree of success." Ibid. p. 19.
[318] Comment by Gerd Haeuslei from a conference by the Swiss Foundation of World Affairs on the topic of Globalization of the International Market, Swiss American Chamber of Commerce, Club 101, New York, December 9, 2004.
[319] Virilio, Paul. *Strategy of Deception.* Trans. Chris Turner. New York: Verso Books, 2000, p. 64.
[320] Ibid. p. 52. We accomplish this with an "initial blurring of the 'military' and the 'humanitarian.'" Ibid. p. 54.

accursed share is excess energy that is wasteful, luxurious, and essentially decadent. But rather spend this share in the name of culture or war, it is given in the name of eventual return, ultimately sustaining the disparity of resources. But the moment of sustainability is the resistant consciousness—"control yourself, take only what you need from it."[321]

Leisure

> The walks he had taken during the last few days had exhausted him; the change from the open air to the warmth of the house, from the sedentary life of a recluse to the free activity of an outdoor existence, had been too sudden.
> - J.K. Huysmans, *A Rebours*[322]

76.

Leisure can exist in varied lengths, hours, days or years. In his notable text *The Theory of the Leisure Class*, Thorstein Veblen describes leisure as "non-productive consumption of time."[323] "Non-productive consumption of time" however, could however be unwilling as with sickness.[324] Leisure is normally a willing time apart from work, and often a deliberate waste of or passing of time. There are also instances in which leisure time could be productive, as in art. But production, no matter how pleasurable, is never the aim of leisure.[325] Leisure is aimless. And leisure is without outside demand, so it is timeless. Importantly, leisure

---

[321] MGMT, *Kids*, 2008

[322] Huysmans, J.K. *A Rebours*. Trans. Havelock Ellis. New York: Dover, 1969, p. 90

[323] Veblen, Thorstein. *The Theory of the Leisure Class*. New York: Dover Publications, 1994, p. 28.

[324] And as Veblem points out "a habitual neglect of work does not constitute leisure." Ibid. 15.

[325] "The leisure of the servant is not his own leisure." Ibid. p. 38.

does not require great wealth, as even the working classes have willing moments of repose.[326] And great wealth does not guarantee leisure as wealth may require work to be maintained, even if it is only in the somewhat passive management of assets.

77.

Does leisure deplete the resources that support it? Does leisure drain reserves? Because in decadence resources are squandered, leisure can further turn the key of decadence. Because leisure is essentially non-productive it can also "conserve what is obsolescent," and lead to breakdown and decay.[327]

78.

Leisure was originally intended as rest in order to later return to work. In our restless culture, we fill leisure with activity. Leisure time is seen as an asset under capitalism so it is not only how much time one has but how time is available for desire fulfillment. The common phrase, "I do not have time for that" is typically not about having time but prioritizing time around personal needs and desires.[328] Whenever one is working for other people's priorities it is "business time," and when one is unwillingly passing time, if detained or sent to prison, it is simply called "wasted time," or just "time."

---

[326] "Abstention from labor is the conventional evidence of wealth." Ibid. p. 26.

[327] Ibid. p. 123. There are entire organizations based on obsolescence and wasteful expenditure, such as conservative foundations for beautification or public spirit, Ibid. p. 212.

[328] "Such questioning is thus the most appropriate manner of access to and of dealing with time in each case mine." Heidegger, Martin. *Der Begriff der Zeit /The Concept of Time*. (German-English edition) Trans. William McNeill. Oxford: Blackwell, 1992, p. 22.

79.

Having abundant "leisure" results from having assets that alleviate needs, and having others who work for you.[329] The working class is always working so to allow for the leisure of someone else.

Tout Va Bien (1972) examines the drudgery of the working class in France. Toward the end of the film a communist is selling books in a supermarket and incites a riot. If the supermarket has already bought the products, and the supermarket is under our government, then as citizens the products already belong to us. But within a capitalist economy, citizens may not "consume freely."[330] And under communism, without competition to motivate, work ultimately had to be enforced, as seen in Chris Marker's *Lettre de Sibérie* (1957). There was no leisure in Siberia, except for that of the French filmmaker.

80.

Leisure wants to take more time than necessary and thus laughs at speed, unless it is speed of pleasure. Technology or, as it was called in prior eras, exploit, transforms an existing resource so to make life more efficient or quicker. Yet though technology appears to accelerate, it is merely a device in service to the slow time of leisure. In the iPod we have quicker access to music in order to decrease the work and increase the leisure time of music listening.

---

[329] Wealth is then not only equity but "personal service and the immediate products of personal service," so to ensure the greatest amount of leisure possible. Veblen, Thorstein. *The Theory of the Leisure Class.* New York: Dover Publications, 1994, p. 25.
[330] Ibid. p. 105.

81.

Industry makes something out of nothing, so the "leisure industry" is to extend time for something unnecessary.[331] *V Magazine* listed a few "men of leisure" and almost all of them were celebrities who feed our leisure industry: Brian Jones, Rudolph Valentino, Mikhail Baryshnikov, Halston, David Bowie, F. Scott Fitzgerald.[332] Their work may have economic demand and exchange, but because they produce leisure material, there is ultimately no urgency or code of ethics other than maximum pleasure. Those in the leisure industry then can work slowly and be self-serving if what they make is pleasurable and good for the leisure of others. It is only the agents who demand a quickly following second album, book or film.

82.

"Colleges have definitively become leisure-class establishments."[333] The premise of academia, beyond high education, is research. The premise of intellectual research is that society needs "thought that is devoted to thought," free from the demands of survival.[334] Thus, intellectual research operates in a quiet field of academic leisure in which scholars are self-directed to pursue whimsy as they feel. Much intellectual research then is unfortunately a decadent endeavor because taste and style are valued over necessity and taking time is valued over production.[335] Even though "knowledge of the unknowable

---

[331] Ibid. p. 8.

[332] "Boys," *V Magazine*, V16, March / April 2002.

[333] Veblen, Thorstein. *The Theory of the Leisure Class.* New York: Dover Publications, 1994, p. 229.

[334] "Knowledge for its own sake, the exercise of the faculty of comprehension without ulterior purpose." Ibid. p. 235.

[335] Even the classics reinforce leisure because they ultimately provide a service to academia. "Inspiring a habitual aversion to what is merely useful," and "consuming the learner's time and effort for no use." Ibid. p. 241.

is still felt to be the ultimate, if not only, true knowledge,"
research is consistently either devoted to re-discovering that
which has been "lost" or exposing the current novelty of
existence itself, but for what end?[336] And because of the ample
allotment of time away from physical labor, academia also
acquires the ambivalence of leisure class.[337] The greatest danger
however for wasted thought is when the thought is
anthropocentric and self-edifying, creating thought without
prosperity.

83.

> My idea about couture is not to cover something with
> embroidery like a Christmas tree–it's how to
> manipulate the material until I find a truth.
> - Jean-Charles de Castelbajac[338]

The leisure class can often grow so distant from work that they
find resolution through the accumulation of objects that "give
evidence of an expenditure of labor," other people's labor.[339]
This is readily apparent in the collection of art, intricate display
objects or something like couture. Fashion is a mark of
conspicuous waste.[340] It is "the insignia of leisure,"[341] and thus

---

[336] Ibid. p. 225.

[337] The ideals of leisure are "transfused among the scholarly classes but with little
mitigation of rigor; and as a consequence there is no class of the community that
spends a larger proportion of its substance in conspicuous waste than these."
Ibid. p. 70.

[338] Speyer, Ariana, Ed. *The Real Thing: Fashion Interviews from Index
Magazine*. New York: Index Books, 2003, p. 80.

[339] Veblen, Thorstein. *The Theory of the Leisure Class*. New York: Dover
Publications, 1994, p. 93.

[340] "In spite of its prestige," explains Roland Barthes, "fashion always feels
guilty of futility." Barthes, Roland. *The Fashion System*. Trans. Matthew Ward
& Richard Howard. Berkeley: University of California Press, 1983, p. 267. We
can also consider that guilt is associated with fashion, linked to shame in Biblical
paradise. The celebration of fashion has largely been the opposite of shame, in

also of decadence. It represents total investment in excess decoration, of excess time invested in planning the design and wasting time on overvaluing it's presentation. Fashion is based on investing only in the moment because the object will not last forever and perhaps by the time it is worn again, is already out of fashion. Contemporary fashion requires leisure time to follow what is currently fashionable, based on knowledge of what is always chic (meaning, "nothing has caused it to go out of fashion, neither months spent gazing at the sea, nor weeks already spent in the hunting field!")[342] Thus fashion requires knowing the codes in the present time and the codes of each and every other time and instance. It is to know how to dress in any circumstance, which is always open to change. So like being famous, one can only be fashionable through an ongoing re-investment.

Different sets of fashion knowledge are obviously associated with different classes, subcultures and regions. For Walter Benjamin, the movement of a fashion code was a "tiger's leap," a leap that "occurs in the arena commanded by the ruling class."[343] By contrast democracy has shown that codes from subcultures can be introduced without consent of the ruling

---

adoration of beauty and pride. But we find the act of dressing is the return to the original event, the confrontation of a naked physical body, a cold universe and exposure to others. This is the state of birth, we are born naked and then dressed *on behalf of* others.
[341] Veblen, Thorstein. *The Theory of the Leisure Class*. New York: Dover Publications, 1994, p. 105.
[342] Quote is from Furbank, P.N. and A.M. Cain. *Mallarmé on Fashion*. New York, Berg, 2004, p. 73. "Dress must be conspicuously expensive and inconvenient; it must at the same time be up to date. No explanation at all satisfactory has hitherto been offered of the phenomenon of changing fashions." Veblen, Thorstein. *The Theory of the Leisure Class*. New York: Dover Publications, 1994, p. 106.
[343] Translation by author. Benjamin, Walter. *Illuminations*. Trans. Harry Zohn. London: Pimlico, 1999, p. 252-253.

class. "Dressing-up" and "dressing-down" not only imply class codes of attire but also that fashion allows a sort of chameleon identity not as tied to class structure as much as fantasy. In most contemporary atmospheres, the lower class worker may still wear a uniform or "dress-up" for work while for the white-collar worker more leisurely attire is acceptable. Leisure clothing, once reserved for the hunt or sport, is now worn everywhere and that is in part because we have more leisure than ever. Missoni and Pucci are now everyday clothing while only a few decades ago they were for holidays. The same could be said of cultural theory, which has allowed formally leisure topics such as fashion, film, television and theme parks, to enter the discussion of thought.

84.

Andy Warhol's television show "Fashion," aired 10 episodes on Manhattan cable and consisted of interviews with models, photographers and friends. The show was not unlike other talk shows where guests do nothing but sit in what look like living rooms that mirror the living rooms of those watching the shows. The talk show is broadcast leisure but television was not originally intended to be a leisure media. Television was, like most media, intended for strategic communication by the government in emergency.[344] This means television is a system that must intentionally waste time until an emergency arises. Thus television must remain free and accessible in order to reach the masses. In this regard anyone at any level, palace or prison, can watch television. But what we find on television is the news, which announces the constant state of emergency warning, and

---

[344] "It is supposed to put events first and its own concerns second. But for some time now it seems either to have lost this respect for itself or to have come to regard *itself* as the event." Baudrillard, Jean. *Screened Out*. Trans. Chris Turner. New York: Verso Books, 2002, 186.

then media about media. Baudrillard suggests it is "talking only to itself or an unidentified audience."[345] We have a self-referential media to the point we even have channels about other channels that show us what television is doing tonight. Of course at any moment television can still be seized by the government (like the radio or the United States highway); we have simply forgotten that like most things we enjoy, it has political potential. Instead we adore television's artifice and formal variety. It is only when we are confronted with a commercial that we are reminded that leisure wants us. The very crux of leisure is that leisure without participants, is nothing but time.

85.
Whenever one becomes an aficionado of a particular expression of leisure, then leisure is hobby. When the hobby begins to satisfy the purpose of the individual, it defines identity. The leisure then is no longer leisure because the individual feels an obligation to maintain it in order to maintain identity. The individual is totally invested and leisure becomes obligation, a form of commitment that no longer provides the undemanding relief of the original event of leisure but instead a sense of work. This is how we become dependent on what does not sustain survival but only pleasure.

Cultivation

> Everything was tasted from grasshopper to ostrich, from dormouse to wild boar; whatever might stimulate the appetite was tried as a seasoning, and as such the cooks used substances which we cannot conceive of,

---

[345] Ibid. p. 187.

like asafetida and rue. The whole known world was put
to gastronomical use.
- Jean Anthelme Brillat-Savarin on Roman cuisine, *The
Physiology of Taste*[346]

86.

Cultivation is a process of development through training and
knowledge acquisition. Cultivation is often the result of a more
detailed use of leisure time, as in music lessons, or culinary
training. Cultivation has the appearance of productive time but is
really a decadent expenditure of time for augmented skill.
Cultivation also includes the socialized development of manners
and taste *in accordance to* whatever is agreed upon as valuable.
One may cultivate a knowledge of dead languages (what Des
Esseintes called "The Decadence"[347]), breeding decorative
animals, gardening flowers, collecting rare objects, as well as a
quickly expendable knowledge of contemporary fashion, film or
other media.[348] Appreciation of art is the form of cultivation par
excellence. Art always signifies expenditure of leisure time
because it requires unproductive time to produce and does not
have tangible use value.

87.

To search out a matter is the glory of Kings.
- Proverbs 25:2[349]

---

[346] Brillat-Savarin, Jean Anthelme. *The Physiology of Taste*. Trans. M.F.K.
Fisher. Washington D.C.: Counterpoint, 1949, p. 287.
[347] Huysmans, J.K. *A Rebours*. Trans. Havelock Ellis. New York: Dover, 1969,
p. 26.
[348] Veblen, Thorstein. *The Theory of the Leisure Class*. New York: Dover
Publications, 1994, p. 29.
[349] *The Holy Bible*. New International Version. Grand Rapids, Michigan:
Zondervan Publishing House, 1996, p. 554.

After ample resources of time and opportunities, one has tasted much and thus develops "taste." Gadamer describes:

> The concept of taste undoubtedly implies a *mode of knowing*. The mark of good taste is being able to stand back from ourselves and our private preferences. Thus taste, in its essential nature, is not private but a social phenomenon of the first order. It can even counter the private inclinations of the individual like a court of law, in the name of a universality that it intends and represents One can like something that one's own taste rejects....Good taste is always sure of its judgment...taste is therefore something like a sense...taste is defined precisely by the fact that it is offended by what is tasteless and thus avoids it, like anything else that threatens to injury. Thus the contrary of "good taste" actually is not "bad taste." Its opposite is rather to have "no taste."[350]

Taste is essential to decadence because it emphasizes particular values over needs, yet taste under democracy has become something highly subjective. Now a bon vivant may come in any style. We have increased the amount of information available, literacy and rights to pleasure, which have resulted in "cultivation for everyone" without regard for the understanding that cultivation was originally intended to develop taste for the *best* of everything. In our decadent society we have a strange phenomenon in which there is a belief of "good taste" but a limited span of cultivation, simply cultivation through media and entertainment, cultivation without essence. Indiscriminant accumulation from mass production has overtaken selective

---

[350] Gadamer, Hans-Georg. *Truth and Method*. Translation revised by Joel Weinsheimer and Donald G. Marshall New York: Continuum, 1999, pp. 36-37.

cultivation of assets guided by good taste.[351] Rather than knowing what is worthy of interest across reality, we now know only what we personally find interesting from the choices of the leisure industry. Thus the masses demonstrate the disposition of "good taste," simply by occupying the seat of judgment overabundance of entertainment or the internet. The press however can still function as a type of tastemaker because of advance access and subsequent pre-selection.

88.

> *EDWARD*: Where on earth do you turn up from?
> *ALEX*: Where on earth? From the East. From Kinkanja–
> an island that you won't have heard of yet. Got back
> this morning. I heard about your party and, as I thought
> you might be leaving for the country I said, I must not
> miss the opportunity to see Edward and Lavinia.
> *JULIA*: What were you doing in Kinkanja? Visiting
> some Sultan? You were shooting tigers?
> *ALEX*: There are no tigers, Julia, in Kinkanja. And there
> are no sultans. I have been staying with the Governor.
> - T.S. Eliot, *The Cocktail Party*[352]

---

[351] Montaigne writes, "I believe the temple of taste is to be rebuilt; but its reconstruction is merely a matter of enlargement so that is may become the home of all noble human beings, of all who have permanently increased the sum of the mind's delights and possessions." De Montaigne, Michel. "What is a Classic," in *Literary and Philosophical Essays*. Ed. Charles Eliot. New York: Collier and Son, 1910, p. 135. Lyotard suggested that "humanity's condition has become one of chasing after the process of the accumulation of new objects (both of practice and of thought.) Lyotard, Jean-François. *The Postmodern Explained to Children: Correspondence 1982-1985*. Trans. Thomas Pefanis. London: Turnaround, 1992, p. 92.

[352] Eliot, T.S. *The Cocktail Party*. New York: Harcourt, Brace and Company, 1950, pp. 159-160.

Heroic legends of adventuresome men fighting natives and unexpected wild animals are something of the past. There is not only increasingly less and less uncivilized territory, but we now approach the hunt with luxury camping gear and maximum safety. In Barbet Schroeder's film *La Vallée* (1972), it is a woman, a French diplomat's wife, who decides to hunt in the South Pacific.[353] She goes to the Mapuga rain forest tribe, in search of exotic feathers purely in the name of decoration. In the hunt, leisure time is transformed to quest, and then quest becomes obsession. The story resembles the German film of the same year *der Zorn Gottes Aguirre* by Werner Herzog, which portrays the hunt as a resolution of desire through capturing. This is what makes the hunt particularly interesting for decadence, and why perhaps it is common to eras of decadence. Hunting resolves the problem of desire for the short term. The hunt however is something that is not supposed to be decadent but rather intended to be grounded in "true" sport and recreation, that is, to recall how to kill and survive. We preserve the skills of hunting now with the internet, academic research, or shopping, seen in the ads "Saks loves treasure seekers."[354]

89.

Contemporary sports are a decadent reminder that sport was a means of keeping citizens active for possible military defense of a tribe. This is why the national anthem is sung at athletic

---

[353] The main character shifts from hunt to wandering. The hunt has an aim and focus of desire. Wandering is rooted in the lack of aim or resting place of desire, thus associated with ennui. Michel de Montaigne explained, "For it is necessary to make a choice, and the first condition of taste, after obtaining knowledge of all, lies not in continual travel, but in rest and cessation from wandering. Nothing blunts and destroys taste so much as endless journeyings." De Montaigne, Michel. "What is a Classic," in *Literary and Philosophical Essays*. Ed. Charles Eliot. New York: Collier and Son, 1910, p. 138.

[354] 2005 campaign for Saks 5th Avenue.

events, a reminder that the strength and skill of the peaceful fight would otherwise be used at war. The competition of sports relies on natural differences in athletic ability relies and invented difference such as colors or mascots. Opposition normally happens with two different tribes of people. The origin of the duel however, as in fencing, wrestling or boxing, is a specific difference of opinion between two people of the same tribe.[355] Today however, even a duel is about nothing, as we have "the large element of make-believe that is present in all sporting activity,"[356] as is the make believe of fashion, travel and so on. The more we invest in one expression of leisure the more it evolves as fantasy.

90.

Gaming is the territory of leisure that operates with a contained knowledge set not translateable to reality. Cultivation normally engages with tangible resources from reality, the abundance of wine or cuisine, the abundance in nature, the variety in music. But gaming wants to exclude reality in exchange for a world of new rules. The world of an aristocrat is a game of rules, a part from reality with safe and symbolic exchanges. Gadamer wrote in "Play as Clue to Ontological Explanation":

> In cases where human subjectivity is what is playing, the primacy of the game over the players engaged in it is experienced by the players themselves in a special way...The attraction that the game exercises on the player lies in this risk. One enjoys a freedom of decision which at the same time is endangered and irrevocably limited....This suggests a general characteristic of the nature of play that is reflected in

---

[355] It is "a final settlement of difference of opinion," Veblen, Thorstein. *The Theory of the Leisure Class*. New York: Dover Publications, 1994, p. 153.
[356] Ibid. p. 157.

playing: all playing is being-played. The attraction of a game, the fascination it exerts, consists precisely in the fact that the game masters the players...the real subject of the game is not the player but instead the game itself. What holds the player in its spell, draws him into play, and keeps him there is the game itself...Every game presents the man who plays it with a task. He cannot enjoy the freedom of playing himself out without transforming the aims of his purposive behavior into mere tasks of the game...The self-presentation of human play depends on the player's conduct being tied to the make-believe goals of the game, but the 'meaning' of these goals does not in fact depend on their being achieved. Rather, in spending oneself on the task of the game, one is in fact playing oneself out.[357]

When we engage in a game, we engage in something unproductive or, as Gadamer describes, seductive. We are drawn into an alternate world in which the only things at risk are the values of the game. So we can play the games of society, sport, fashion, politics, but we are as Gadamer expresses, also played by them, as they dominant our time. When we achieve the goals of the game, we obtain a semblance of meaning and if that meaning is allowed to penetrate reality, to ascribe status or significance to being outside of the game, we are then under the influence of fantasy and supremely decadent.

91.

Decadence is to live always inclined to death. Therefore the healthy practice of cultivation is exchanged for a passive decay. The word "cultivation," refers to farming and improving the harvest and is the luxury of the leisure class, to have time to

---

[357] Gadamer, Hans-Georg. *Truth and Method*. Translation revised by Joel Weinsheimer and Donald G. Marshall, New York: Continuum, 1999, pp. 106-108.

make the most of what one has. But from the decadent
perspective leisure is like anything else, caught in illusion and
bound to disappearance. If there is a vanishing point of
decadence, it is perhaps just this moment, when the fortune of
time is laid out like a feast on a long banquet table and one
chooses to sit and watch the flies gather and fruit rot, to see time
decay before one's eyes.

Luxury

FRANNY: College was just one more place where
people were dedicated to piling up treasure on earth and
everything. I mean treasure is treasure, money,
property, culture or even just plain knowledge–when
it's knowledge for knowledge sake it's worst of all.
ZOOEY: There is no difference at all between the man
who's greedy for material treasure or even intellectual
treasure and the man who's greedy for spiritual
treasure...you talk about piling up treasure... aren't you
trying to lay up some kind of treasure? Something
every bit as negotiable as all the other material
things?... Is there a difference in which side someone
lays up his treasure–this side, or the other?...
FRANNY: You're saying I want something from the
Jesus Prayer–which makes me just as acquisitive, in
your word, really as somebody who wants a sable coat,
or to be famous, or to be dripping with some kind of
crazy prestige. I know all that... Just because I'm
choosy about what I want–in this case enlightenment or
peace instead of money or prestige or fame–doesn't
mean I'm not egotistical or self-seeking like everybody
else...
- J.D. Salinger, *Franny and Zooey*[358]

---

[358] Salinger, J. D. *Franny and Zooey.* New York: Little, Brown and Company,
1955, p.145-148.

92.
What is luxury? Luxury comes from the Latin term "luxuria"
which means extra of life and is thus commonly associated with
wealth and excess. Yet even a peasant may use the term to
describe that which is exceptional. The "luxury market" is
simply regulated by limited quantities. There are then
circumstantial luxuries whenever a resource is in short supply.
And because of mortal finitude, for example, we also call
something like time a luxury. Calling anything a luxury is
subjective until it becomes shared opinion, the result of testing
or ages of tasting. The aristocratic ethic suggests that only after
one has been cultivated and developed taste, can one recognize
luxury at first sight.

93.

> Cast but a glance at riches, and they are gone, for they
> will surely sprout wings and fly off to the sky like an
> eagle.
> - Proverbs 26:5[359]

Luxury is often considered divine. We give luxury a special
place in this world, regarding its rarity almost like a miracle.[360]
A miracle however is a bi-product of truth, something that was
unseen and then reveals its existence. Luxury is a byproduct of
illusion; something seen and valued for its invisible qualities
such as status. Theodor Adorno wrote about how gemstones

---

[359] *The Holy Bible*. New International Version. Grand Rapids, Michigan:
Zondervan Publishing House, 1996, p. 555.
[360] "An arduous thing is called a miracle, not because of the excellence of the
thing wherein it is done, but because it surpasses the ability of nature. So, too, a
thing is called unusual." Aquinas, Thomas. *Summa Teologica*, in *Half Hours
with the Best Thinkers*, Ed. Frank J. Finamore. New York: Gramercy Books,
1999, p. 67.

were once thought to have magic powers; however, even when the superstition faded, they continued to attract interest. He describes that the "primeval history of luxury... has migrated into all art... but the magic has survived... as the power of radiant things over men... as radiant things give up their magic claims... they become transformed into images of gentleness, promises of happiness...this is the primeval history of luxury, that has migrated into the meaning of all art. In the magic of whatever reveals itself in absolute powerlessness of beauty, at once perfection and nothingness, the illusion of omnipotence is mirrored negatively as hope."[361] Luxury then is an empty promise. It alludes to the infinite, and infinite enjoyment, but the reality is that it is an object to be used and maintained.

94.

> Energy is always in excess; the question is always posed in terms of extravagance. The choice is limited to how wealth is to be squandered... For if we do not have the force to destroy the surplus energy ourselves... it is this energy that destroys us.
> - George Bataille, *The Accursed Share*[362]

Even though luxury is associated with something in limitation, both exaggeration and extravagance are connected to it. Yet excess is not always luxury. One can think easily of an excess nuisance, and sometimes the accumulation of luxury results in bothersome excess. But it is often the accursed share that is traded for luxury goods. By using personal excess to acquire luxury, one is simply transferring the curse. Thus excess and

---

[361] Adorno, Theodor. *Minima Moralia*. Trans. E.N. Jephcott. New York: Verso Books, 1997, p. 224.
[362] Bataille, Georges. *The Accursed Share*. Trans. Robert Hurley. New York: Zone Books, 1988, pp. 23-24.

luxury are intertwined and in our augmented state of survival we have made them our anthropocentric destiny. Yet it means nothing more than more responsibility. Jean-Luc Nancy writes that "the proliferation of large numbers in our culture, our interests and our ends also defines the exponential growth of such responsibility...the true 'measure' of the universe is found in the 'excessive responsibility' we have for it."[363]

95.

> Do not store up for yourselves treasures on earth, where moth and rust destroy, and where thieves break in and steal. But store up for yourselves treasures in heaven, where moth and rust do not destroy, and where thieves do not break in and steal. For where your treasure is, there your heart will be also.
> - Matthew 6:19-21[364]

Old guard luxury is *both* product and experience. It is the top shelf of exchange that involves consistent delivery of premium quality through heritage of craftsmanship, an original and singular designer, values of a creator that create recognizable style, limited production run, selective placement with emotional appeal, premium pricing and global reputation.[365] Luxury is about the investment of time into a product and the time required to maintain it. Dianna Vreeland described that before the World Wars, couture was personally tailored by the designer who made

---

[363] Nancy, Jean-Luc. *Being Singular Plural*. Trans. Robert D. Richardson and Anne E. O'Byrne. Stanford: Stanford Univ. Press, 2000, pp. 177-178.

[364] *The Holy Bible*. New International Version. Grand Rapids, Michigan: Zondervan Publishing House, 1996, p. 841.

[365] Explanations of luxury based on descriptions throughout the book of Pamela Danzinger, *Let Them Eat Cake: Marketing Luxury to the Masses and the Classes*. New York: Kaplan Business, 2004.

it and "there's never been such luxury since."[366] Bergdorff
Goodman began as a tailor who introduced luxury ready-to-wear
in 1899, but then in 1906, the store opened one of the first
American fur salons, a cold storage service that continues to this
day. Whether tailoring or storing, luxury requires work. The
luxury consumer however wants to be aligned with leisure, not
work. Luxury service then is management of existing decadence,
taking over the burden of maintenance and care.

96.

Luxury service was intended to provide each client with
exclusive attention, which meant appointments and waiting lists,
for complete attention. In *A Rebours*, Des Esseintes hires a
jeweler so to have "his turtle's back glazed over with gold."[367]
But he soon decides "it would not be really complete and perfect
until it was encrusted with stones,"[368]gemstones that
complimented the colors in his rugs. The turtle signifies the
decadent decline of French aristocracy. A turtle is known for
longevity, but in Huysmans' novel after the turtle is over-
decorated it dies. It is *death by decoration*: "it had not been able
to support the dazzling luxury imposed on it, the shining
garment in which it had been clad."[369]

Custom attention is still part of the agenda of European
corporations Moët Hennessy Louis Vuitton (LVMH),
Richemont, Gucci Inc., and Armani, which collectively
supervise the majority of America's imported luxury brands. In
America, through democratic capitalism, and our decadence, we

---

[366] Vreeland, Diana. *D.V.* New York: De Capo Press, 1984, p. 14.
[367] Huysmans, J.K. *A Rebours*. Trans. Havelock Ellis. New York: Dover, 1969,
p. 40.
[368] Ibid. p. 40.
[369] Ibid. p. 49.

have made luxury increasingly accessible. There has not only been a dissemination of luxury brands and products but a new type of luxury, an expansive product base that creates consumer opportunity, tells a story, and is relevant to basic needs and consumer values (not the creator's values). The new luxury is whatever makes *everyone's* world better.[370] The risk of mass luxury is that it is ultimately not possible to maintain the quality because the quality requires taking considerable time for each instance.

97.
Manmade luxury is what we are not willing to do or cannot do for ourselves in terms of craftsmanship, service or knowledge. In this way luxury is based upon actualization, each contributing to and then benefiting from excellence in skill. Luxury involves a gaze of adoration, of admiring the fruits of labor, though not our own. If we consider the time invested in thought, it is a luxury to learn. But with its contemporary availability, knowledge is not a luxury, it is abundant and free and thus in a state of decadence.[371]

98.

> How the gold has lost its luster.
> - Lamentations 4:1[372]

---

[370] Explanations of luxury based on descriptions throughout the book of Pamela Danzinger, *Let Them Eat Cake: Marketing Luxury to the Masses and the Classes*. New York: Kaplan Business, 2004.

[371] "Education gives man nothing which he might not educe out of himself; it gives him that which he might educe out of himself only quicker and more easily." Lessing, Gotthold. "The Education of the Human Race," in *Literary and Philosophical Essays*. Ed. Charles Eliot. New York: Collier and Son, 1910, p. 195.

[372] *The Holy Bible.* New International Version. Grand Rapids, Michigan: Zondervan Publishing House, 1996, p. 608.

Manmade luxury is great skill that signifies the believed human sovereignty over the earth. The excellence creates an illusion of ultimate value that in time declines. Voltaire describes, "decadence is produced by facility in making and by laziness in making well, by the satiety with beauty and the taste for the bizarre."[373] There is a risk in believing a life of luxury as the pinnacle of human existence. In describing the characters in *The Beautiful and Damned*, the commentator Edmond Wilson explained that "in the end you do not believe they ever were people who wanted the opportunities for fineness that the freedom of wealth provides; you believe them only people who wanted luxury. They are pitiful, and their pathos is brilliantly realized, but they are not tragic."[374] Decadence continually resolves desire via subjective means taken to the last extreme. Decadence then is not a tragedy, and we cannot feel for the decadents' suffering. Decadence only knows travesty.

99.

> What I'm doing is about as close as you're going to get, in the twentieth century, to the quality of Versailles. Everything is made to order. For example, we had the finest craftsman in Italy hand carve twenty-seven solid marble columns for the living room. They arrived yesterday and they're beautiful. I can afford the finest workmanship, and when it comes to my own apartment, I figure, why spare expense? I want the best, whatever it takes.
>
> - Donald Trump, *Trump: The Art of the Deal*[375]

---

[373] Jencks, Charles. *Le Corbusier and the Continual Revolution in Architecture.* New York: The Montacelli Press, 2000, p. 114.

[374] Fitzgerald, F. Scott. *The Beautiful and Damned.* New York: The Modern Library, 2002, p. 384.

[375] Trump, Donald. *Trump: The Art of the Deal.* Boston: G.K. Hall & Co., 1989, p. 42.

"Luxury," described Coco Chanel, "is the absence of vulgarity."[376] It is an investment in refinement, for superior quality. The idea that luxury is refinement seems to go against the idea that luxury is more than normal, exceptional and essentially a prize of greed. The Roman historian Titus Livius (Livy) described decadence of the Roman state as suffering from two opposing vices, luxury and avarice.[377] Yet rather than opposing, they feed one another.

100.

Simone Weil writes, "most of those who seek riches connect the thought of luxury with them. Luxury is the finality of riches. Moreover luxury itself represents beauty for a whole class of men. It provides surroundings through which they can feel in a vague fashion that the universe is beautiful."[378] This is the essential scene of decadence, a negotiation of resources toward a beautiful ambiance, which is simply an artifice of appearances. The expression of beauty is subjective but the investment is toward a complete environment, a paradise.

L'Année dernière à Marienbad (1961) is film as luxury ambiance. *X wanders through the hotel's corridors cataloging items he sees*: "Empty salons. Corridors. Salons. Doors. Doors. Salons. Empty chairs, deep armchairs, thick carpets. Heavy hangings. Stairs, steps. Steps, one after the other. Glass objects, objects still intact, empty glasses. A glass that falls, three, two, one, zero. Glass partition, letters." There is so much yet only

---

[376] Quote was part of the wall display without source, at the Chanel exhibition at the Metropolitan Museum of Art in Spring 2005.
[377] Livius, Titus. *The History of Rome*, Vol. 5. Ed. Ernest Rhys. Trans. Canon Roberts. London: Dent & Sons, 1905, Book 34.
[378] Weil, Simone. *Waiting for God*. Trans. Emma Craufurd. New York: G.P. Putnam's Sons, 1951, p. 167.

objects. The great luxury ambiance is opulence–an atmosphere abundantly filled with beauty and pleasure. The fantasy of opulence is the agenda of Condé Nast, which produces magazines with a mise-en-scène of luxury. Condé Nast, however, emphasizes advertisers over content and is true to the magazine's origin as a commercial catalog. It is selling global brands whose goods are available locally. But the aim is creating an imaginary lifestyle, where luxury coalesces in one unifying ambiance. This is also the case with private publications like *Visionaire* and *Self-Service*, which arbitrate advertiser content in order to force ambiance. The intention of the magazine is that it will function like film or a book, a world that you enter...

101.

> While he was in Bethany, reclining at the table in the home of a man known as Simon the Leper, a woman came with an alabaster jar of very expensive perfume, made of pure nard. She broke the jar and poured the perfume on his head. Some of those present were saying indignantly to one another, "Why this waste of perfume? It could have been sold for more than a year's wages and the money given to the poor." And they rebuked her harshly. "Leave her alone," said Jesus. "Why are you bothering her? She has done a beautiful thing to me.
> - Mark 14:3-6[379]

With luxury we discover the pinnacle moment of decadence. We esteem resources that will make this life as pleasant as possible.

---

[379] *The Holy Bible*. New International Version. Grand Rapids, Michigan: Zondervan Publishing House, 1996, pp. 858-859.

Privileging luxury obviously hinges on a denial of any life but this, of any value but that of the market. We are not free in luxury because we answer to whatever it is that is worth more than what we have. Desire urges us to give up our resources in exchange for the luxury object or experience, failing to realize it is all only a symbolic exchange and that the value has been assigned by some authority. Baudrillard writes, "God is the general equivalent in whose name everything changes and is exchanged. In the absence of God, everything can become freely," and thus today we have a "free market" where everything is freely sold at a price.[380]

102.

> Virtue (e.g. in the form of truthfulness) as *our* noble
> and dangerous luxury; we must not refuse the
> disadvantages it brings with it.
> - Friedrich Nietzsche, *Will to Power*[381]

Diana Vreeland described, "there is nothing common about swans," and despite that swans are natural and quite common, with decadence there is exaggerated importance given to the everyday.[382] Our contemporary decadence gives importance to all things anthropocentric. We elevate every aspect of human identity and make each and every one of us into a rare specimen. This is because we assume the greatest luxury is not an object but human life and maximizing life by quantity or quality. We have excess in the number of our events and activities, though

[380] Baudrillard, Jean. *Impossible Exchange*. Trans. Chris Turner. New York: Verso Books, 2001, p. 131.
[381] Nietzsche, Friedrich. *The Will to Power*. Trans. Walter Kaufmann. New York: Random House, 1968, p. 498.
[382] Vreeland, Diana. *D.V.* New York: De Capo Press, 1984, p. 23.

we have amassed primarily "noncumulative experience."[383]
Those who already live with extreme tangible luxuries, may add
to the list intangible values, such as virtue. Thus we now have
excess vices and excess virtues and we treat them both with
decadence, quickly embracing them and easily dismissing them.
Thus decadence may be less about exploiting inheritance,
privileges and fortune, and rather simply accumulating dead end
values that fail to unify human existence other than in our
demise.

---

[383] Habermas, Jürgen. *The Structural Transformation of the Public Sphere.*
Cambridge, Massachusetts: The MIT Press, 1989, p. 167.

V. Vanitas

Whenever people and civilizations get degenerate and materialistic, they always point at the outward beauty and riches and say that if what they were doing was bad, they wouldn't being doing so well, being so rich and beautiful.

- Andy Warhol, *The Philosophy of Andy Warhol* [384]

[384] Warhol, Andy. *The Philosophy of Andy Warhol.* New York: Harcourt Brace & Company, 1975, p. 70.

Beauty

> Beauty alone confers happiness on all, and under its
> influence every being forgets that he is limited... Taste
> does not suffer any superior or absolute authority, and
> the sway of beauty is extended over appearance... taste
> ever   maintains   its   power   over   remote
> borders...particular desires   must   renounce   their
> egotism.
> - Friedrich Von Schiller, "The Aesthetic Education of
> Man"[385]

103.

Beauty is enigmatic and awe giving. It is an indeterminate
quality of a some thing that attracts us and asks to be
acknowledged. It can be stable, accessible each time a particular
thing is approached, like a beautiful site over courses of
centuries. But, more often beauty appears as a passing event and
is in all instances subject to change or decay.[386] Thus beauty is a
constant vanishing point.[387] "There's no beauty without
poignancy and there's no poignancy without the feeling that it's
going, men, names, books, houses—bound for dust—mortal,"
wrote Fitzgerald.[388] Yet whenever beauty reaches a limit it

---

[385] Von Schiller, J. C. Friedrich. "Letters Upon the Aesthetic Education of Man,"
in *Literary and Philosophical Essays*. Ed. Charles Eliot. New York: Collier and
Son, 1910, p. 312.

[386] "Beauty in danger becomes more beautiful," Warhol, Andy. *The Philosophy
of Andy Warhol*. New York: Harcourt Brace & Company, 1975, p. 65.

[387] "We are drawn to it without knowing what to ask of it. It offers us its own
existence. We do not desire anything else, we possess it, and yet still desire
something. We do not in the least know what it is. We want to get behind beauty,
but ...it is like a mirror that sends us back our own desire for goodness. It is a
sphinx, an enigma, a mystery which is painfully tantalizing. We should like to
feed upon it but it is merely something to look at." Weil, Simone. *Waiting for
God*. Trans. Emma Craufurd. New York: G.P. Putnam's Sons, 1951, p. 166.

[388] Fitzgerald, F. Scott. *The Beautiful and Damned*, New York: The Modern
Library, 2002, p. 141.

appears somewhere else. It continually breaks through again and again in an ongoing dialogue with humanity. Its constant re-appearance intensifies its contemporary attraction and role in decadence. It is an expendable resource that keeps re-appearing, allowing for continued decadence. Contemporary magazine culture thrives off beauty as the latest event upon which to report–what it looks like, how to get it, who already has it, declaring "what's hot" before it's already gone. In the phenomenon of "what's hot," we witness beauty as an invitation to possess it and its limit. But the hot version of beauty is only a mirage, nothing beyond its moment.

104.

> The beauty of the world is not an attribute of matter in itself. It is a relationship of the world to our sensibility, the sensibility that depends upon the structure of our body and our soul...the beauty we experience is designed and destined for our human sensibility.
> - Simone Weil, *Waiting for God*[389]

Beauty is a dialogue with the senses, in every way. The tangible aspects of beauty, give way to the assumption that beauty has immaterial value, that it is a form of perfection offering everything from joy to healing. The continual elevation of beauty in every historic era is also used to point to its everlastingness. Thus, as perfect and eternal, beauty is regarded as divine. In decadence, the divinity of beauty is only interesting for its infinite supply. Beauty yields to the incessant demand from desire. Thus beauty also frustrates desire. The vanishing point of desire is normally reached through consumption. In the

---

[389] Weil, Simone. *Waiting for God.* Trans. Emma Craufurd. New York: G.P. Putnam's Sons, 1951, p. 164.

case of beauty, the vanishing point is reached unpredictably yet there is a guarantee of more to come: Never enough but always more, as if it were the essence of desire itself.

105.

> Death and Destruction are never satisfied, and neither are human eyes.
> - Proverbs 27:20[390]

Decadence typically takes an interest in surface, or at least in affirmation of the surface as meaningful. This is perhaps the gift of decadence, validation that the indexical is more than referential but rather substantial. "The beauty of the world is the mouth of a labyrinth," explained Weil.[391] It is naïve to think that the appreciation of beauty stops at the surface. Is it not what is below the surface also beautiful?[392] The beauty lover loves beauty to its core. But like being in a labyrinth, we chase beauty as it constantly leaves us. C.S. Lewis described the struggle we encounter whenever we try to fix beauty:

> The books or the music in which we thought the beauty was located will betray us if we trust to them; it was not *in* them, it only came *through* them, and what came through them was longing. These things—the beauty, the memory of our own past—are good images of what we really desire; but if they are mistaken for the thing itself they turn into dumb idols, breaking the hearts of their worshippers. For they are not the thing itself; they

---

[390] *The Holy Bible*. New International Version. Grand Rapids, Michigan: Zondervan Publishing House, 1996, p. 556.
[391] Weil, Simone. *Waiting for God*. Trans. Emma Craufurd. New York: G.P. Putnam's Sons, 1951, p. 163.
[392] "Any exaggerated emphasis on surface for the sake of itself is decadent." Serra, Richard. *Writings/Interviews*. Chicago: University of Chicago Press, 1994, p. 23.

are only the scent of a flower we have not found, the echo of a tune we have not heard, news from a country we have never yet visited.[393]

What Lewis describes has an important relationship to desire and decadence. In extreme desire, to the point of expenditure of all resources, we believe we have located a resolution for desire. However, Lewis suggests that we can only locate the vanishing point, from which beauty emerges and disappears. We try to negotiate our desire with the immediate manifestation of beauty before us. The effort is to resolve the total basis of desire in many manifestations that together could be enough to please, "beauty as the sum of several parts."[394] This idea explains the consciously decadent styles and their ornate detail, which are only unified by one very subjective vision. With the subjectivity of beauty, anything can become an object of adoration.[395] Each part is a culminating point of desire but none can individually satisfy even in utmost ornamentation.

106.

The 17th century painter Anthony Van Dyck was a master of painting fabrics, a skill that led to his fame among the English court. The representation of fashion is integral to the

---

[393] Lewis, C.S. "The Weight of Glory," originally a sermon at the Church of St. Mary the Virgin, Oxford, on June 8, 1942. *The Essential C.S. Lewis*. Ed. Lyle W. Dorsett. New York: Simon & Schuster, 1988, p. 363.

[394] Fitzgerald, F. Scott. *The Beautiful and Damned*, New York: The Modern Library, 2002, p. 354.

[395] "There are also a number of seductive factors which have nothing whatever to do with beauty but which cause the things in which they are present to be called beautiful through lack of discernment; for these things attract love by fraud, and all men, even the most ignorant, even the vilest of them, know that beauty alone has a right to our love. The most truly great know it too. No man is below or above beauty. The words which express beauty come to the lips of all as soon as they want to praise what they love." Weil, Simone. *Waiting for God*. Trans. Emma Craufurd. New York: G.P. Putnam's Sons, 1951, p. 165.

"conspicuous waste" and showmanship of beauty in decadence.[396] The same practice is observed today in the work of Vanessa Beecroft. In her assembly of hundreds of young women, they are either clothed in couture or nothing at all; it is beauty in excess.[397] Really Beecroft's art is beauty pageant on demand.[398] The performances require extensive planning and are a *work* of art, recalling that "we must labour to be beautiful."[399] For each work, she orders the models in lines or scatters them, disguises them or unveils them. As a result, we observe only a surface of passing style. The actual event is nothing but standing and walking; it is beauty as justification. The performance resembles our ceremonies, like a still life of a restless life, of events without purpose other than the purpose of looking good–walking the red carpet at an award's show, a biennial or concert, all where the value of the occasion is in relationship to its aesthetic presentation. The same showmanship is observed on the fashion runway where we find beautiful models, "useless and expensive,"[400] thus symptoms of cultural decoration like living

---

[396] Packard, Vance. *The Status Seekers*. New York: Simon and Schuster, 1959, p. 106.

[397] As a project for this text, *Terminal 5* included a production of the work of Vanessa Beecroft in VB54.

[398] Juergen Teller describes photographing contestants, "I had to ask the Miss World organization... suddenly the red carpet rolled out and I had all eighty-eight Miss World contestants in front of me...they looked just like each other." Speyer, Ariana, Ed. *The Real Thing: Fashion Interviews from Index Magazine*. New York: Index Books, 2003, p. 89.

[399] Yeats, W. B. *The Yeats Reader*. Ed. Richard Finneran. New York: Scriber, 1997, p. 41. "Adam's Curse, "To be born woman is to know...that we must labour to be beautiful." "If beauty or comfort is achieved,–and it is more or less fortuitous circumstance if they are–they must be achieved by means and methods that commend themselves to the great economic law of wasted effort." Veblen, Thorstein. *The Theory of the Leisure Class*. New York: Dover Publications, 1994, p. 51.

[400] Veblen, Thorstein. *The Theory of the Leisure Class*. New York: Dover Publications, 1994, p. 90.

fashion accessories.[401] The beauty worship is also a performance of attractive body forms, which then addresses not only the luxury in fabrics but the new luxury in transforming the body using wealth to make oneself more beautiful.

107.

> Nature has had her day...there is not one of her inventions, deemed so subtle and so wonderful which the ingenuity of mankind cannot create.
> - J.K. Huysmans, *A Rebours* [402]

In our decadence, rather than wait for beauty's next arrival we continually embellish it and surround ourselves with re-creations. Humanity stylishly displays beauty, giving it total territory, any territory.[403] We are constantly beautifying the world, almost in an effort to merge with it.[404] We are filling every gap with some type of beauty, natural or constructed. This is a process of beautification.

"The beautiful in nature and art," writes Gadamer, "is to be supplemented by the whole ocean of the beautiful spread

---

[401] There is also "fashion week," always occurring somewhere around the world. "There are eighty-five shows and everybody is exhausted and everybody is fabulous–'Where am I seated, what should I wear today?'" described APC designer Jean Touitou. Speyer, Ariana, Ed. *The Real Thing: Fashion Interviews from Index Magazine*. New York: Index Books, 2003, p. 4.

[402] Huysmans, J.K. *A Rebours*. Trans. Havelock Ellis. New York: Dover, 1969, p. 22.

[403] "Beautiful jails for beautiful people." Warhol, Andy. *The Philosophy of Andy Warhol*. New York: Harcourt Brace & Company, 1975, p. 71.

[404] "We want something else which can hardly be put into words–to be united with the beauty we see, to pass into it, to receive it into ourselves, to bathe in it, to become part of it. That is why we have peopled air and earth and water with gods and goddesses and nymphs and elves–that, though we cannot, yet these projections can, enjoy themselves that beauty, grace and power of which Nature is the image." Lewis, C.S. *The Essential C.S. Lewis*. Ed. Lyle W. Dorsett. New York: Simon & Schuster, 1988, p. 4368.

throughout the moral reality of mankind."[405] Does beauty need expansion?[406] Why do we feel we must obtain or sustain both pleasure and beauty in our world? It is some kind of effort to sustain pleasure *instead* of feeling itself. Doesn't beauty need us to praise it?[407] Why does man made beauty expand territory, without the capacity to expand its own meaning? Natural beauty, in its magnitude and eternal status, is the backdrop to our limited, contextual expressions that try to fix beauty. We collectively advance beauty as utmost value. We then gracefully negate and disguise whatever is deemed not beautiful in this moment. We even complain about the ugly, though it is subjective and before long, the ugly is considered beautiful again. And as much as we have spent decades expounding on the perverse for example, it seems that we always return to the Apollonian. We have proven again and again with each decadent era that we not only believe in the philosophy that "all cognition should begin with the study of the beautiful,"[408] but that it should also end there.

108.

Aristocracy has traditionally aimed to provide examples of "what are the right and beautiful habits of life."[409] This is

---

[405] Gadamer, Hans-Georg. *Truth and Method.* Translation revised by Joel Weinsheimer and Donald G. Marshall New York: Continuum, 1999, pp. 38-39.

[406] "All these secondary kinds of beauty are of infinite value as openings to universal beauty. But if we stop short at them, they are, on the contrary, veils; then they corrupt. They all have in them more or less this temptation." Weil, Simone. *Waiting for God.* Trans. Emma Craufurd. New York: G.P. Putnam's Sons, 1951, p. 165.

[407] "All beauty is incomplete if there is no one there to praise it." Snell, Bruno. *The Discovery of the Mind: In Greek Philosophy and Literature.* Trans. T. G. Rosenmeyer. New York: Dover, 1982, p. 78.

[408] Hölderlin, Friedrich. *Essays and Letters on Theory.* Trans. Thomas Pfau. New York: State University of New York Press, 1988, p. 47.

[409] Veblen, Thorstein. *The Theory of the Leisure Class.* New York: Dover Publications, 1994, p. 121.

accomplished through a restraint of resources, thus suggesting restraint in behavior and appearance is beauty, or that beauty is simply what obeys.[410] Virtue is a method of controlling desire, moderately and with reason.[411] In 1474, Leonardo da Vinci painted a portrait of noblewoman Ginevra de'Benci. On the back of the portrait is the inscription, "Virtutem Forma Decorat" which has been understood to mean "beauty adorns virtue." The phrase could also mean "virtue is the form of beauty." Because beauty is associated with goodness, it is often assumed that beauty is a virtue of its own or that associating with beauty makes one good. This sanctification of beauty is what allows beauty to rise to a place of otherwise unjustified social esteem. Beauty also somehow seems to have the power to redeem, to make the ugly better, which leads unfortunately to using beauty as a means and end.[412] "For only beauty should preach repentance," explained Nietzsche.[413]

Style

> A "classic" is a successful book that has survived the reaction of the next period or generation. Then it's safe, like a style in architecture or furniture. It's acquired a picturesque dignity to take the place of its fashion.
> - F. Scott Fitzgerald, *The Beautiful and Damned* [414]

---

[410] "Beauty," considered Nietzsche, is "the highest sign of power." Nietzsche, Friedrich. *The Will to Power*. Trans. Walter Kaufmann. New York: Random House, 1968, p. 422.

[411] Ibid. p. 238.

[412] Ibid. p. 424.

[413] Nietzsche, Friedrich. *Thus Spoke Zarathustra: A Book for All and None*. Trans. Walter Kaufman. New York: The Modern Library. 1992, p. 92.

[414] Fitzgerald, F. Scott. *The Beautiful and Damned*, New York: The Modern Library, 2002, p. 39.

109.

Cultivation aims for excellent taste. There is a process of encountering the full spectrum of aesthetics which allows one to recognize the best. The idea of a "best" however is to believe to have resolved the absolute point of beauty and thus desire. The best taste is a type of "salvation by form" that generates a fixed style.[415] The result of consistent preference for a particular style of beauty, is that one soon grows disenchanted. One either grows tired of a style or stubborn in style. Thus, "the 'styles' are a lie," explained Le Corbusier.[416] The charm wears off and the person must then re-decorate with a new expression. The other outcome of steadfastness to a style such as "classic," or as seen in the last century a preference for minimalism, is a constant closure to and negation of all other forms of beauty which naturally fill existence.

110.

> You seriously think you'll never get old that you'll be forever good-looking, and they'll keep you here forever and ever.
> - Fyodor Dostoevsky, *Notes from Underground*[417]

The appreciation of beauty in decadence is usually an endless romance with a particular direction of style. The investment in a decadent style however does not consider the passage of time, that it will get old and in time become aged and weathered. We associate set or fixed styles with former eras, as in "Second

---

[415] We must further consider the limits of "salvation by form." Lecture with Jean Baudrillard, European Graduate School, Saas-Fee Switzerland, June 12, 2004.
[416] Conrad, Ulrich. *Programs and Manifestoes on 20th-century Architecture.* Cambridge: MIT Press, 1997, p. 60.
[417] Dostoevsky, Fyodor. *Notes from Underground.* New York: Vintage Books Random House, 1993, p. 99.

Empire," "Mission," "Colonial," or "Puritan," furniture and décor. We can describe previous expressions of style but are often unable to name contemporary expressions with the same clarity, or more importantly in acknowledging our own preferences. The exception is in the style media who trendspot and name the style of the moment. These trend reporters are like bounty hunters on beauty. They acknowledge that beauty is an event and they have seen its current style. The comeback of fashion styles evidence the collective unconscious, exposing shared memory and presence. The turnover of style is justified by its connection to humanity and the greater need for ongoing relevance.

111.

There are then fixed styles and also the event of style, which is willingness to put any resource at risk in a continual freedom of expression. Style is gesturing with whatever is available. "It is not the author's viewpoint," writes Schirmacher, "or his or her aesthetic judgment that style expresses. Style is a game playing with time and language in which you discover and forget the self. Style is neither an identification tag nor a tool of power but a composition never made before, in a language free of fixed meaning but still meaningful to you."[418] Thus style involves a play with what appears in openness and action.[419] When a

---

[418] Schirmacher, Wolfgang. Homo Generator: Media and Postmodern Technology. Ed. G. Bender, T. Duckrey. *Culture on the Brink: Ideologies of Technology.* The New Press. New York, 1994/1999. Quote appears from lecture at http://www.egs.edu/faculty/schirmacher/schirmacher-homo-generator.html. A similar concept was suggested by Maslow who proposed that health is the balance between spontaneity and intellect, an inward discretion over when to allow openness. Maslow, Abraham. *Toward a Psychology of Being.* New York: Van Nostrand Reinhold, 1968, pp. 197-198.

[419] "Style is openness, a life search that *'de-appropriates'* (Avital Ronell) given realities. The gaze as exchange of seeing and being seen, the ear as confluence of hearing and being heard, and writing as expression and learning do not need

particular action proves successful, as in the great stroke of the paintbrush, the same action may be tried again, rather than new openness and action. Consistent style choices begin to appear like a pattern, and thus soon the style is mistaken for identity. While it is true that each style is an aspect of being, fixing that aspect is not being in total. For example, the "classic" is considered a style-less, timeless form. It is consistent with a certain idealized form of being that does re-appear but not in all instances. Seeking to express the classic style or status quo every time is an effort to normalize the differences in being. This is why corporations communicate with classic style, to neutralize both employees and the customers. We have grown to accept the mass produced corporate style is neutral and best for all, and should not be questioned = democratic capitalism.

112.

> Today it is true, our task is to "fill in the background," but we must not neglect the delightful trifles which are the finishing touches dictated by Good Taste.
> - Stéphane Mallarmé, *La Derniére Mode* [420]

Because decadence seeks to resolve desire in particular style, decadent taste usually results in very bad style that is dead and blind to whole being. Gadamer describes the potential for overdetermining style:

---

recording but aspire to fulfillment." Schirmacher, Wolfgang. "Homo Generator: Media and Postmodern Technology." *Culture on the Brink: Ideologies of Technology.* Ed. G. Bender, T. Duckrey. New York: The New Press. 1994/1999. Quote appears from lecture at www.egs.edu, http://www.egs.edu/faculty/schirmacher/schirmacher-homo-generator.html.
[420] Furbank, P.N. and A. M. Cain. *Mallarmé on Fashion.* New York, Berg, 2004, p. 73.

The phenomenon of taste is an intellectual faculty of differentiation...good taste is distinguished by the fact that it is able to adapt itself to the direction of taste represented by fashion or, contrariwise, is able to adapt what is demanded by fashion to its own good taste. Part of the concept of taste, then, is that one observes measure even in fashion, not blindly following its changing dictates but using one's own judgment. One maintains one's own "style"–i.e., one relates that demands of fashion to a whole that one's own taste keeps in view and accepts only what harmonizes with this whole... Thus taste not only recognizes this or that as beautiful but has an eye to the whole, with which everything that is beautiful must harmonize. ...(taste) constitutes a special way of knowing. Like reflective judgment, it belongs in the realm of that which grasps, in the individual object, the universal under which it is to be subsumed. Both taste and judgment evaluate that object in relation to a whole in order to see whether it fits in with everything else.[421]

There is an inclination to negotiate all appearances of beauty into a specific pre-determined "good style." But we must remain conscious of the mediation of aesthetics as mediation of singular and collective. This is why there is personal style and trend. But neither is the truth, as both are in dialogue with the truth, and what Gadamer suggests is to consider "the object in relation to the whole," as they are both necessary in understanding.

113.

Decadence involves extreme use of resources with a strong attraction to assert something is "beautiful," no matter how

---

[421] Gadamer, Hans-Georg. *Truth and Method*. Translation revised by Joel Weinsheimer and Donald G. Marshall New York: Continuum, 1999, pp. 37-38.

depraved.[422] For Nietzsche the interest in "becoming more beautiful," leads toward a "high point of the development: the grand style."[423] If we can ever step outside a decadent definition of beauty, the awareness leads to a lateral move of one style for another. Style is a partial expression of beauty but is accepted as absolute beauty in the same way that in decadence partial truths are used in place of total absolute truth. A decadent style expresses fragmented values that are taken in total as ideology. Gadamer expressed such a view:

> The history of the idea of taste follows the history of absolutism from Spain to France and England...Taste is not only the ideal created by a new society, but we see this ideal of "good taste" producing what was subsequently called "good society." It no longer recognizes and legitimates itself on the basis of birth and rank but simply through the shared nature of its judgments or, rather, its capacity to rise above narrow interests and private predilections to the tithe of judgment.[424]

Historically, the judgment of quality was not taken lightly, and not allowed to be carried out by the un-informed. Only those with power could deem what was worthy and that judgment was total for all. It was not only the concentration of wealth that angered the citizens against "Louis the Last" but it was the concentration of judgment. In democratic capitalism, the assertion of taste and expression of style is free. Now all types of taste and style are validated and expressed. We now taste test

---

[422] Warhol, Andy. *The Philosophy of Andy Warhol*. New York: Harcourt Brace & Company, 1975, p. 72.
[423] Nietzsche, Friedrich. *The Will to Power*. Trans. Walter Kaufmann. New York: Random House, 1968, p. 420.
[424] Gadamer, Hans-Georg. *Truth and Method*. Translation revised by Joel Weinsheimer and Donald G. Marshall New York: Continuum, 1999, p. 36.

every product and participate in voting for music stars, but we
have forgotten the power of judgment. It is no longer feared and
we cannot understand the privilege of an informed refusal. It's
"yes to all."[425]

114.

> It is all right to decorate construction but never
> construct decoration.
> - Robert Venturi and Denise Scott Brown, *Learning
> from Las Vegas*[426]

Because decadence is a process of expending resources, it
normally tends toward an expressive, baroque style. "Baroque"
comes from the Portuguese word for the natural variation in
pearls. It signifies enough material for an uneven form. The
baroque also points to our inability to grasp the natural world,
full of both form and formless. It can also refer to the very
specific historic period of the 17th century in Rome when the
Catholic Church was excessive in aesthetic production, and it is
used to describe something theatrical as in a jest or a dream, like
a reflection in a carnival mirror showing elaboration without
reason. The baroque can also simply mean repetition and
exaggeration as in *Finnegan's Wake* (1939) or Blanchot's
Infinite Conversation (1993). Kierkegaard refers to himself as
"the Baroque thinker."[427] Could then we also regard Carl
Andre's excessive bricks as baroque minimalism?[428] There is

[425] Work of art by Sylvie Fluery, 2002.
[426] Venturi, Robert, et al. *Learning from Las Vegas*. Cambridge: MIT Press,
1971, p. 163.
[427] Kierkegaard, Søren. *The Point of View*. Trans. Walter Lowrie. London:
Oxford University Press, 1939, p. 62
[428] Term used in conversation with James Westcott, online editor of Art Review,
September 2006.

nothing ornate about the medium but the gesture is excessive. Matthew Barney, Sylvie Fluery, and Tom Sachs are overtly excessive and in dialog with the drama of mass production. Banks Violette has used the gallery and museum as a theater stage, evoking the historic notion of the baroque.[429] The forced ambiance is decadent in form and meaning. Vivienne Westwood, Jean-Charles de Castelbajac, John Galliano, and Alexander McQueen favor the drama of performance and excess. The baroque then is simply an excessive gesture, with perhaps an added understanding of its own excessiveness. It is unabashed and over the top without concern of implication.

115.

In a traditional museum the installation of furniture is intended to bear representation of the style of particular periods. We walk into a room of furniture from another era, and we feel like we could be there. It creates an impression and at best elicits fantasy. The contemporary gallery, like a retail space wants to constantly turnover style, in order to attract customers. The commercial gallery, really a product of the mid-20th century, promises to be erased again and again, providing a blank slate for the artist–an empty parentheses.

{{{{{{{{{{{{{{{{{{{{{{{{{ }}}}}}}}}}}}}}}}}}}}}}}}}

In her work, *Commemorative Toile* (1993), Renée Green decorated the Galerie Metropol in Vienna Austria with ornate wallpaper and furniture. The furniture was arranged along with

---

[429] "Like many contemporary artists, Violette embraces this 'perverse' notion of theater and staging, yet the baroque theatricality and decentered complexity of his typical source material are filtered through a Minimalist language of formal gestures." Momin, Shamim. *Banks Violette*. New York: Whitney Museum of American Art, 2005, p. 17.

small black boxes labeled "AMBIANCE." The installation
pointed to contemporary art as constant installation dominating
total gallery territory. Mike Kelly's *Day is Done* (2005)
installation at Gagosian Gallery made a similar gesture by
consuming total gallery territory with carnival like booths for
performances of high school events. The ambiance of the art
world is like any other site of decadence, a point for
performance and artifice. But what a dream to have as Le
Corbusier wanted, the capacity to always start again at zero. But
what zero? The zero of commercial territory? That is the
storefront. The turnover of style translates to turnover of
merchandise that will accumulate and contribute to the ultimate
decay. The gallery will die with capitalism.

116.

> I have always argued for my favorite architecture:
> beautiful, light, varied, imaginative, and awe-inspiring.
> These are words that, much to my delight, I found later
> in a Baudelaire poem: "L'attendu, l'irrégularité, la
> surprise et l'étonnement son tune partie essentielle et
> une charactéristique de la beauté"...I defended my
> architecture and my fantasies.
> - Oscar Niemeyer, *The Memoirs of Oscar Niemeyer* [430]

With minimal ornamentation, modern architecture decorated the
urban and suburban landscape of the 20th century. What we find
is not minimal production but maximum production of
minimalism. The work of Oscar Niemeyer is driven by fantasy
of a monumental world of fantastic ease. His poured concrete
surfaces are true integrity of core to surface. The forms are

---

[430] Niemeyer, Oscar. *The Curves of Time: The Memoirs of Oscar Niemeyer*.
London: Phaidon, 2000, p. 168 & p. 170.

extreme, though controlled, and for that reason he has been called baroque. He explains that

> The criticisms did not bother me at all. I knew that someday critics would tire of their tedious sameness and start looking for something else. Now its postmodernism they have turned to; they have accepted all the novelties they once rejected, only now these are a thousand times more conspicuous. Le Corbusier alone refused to jump on the bandwagon. I remember him once remarking, "Oscar, what you are doing is baroque, but it's very well done." And again several years later, "They say my work is baroque too."[431]

Niemeyer pursued more irregular shapes and curves than Le Corbusier and also survived the entire 20th century continuing his work from an office in Copacabana well past age 100. His decadent style speaks of a particular moment in history but his attitude is reverence for the vitality in truth that the most genuine expression of style can achieve.[432] However today the style is fixed and dead. Today, it is no longer possible to design the future Niemeyer envisioned because being has already moved forward to the next future.

117.

In contemporary thought, we the style of idea presentation is fixed, not only by the book or type forms but also by the lecture. *"Towards a new style of philosophy,"* Badiou says. "My position is to break with these frameworks of thought, to find another philosophical style, a style other than that of interpretation, of

---

[431] Ibid. p. 63.
[432] "I was convinced that truth could not be slighted; one day it will triumph and be lasting and irrefutable. I realized that the universe was not made for us." Ibid. p. 162.

logical grammarian analysis, or of polyvalence and language games—that is to rediscover, a dedicated style, a style in the school of Descartes for example."[433] Why do we need a new style? What about truth? We do not instigate revolution by discussing the uniforms of the opposition or changing our uniforms. We attack, with a brilliance all our own that communicates the same truth as before. As thinkers we are undeniably subject to style forms of language, which are plural and always in flux. To call for the new style of thought or theory is to bring attention to particular value sets that deny absolute value. Every generation wants to claim an influence and style is one way in which they can be remembered but it is also the way in which they will be seen as historic and limited in understanding.

Fashion

> Life is a masquerade, you explain, and for you this is inexhaustible material for amusement...for every revelation you make is always an illusion...your occupation consists in preserving your hiding place, and that you succeed in doing, for your mask is the most enigmatic of all. In fact you are nothing; you are merely a relation to others, and what you are you are by virtue of this relation.
> - Søren Kierkegaard, *Either/Or*[434]

---

[433] Badiou, Alain. *Infinite Thought*. Trans. Justin Clemens. New York: Continuum, 2003, p. 50.

[434] Kierkegaard, Søren. "Vol. II: Equilibrium Between the Aesthetical and the Ethical in the Composition of Personality." *Either/Or: A Fragment of Life.* in *A Kierkegaard Anthology.* Ed. Robert Bretall. New York: The Modern Library, 1946, p.99.

118.

Clothing is most simply a covering over of the body. A designer creates fashion by shaping the form into an object that is valued for its aesthetic appearance and symbolic meaning. With fashion at large, we are constantly furthering our fascination with visual presentation and values, engaging in a dialog with others and with context.

119.

If style is the varied expression of beauty then fashion is the complete dedication to the turnover of style.

120.

French artist Louis Arogon described that, "Fashion is the word that lovers of weakness and those who revere reassuring divinities have invented as a sort of mask to disfigure the future."[435] Yet it is fashion that expresses the times, in concert with collective consciousness, revealing being. The law of fashion is constant play, a play that defies rules but reveres exceptions.[436] The "classic" is a constant state of exception to fashion du jour because it is always acceptable, exempt from the current mode.

121.

I'm always intrigued by the performance. I think of the clothes as mostly costumes in some ways. They're

---

[435] "One must accept the challenge; one has to accept that fashion, in the most discredited meaning of the word, women's fashion, this frightening and frivolous history of changing hats, may become the vulgar symbol of what disqualifies any activity one day." Lehmann, Ulrich. *Tigersprung: Fashion in Modernity.* Cambridge, Massachusetts: MIT Press, 2000, pp. 301-302.
[436] "Play is always lost when it seeks salvation in games," Derrida, Jacques. *Dissemination.* Chicago: The University of Chicago Press, 1981, p. 158.

usually the last things that we think about after we've come up with the overall concept. It's a piece of the whole not the whole itself.

- Tara Subkoff on the runway presentations for *Imitation of Christ*[437]

Clothing is worn; fashion is performed.

122.

"We all want *one* thing. That little red ribbon of the Légion d'Honneur," wrote Diana Vreeland.[438] Fashion is desire for the signifier. The exchange of signifiers in wearing involves claims to values, as in the honor of a ribbon, or negation of a punk's safety pin. Postmodern fashion is a "free use of the proper" in the sense it requires a fluency of existing codes. The process of mixing codes is a contamination that creates equivalency among forms. Only when the fashion code is regarded in context, that is for example the ribbon of honor with the ritual ceremony, is it an absolute. The dilution of fashion codes explains the power of the brand. The brand continually re-asserts itself as purified code and thus satisfies the desire for absolutes.

123.

According to Gilles Lipovetsky, fashion has functioned as sanctioned mockery. He describes the atmosphere of the 19th Century:

> As fashion and the people engaged in it were winning their own letters of nobility, people engaged in intellectual pursuits–philosophers, writers, poets–were also acquiring immense prestige. They were sometimes

[437] Speyer, Ariana, Ed. *The Real Thing: Fashion Interviews.* New York: Index Books, 2003, p. 119.
[438] Vreeland, Diana. *D.V.* New York: De Capo Press, 1984, p. 195.

viewed as the 'equal of kings,' and they took on the preeminent roles of guides, educators and prophets to the human race. Just as fashion took over as arbiter of elegance, intellectuals, poets and later scientists claimed the right to legitimate values...However, alongside this triumph of intellectuals and artists with a mission, another phenomenon emerged...artists began to offer ambivalent, mocking representations of themselves...this tragic aspect of artistic representation contrasts with a triumphant, wholly positive image of fashion and the great couturier...who understands mockery as a necessary game.[439]

Whatever was sought by the rebellious artist was already at play in fashion. Art is always already obsolete.[440] Fashion functions in the real world where it aims to participate. It never needs to justify ownership for beauty alone, the way that art does. And fashion by the very nature of it, has already moved on before we do. In this way the social enactment of fashion is like a charade of being, always hovering on the vanishing point, taking pleasure in the moment and simultaneously throwing it away for the next one.

124.

Fashion is clothing that is accepted as actually carrying meaning that is understood by others. For a solider to wear a military coat relies on his assumption that the actual coat is party to power and will be recognized as powerful by others. For a civilian to wear a military coat expresses value of power but negates the

---

[439] Lipovetsky, Gilles. *The Empire of Fashion*. Tans. Catherine Porter. Princeton: Princeton University Press, 1994, p. 73.
[440] Belle Epoque designer Paul Poiret remarked, "The spirit of contradiction in fashion is so frequent and so regular that one can see in it almost a law." Poiret was known for throwing elaborate themed parties. Poiret, Paul. *King of Fashion: The Autobiography of Paul Poiret*. Trans. Stephen Haden Guest. Philadelphia: Lippincott, 1931, p. 295.

particular authority of the military, demoting it to decoration. The military coat still signifies the military but it enters the charade, a game of value assertion called fashion. It all goes one step further in the sense that a new coat made in the style of the military relies only on a memory of the real, revealing fashion as index.

Fixed styles attempt to petrify a fashion expression.[441] Fixed styles seek to retain meaning, or rather rely upon the fact that others continue most easily with existing codes. The military coat tries to remain consistent in appearance to preserve the recognition of its power. The style only signifies if the person who sees the coat can understand not just that the coat is from the military but that the coat equals power, prestige, protection and death.

125.

The greater play of meaning in fashion depends upon fluency or a "free use of the proper."[442] Yet the fluency is not only based upon real world referents but a contrived "system of meaning," that is really more of a "supervised freedom," for the dresser, because the fashion industry can shift a code or invent a new meaning through media at any time.[443] Suddenly then we can

---

[441] "Style thereby protects the presence, the content, the thing itself, meaning, truth–on the condition at least that it should not *already* be that gaping chasm which has been deflowered in the unveiling of the difference." Derrida, Jacques. *Spurs*. Chicago, The University of Chicago Press, 1978, p. 39. The situation can become more complex however when style is separated into genre or categories such as "styles" of music. In this instance there is like a meta-code that can lead to assumptions that overdetermine individual expression.
[442] "Free Use of the Proper ("der freie Gebrauch des Eigenen,") Hölderlin, Friedrich. *Essays and Letters on Theory*. Trans. Thomas Pfau. New York: State University of New York Press, 1988, p. 150.
[443] Barthes, Roland. *The Fashion System*. Trans. Matthew Ward & Richard Howard. Berkeley: University of California Press, 1983, p. 161.

have what Roland Barthes describes as "California style," an invented style constructed for warmer weather, the seaside, celebrities, sunsets and other American dreams.[444] Fashion is a system of relevance to the collective conscious and unconscious which is full of fantasies.

126.

Fashion is a live performance with one another with varying subtlety of value assertion. We engage in an unspoken dialogue. But to regard that dialogue as real is to forget the nakedness of humanity. In his book *Anthropology from a Pragmatic Point of View*, Immanuel Kant expressed:

> It is a natural inclination of man to compare his behavior to that of a more important person (the child compares itself to grown-ups, and the lowly compares himself to the aristocrat) in order to imitate the other person's ways. A law of such imitation, which aims at not appearing less important than others, especially when no regard is paid to gaining any profit from it, is called fashion. Therefore it belongs under the title of vanity, because in its intention there is no inner value; at the same time, it belongs also under the title of folly, because in fashion there is still a compulsion to subject oneself slavishly to the mere example which many in society project to us. To be in fashion is a matter of taste; he who clings to custom which is out of fashion is said to be old-fashioned; and he who even attributes value to being out of fashion is an odd person. But it is always better, nevertheless, to be a fool in fashion than a fool out of fashion, if one chooses to brand this vanity at all with such a hard name, a title which the mania for fashion really deserves whenever it sacrifices true uses or even duties to such vanity. All fashion are, by their very concept, mutable ways of living. Whenever the

---

[444] Ibid. p. 195.

play of imitating becomes fixed, imitation becomes usage, and that means the end of taste. Novelty makes fashion alluring; and to be inventive in all sorts of external forms, even if they often degenerate into something fantastic and even detestable, belongs to the style of courtiers, especially the ladies, whom others then follow avidly. Those in low social positions burden themselves with these fashions long after the courtiers have put them aside. Therefore, fashion is not properly a matter of taste (for it may be extremely antagonistic to taste), but a matter of mere vanity in order to appear distinguished.[445]

Fashion is an open invitation but one must know the rules of the game, which involve appropriateness, contemporary relevance and the distinguishing expression described by Kant. Those who take part in fashion make their awareness of the rules visible which often means similarity and imitation is what is recognized over personal style. There is however always the possibility of the surprise of the new, which appears to break the cycle of imitation and can disrupt personal style. The new is simply an idea made visible by fashion that is then replayed and appropriated by the imitation known as trend. The trend is a weak aftermath of the original event of the new. The "new" (so frequently considered synonymous with fashion) is simply the ongoing acquaintance with total being. Out of a race to keep a pace with others and also the self, one finds the new as necessary to personal expression. Thus, when one does not know the self at all, the trends of fashion satisfy the desire for consciousness but deny distinguishing expression, thus working like ideology over truth.

---

[445] Kant, Immanuel. *Anthropology from a Pragmatic Point of View.* Trans. by Victor Lyle Dowdel. *Carbondale, IL:* Southern Illinois University Press, 1978, p. 148.

127.

> Fashion retains its full 'kingship of a day' over them,
> though subject to customs which alter over the
> years...As for the law for this winter it remains
> uncertain. We are thus still under summer rule which, I
> take it, you know?
> - Stephané Mallarmé, *La Dernière Mode*[446]

It is old fashioned to assume that we all want to be kings. There is a certain degree of posturing and negation among youth that dismisses the market value of beauty and prizes the anti-aesthetic. The punk movement for example presents unresolved angst as its decoration. The subjects negate accepted values on a superficial level. The investment into surface is why a punk is more similar to an overdressed aristocrat than to common man, because the punk and the aristocrat both appreciate the performance of appearances. There is also the decadent expression of dandyism, known today as the hipster, with an accentuation of depravity and a "magical relation to a poverty."[447] Poverty and depravity become grandeur. The photographs of hipster Dash Snow of abject youths living a life of casual intensity have transformed squalor into dream world. There is a blank, dismissive attitude that reveals decadence can simply be a costume of refusal, a willing stigmata.[448] It is a performance of giving the self over to the desire for nothing.

---

[446] Furbank, P.N. and A.M. Cain. *Mallarmé on Fashion*. New York, Berg, 2004, p. 95 and p. 214.
[447] Hebdige, Dick. *Subculture: The Meaning of Style*. New York, Routledge, 1979, p. 49.
[448] Ibid. p. 2.

128.

Goya's interest in costume rose from his exposure to aristocracy.[449] His deliberate use of masks and capes in the "Caprichos" was an attempt to make the staging of the royal court into the farce they could not see for themselves.[450]

In Stanley Kubrik's *Eyes Wide Shut* (1999), the characters are discussing if a dream can be real. Alice expresses her uncertainty "that the reality of one night, let alone that of a whole lifetime, can ever be the whole truth." *Eyes Wide Shut* is not only a mockery of the media industry but also a consideration of the everyday game of disguise.

Life has become a decadent costume party of our own invention in which people assume a role and dress accordingly. While under democratic capitalism we can freely dress ourselves, the costume alone cannot produce a social status shift because it is only a necessary tool of social position, not the necessary invitation.

129.

In Roger Vadim's *La Curée* (1966) a woman has left her aristocratic husband for his wayward son. She eventually decides to return to the good life, arriving at her ex-husband's home in the middle of a masquerade party. The woman walks through rooms of the house where she once resided, now filled with people in costumes. Suddenly her estranged husband sees her

---

[449] "Aristocracy results from the rule of the game." Lecture with Jean Baudrillard, European Graduate School, Saas-Fee Switzerland, June 12, 2004.

[450] "El Pelele" (1791-2) is understood to mock the king as a toy of collective whimsy, always at the people's command. In the tapestry "La Gallina Ciega" (1788-1789) there are a group of children playing Blind Man's Bluff. The figure in the middle is willingly blindfolded.

and escorts her outside where she then watches the party through a window. The scene is not only a comment on the charade of aristocracy but a comment on the spectacle of film. We have left the real world for a younger, impoverished son in media. When we grow hungry for the reality we previously enjoyed, we return to it only to find it now also seems to also be a charade, and one at which we are not at home in anymore.

The original story of *La Curée*, a title that means "kill of the hunt," was written by Emile Zola in 1871-72. The real charade of the story is that Zola was unknown and living in poverty at the time. Though he toured a few aristocratic homes he had never experienced any of the life he wrote about. Neither had any of the critics, obviously, who reviewed the book as "realistic."

130.

What embellishes and obscures, not only by costumes but laugh tracks on television or decorated covers on books? Writing itself functions like a decoration on a surface. Do we ever cease to be attracted to the trace of the pen or the typeface in print? We adore the covering over of a blank space. We love to imagine the meaning of the words. This word, the meaning–what meaning of what word? The one you read now that echoes in your head Where could it go next? What will it look like next? Will it please you? Or fail you? Or entertain you? Do you need to further decorate it? To correct it? To pause and make it something else? What of this game, the masquerade of meaning? Why is there a styling of thought? What is a naked word?

131.
The question of the masquerade is are we concealing or revealing? How do we know the difference? Do we ever completely conceal? Do we ever completely reveal? Kierkegaard wrote, "Do you not know that there comes a midnight hour when everyone has to throw off his mask? Do you believe that life will always let itself be mocked? Do you think you can slip away a little before midnight in order to avoid this? Or are you not terrified by it? I have seen men in real life who so long deceived others that at last their true nature could not reveal itself... In every man there is something which to a certain degree prevents him from becoming perfectly transparent to himself... But he who cannot reveal himself cannot love, and he who cannot love is the most unhappy man of all."[451]

The need to unveil the truth by a minimalist style, that was itself contrived, was a modernist proposition. In postmodernity, the world still plays a grand charade. The role of thought is not to minimize the masquerade, but to make known that an elaborate masquerade cannot hide the already unmasked truth.

Aura

> Yesterday they were diverted from the truth of history–
> today they are diverted from the truth of their own
> desires.
> - Jean Baudrillard, *Seduction*[452]

[451] Kierkegaard, Søren. "Vol. II: Equilibrium Between the Aesthetical and the Ethical in the Composition of Personality." *Either/Or: A Fragment of Life.* in *A Kierkegaard Anthology.* Ed. Robert Bretall. New York: The Modern Library, 1946, p. 99-100.
[452] Baudrillard, Jean. *Seduction.* Trans. Brain Singer. New York: St. Martin's Press, 1990, p. 175.

132.

In the early 20th century, Walter Benjamin explained the relation between mechanical reproduction and the loss of the aura. Aura is the singular presence and authority of an original object. Technology could possibly preserve skill, but the original essence of things was supposed to disappear.[453] By contrast, aura survives today in the authority and presence of the image. The photograph expands original authority to the point that there can no longer be an event without images.[454] These images of our era are images of ourselves; we are obsessed with the anthropocentric aura, in the greatest decadent vanity known to man. Never before were there more mirrors, cameras or recording devices allowing every trace to be noted and re-considered.

133.

Aura is radiation. Adorno describes it as emanating from luxury. But aura can also beam from ordinary things, especially if the object is associated with something greater. Souvenirs for example are desirable because they suggest access to original locations, to truth. Aura involves a restless reflection, nostalgia for original truth. If we consider for example Eve in paradise it was not the truth about the fruit that seduced her but her contemplation of what could be true. The snake gives a doubt, "You will not surely die," prompting her to think something else

---

[453] Benjamin, Walter. "The Work of Art in the Age of Mechanical Reproduction," in Mast, Gerald, et al. *Film Theory and Criticism.* Oxford: Oxford University Press, 1992, p. 665-681.
[454] "There is no event without images." Lecture with Jean Baudrillard, European Graduate School, Saas-Fee Switzerland, June 12, 2004. I would suggest however there is no event without representation, which could be by story, sound or other expression.

could be true.[455] Could it be true that the fruit would kill her? Could it be true that she gains knowledge? The contemplation was not about right or wrong but about the possibility that seemed to exist in the object.

134.

Fashion has an aura of status and beauty. Tourism has the aura of an "other." Possession of objects with aura does not however result in power over aura, rather it is being under its influence. Power over aura comes in differentiating the real from the aura. That is why the internet does not have power or control anything by containing all the knowledge of the world. It contains information, like a library but it does not discern thus has no power.

Power comes in witness to truth and thus indifference to aura. In academia, the citation appears to reference truth and thus creates an aura of truth, which in turn constantly distracts from the presence of truth. "'Truth,' "can only be surface" wrote Derrida, "But the blushing movement of that truth which is not suspended in quotations marks casts a modest veil over such a surface. And only through such a veil which thus falls over it could 'truth' become truth, profound, indecent, desirable."[456] The citation satisfies our need for authenticity, too well.[457]

---

[455] Genesis 3: 4. *The Holy Bible*. New International Version. Grand Rapids, Michigan: Zondervan Publishing House, 1996, p. 3.

[456] Derrida, Jacques. *Spurs*. Chicago, The University of Chicago Press, 1978, p. 59.

[457] In fiction and art we assume total deception and thus no citation is needed. For Derrida, poetry was imitation, and thus not truth. "Painting and poetry are of course far away from truth," Derrida, Jacques. *Dissemination*. Chicago: The University of Chicago Press, 1981, p.137.

135.

> I am an unbeliever who has a nostalgia for a belief.
> - Pier Paolo Pasolini, 1966[458]

In our contemporary era, the camera is the globally shared dominate worldview and film is a constant production of aura.[459] The film leaves no trace in reality, no consequence. The sets are dismantled and people return to their lives. The film itself is a luminescent trace, a remembrance of a private original event that the viewer missed while living elsewhere. The event was obviously important enough that it warrants checking out of our present reality for hours. "Films want you to forget yourself," said Chantal Akerman.[460] Aura wants us to forget ourselves and abide in fantasies.

136.

Aura is the mist emitted by a fashion magazine. It is the subtle show of beauty and seduction from one page to the next that draws us further into the dream world. While aura may be something associated with power in past eras, aura is now about putting down weapons and bathing in pleasure for as long as possible. This is the basis of virtual reality.

137.

Aura survives as something indeterminate not bound to an object but rather to a much grander continuation of illusion. We do not

---

[458] Wikipedia, http://en.wikipedia.org/wiki/Pier_Paolo_Pasolini#Quotes

[459] "The relation of thought to the current moment in art is one of a localized prescription and not a description. Everything depends upon the point at which one is subjectively situated, and upon the axioms which are used to support judgments. The point at which we choose to situate ourselves is called *L'Art du Cinema*." Badiou, Alain. *Infinite Thought*. Trans. Justin Clemens. New York: Continuum, 2003, p. 109.

[460] Comment in lecture at the European Graduate School, June 2002.

even need objects to have aura. Without a record album, a digital immaterial version of a song is still enigmatic. All media is now simply the time it takes to transfer the file so the aura then survives by myth. Aura is facilitated by myth but it is not the same thing.[461] Myth is a story, a legend like history. "Desire," for example, "is a myth,"[462] a story seeking conclusion. Modernity is a myth that wants no conclusion.[463] We know that aura can be used to further myth and divert. The Third Reich is an example of a political entity able to use aura to distract from truth, as is Phillip Morris with the Altria initiative.[464]

138.

It is not that the aura is decadent, but that decadence desires aura to fill the role of truth. In contemporary decadence the democratic capitalist dissipation of excess wealth, power, and manufactured objects coincides with the dispersion of excess information. Now information spread through advertising, mass media and the internet, extends aura, as evident in fame, subcultures, and the work of art. The great event in our time is information as ongoing performance.[465] Even the work of art does not need to be original but needs an aura of information. There is such an abundance of aura we now demand that it also be pleasurable and stylish. We know that there is such a thing as

---

[461] Myth was "Roland Barthes way of complicating the Marxist term 'ideology.'" Barnard, Malcolm. *Fashion as Communication.* New York: Routledge, 1996, p. 194.

[462] Baudrillard, Jean. *Seduction.* Trans. Brain Singer. New York: St. Martin's Press, 1990, p. 93.

[463] "Modernity is a myth." Lecture with Jean Baudrillard, European Graduate School, Saas-Fee Switzerland, June 12, 2004.

[464] Philip Morris made itself a tobacco subsidiary of a general company it invented called Altria (altruistic) in order to improve public relations.

[465] "Art has become performance," and also discussion of information as an event. Lecture with Jean Baudrillard, European Graduate School, Saas-Fee Switzerland, June 12, 2004.

boring aura and we do not want it.[466] It needs social connectedness, public interest, fame or controversy.[467] If it does not have some type of hype, or some "aura of derision," then it is not sexy or relevant, even if it does have aura of originality.[468]

139.

The interest in social aura is like all the illusions of democracy–shared. The invention of a fashion industry has helped to define aura in America. Robert Riley wrote that after France fell in World War II, America led the avant garde, in fashion and art but that "much of the triumph of American design proved to be publicity."[469] The originality is the designer's name and public image. In describing her work in fashion, Gloria Vanderbilt explained that "most of the creativity involved is in projecting an aura."[470]

140.

Benjamin explains that among the homes of the bourgeoisie, it all aura.[471] This is because they have layered the decoration of the home so that the belongings are representative of more than

---

[466] John Baldessari's "I will not make any more boring art" is just one example of the rejection.

[467] "But perhaps deep down we are merely playing out the comedy of art," Baudrillard suggests "as other societies have played out the comedy of ideology." Baudrillard, Jean. *Screened Out.* Trans. Chris Turner. New York: Verso Books, 2002, p. 182.

[468] Baudrillard, Jean. *Screened Out.* Trans. Chris Turner. New York: Verso Books, 2002, p. 183.

[469] Riley, Robert and Walter Vecchio. *The Fashion Makers.* New York: Crown Publishers, 1968, p. 3.

[470] Vanderbilt, Gloria. *It Seemed Important at the Time.* New York: Simon & Schuster, 2004, p. 121.

[471] "There is no speck on which the inhabitants have not left their trace," filling every space with some object. It results in a world of "habits which suit the interior inhabited, rather than they do the inhabitants themselves." Benjamin, Walter. "Experience and Poverty," *Walter Benjamin: Selected Writings, Vol. 2 1927-1934.* Cambridge: Harvard University Press, 1999, p. 734.

an individual dweller's singularity. It is a stifling condition of too much indiscriminate aura. Benjamin prefers to live as Brecht calls for in his *Reader for City Dwellers*, "cover your tracks," (Verwisch die Spuren), really meaning to *leave no trace*.[472] In Paul Scheerbart glass houses it is impossible to leave a trace– nothing can be hidden or permanently affixed. "What is made of glass has no 'aura,'" explained Benjamin, and thus "glass is, foremost, an enemy of secrets. It is also the enemy of property."[473] Does this mean that aura is lover of secrets and possessions?

Today however glass enhances aura and illuminates the "atmospheric medium."[474] Glass gives an illusion of total transparency or truth, but creates distance, like a museum display, thus enhancing aura.[475] The fascination with mirrors and vanity is also powerfully associated with great epochs of decadence. "The glass is watching us," it gives us a performance, wrote Borges:

> Nos acecha el crystal. Si entre las cuatro
> Paredes de la alcoba hay un espejo,
> Ya no estoy solo. Hay otro. Hay el reflejo
> Que arma en el alba un sigiloso teatro.[476]

---

[472] Benjamin, Walter. "Experience and Poverty," *Walter Benjamin: Selected Writings, Vol. 2 1927-1934.* Cambridge: Harvard University Press, 1999, p. 734.

[473] Ibid. p. 734.

[474] Benjamin, Walter. *One-Way Street and Other Writings.* Trans Edmund Jephcott and Kingsley Shorter. New York: Verso, 1997, p. 247.

[475] Joseph Paxton's Crystal Palace (1850-1936) was a prefabricated wrought iron building of glass created in London for the Great Exhibition of 1851. The excessive structure lasted only 80 years before it caught on fire and disappeared.

[476] From "Los espejos," Mirrors: The glass is watching us. And if a mirror / hangs somewhere on the four walls of my room / I am not alone. There's an other, a reflection / which in the dawn enacts its own performance. Borges, Jorge Luis. *Selected Poems.* Ed. Alexander Coleman. New York: Viking Penguin Group, 1999, pp. 104-105.

141.

Benjamin describes a mountain in the distance. In decadence
there is a desire for distance, a want to separate from the excess
that surround us.[477] In contemporary culture, despite the
breaking down of boundaries in social spaces and reality TV, we
continually maintain distance between the viewer and the world,
either by a screen or velvet ropes.

Benjamin explains, "to pry an object from its shell is to destroy
aura."[478] For the man-made object that shell is history.[479] The
aura of a historic object is in our knowledge that its full meaning
is somewhat inaccessible, thus it is mysterious–present, but also
distant. Christ is the great story of aura. His story is a cycle that
offers meaning because he is always present but also distant. The
celebrity follows this model, to constantly build presence with
distant mystique.[480] Magazines give an illusion of proximity to
celebrities, but we are really distant and only basking in aura.[481]

---

[477] Benjamin, Walter. "The Work of Art in the Age of Mechanical
Reproduction," in Mast, Gerald, et al. *Film Theory and Criticism*. Oxford:
Oxford University Press, 1992, p. 668.
[478] Ibid. p. 669.
[479] Benjamin affirms that the "uniqueness of a work of art is inseparable from its
being imbedded in the fabric of tradition...An ancient statue of Venus, for
example, stood in a different traditional context with the Greeks, who made it an
object of veneration, than with the clerics of the Middle Ages, who viewed it as
an ominous idol. Both of them, however, were equally confronted with its
uniqueness, that is, its aura." Ibid. p. 669.
[480] More than any paraphernalia, autographs are the trace of a famous person, a
mark that references all of the indeterminate events, the famous and unfamous
influences, that have contributed to this identity that has in some instances
passed without photograph.
[481] "Their place is taken by popular advertiser-financed illustrated magazines
distributed by subscriber services–themselves witness to a culture that no longer
trusts the power of the printed word." Habermas, Jürgen. *The Structural
Transformation of the Public Sphere*. Cambridge, Massachusetts: The MIT
Press, 1989, p. 163.

142.

In commercial products it seems that the more information on the exterior of a product the more it appears like propaganda. Aura is nothing but a word. The commercial logo for example is a signifier that represents both demand and possession simultaneously, like a contract between the purveyor and consumer in which both take pride. In acquiring the logo, the consumer feels like they access aura. Yet the purveyor increases presence by entering the consumer's world.[482] This is not only visible in fashion's transit to home and lifestyle, but of the transcendent ability of a commercial logo, and its aura, extending even the keys to a consumer's entire life in a designer keychain.[483] Aura wants to increase the territory of illusion.[484] Authors Halbertal and Margalit describe the role of power and symbolic presence in territory: "Another important element is the ability to have symbolic presence, the ability to have not only power but also omnipresence...any simultaneous presence in many places, or even the possibility of such presence, is an essential attribute of a deity, perhaps even the most important attribute."[485] The brand or logo, extends aura which extends an

---

[482] "The world fashioned by the mass media is a public sphere in appearance only. By the same token the integrity of the private sphere, which is the promise to their consumers, is also an illusion." Habermas, Jürgen. *The Structural Transformation of the Public Sphere*. Cambridge, Massachusetts: The MIT Press, 1989, p. 171.

[483] Debord describes that "keychains that are not paid for but come as free gifts with the purchase of some luxury product, or are then traded back and forth in a sphere far removed from that of their original use, bear eloquent witness to a mystical self-abandonment to the transcendent spirit of the commodity." Debord, Guy. *The Society of the Spectacle*. Trans. Donald Nicholson-Smith. New York: Zone Books, 1994, p. 44.

[484] Benjamin had speculated that mechanical reproduction "helps men achieve a control over works of art," Benjamin, Walter. *One-Way Street and Other Writings*. Trans Edmund Jephcott and Kingsley Shorter. New York: Verso, 1997, p. 252.

[485] Halbertal, Moshe and Avishai Margalit. *Idolatry*. Trans. Naomi Goldblum. Cambridge, Massachusetts: Harvard University Press. 1992, p. 228.

illusion of power. So despite Benjamin's fear, we now have too much aura, a saturation of it. We find it, however, losing not its presence but only its capacity to interest us. The spell of aura is breaking down, because it has grown so familiar. The density of aura, density of illusion, makes media seem like a charade. We do not then "give of ourselves in exchange for the satisfaction of media's promises."[486] We already see through media's promises and know they will not quench desire. Aura is ever-present but we are dispelling its pretense.

---

[486] Comment from the abstract of "The False Economy of Our Desires," by Jacqueline Guzda for the European Graduate School, 2003.

VI. Attraction

For me, an amorous subject, everything which is new, everything which disturbs, is received not as a fact but in the aspect of a sign which must be interpreted...*Everything signifies*.
- Roland Barthes, *A Lover's Discourse*[487]

[487] Barthes, Roland. *A Lover's Discourse*. Trans. Richard Howard. New York: Vintage Classics, 1977, p. 173.

Surprise

> Emotion is surprise through sensation, whereby the
> composure of mind is suspended.
> - Immanuel Kant, *Anthropology from a Pragmatic
> Point of View*[488]

141.

Being pivots on seemingly chance events and thus we have
constant interruptions. An invitation is a welcome surprise, as it
is an opening in being, an opportunity to an event yet to come.
The invitation speaks of a greater force, an event not of our own
making, an honor of destiny. It is a vanishing point on the
horizon of being, beyond us, not of our choosing, to which
things may begin or end. The "new" is a surprise invitation, as is
beauty, as is a performance; they invite us to share in being. A
"question" is an invitation that arrives in conversation. We can
refuse an invitation–being is suspended. There is the
disappointment we have when we discover everyone has been
invited. We want to have a world of surprises to ourselves, to be
special recipients. This rises not only from psychological
insecurity but a human nature to regard the unexpected event as
the essential truth of being, that is of a particular being. We want
the rupture we feel to be the rare light of truth.

142.

> What, then, is the surprise?... The surprise is not
> anything. It is not some newness in Being that would be
> surprising in comparison to the Being that is already

---

[488] Kant, Immanuel. *Anthropology from a Pragmatic Point of View*. Trans. by
Victor Lyle Dowdel. *Carbondale, IL:* Southern Illinois University Press, 1978, p.
156.

given. When there is the event, it is the "already" that
leaves up, along with the "not yet."

- Jean-Luc Nancy, "The Surprise of the Event"[489]

The surprise is especially meaningful to decadence because it
affirms desire.[490] A disruption of no permanent harm appears
only to intensify life.[491] It may be taken as a disruption from
pleasure, unless the disruption is found to be pleasure, and then
we want the surprise again and again. The surprise is like luxury,
at first extraordinary, then regularly anticipated. Even the new
does not stop decadence, since it is immediately incorporated
and consumed by decadence. The new simply announces itself
like an uninvited guest. This is the genuine surprise of the new,
the singular intersection in time which attracts us again and
again. The new possesses the moment. What is this thing before
us, this mysterious object that holds all the potential for
tomorrow, will it go all the way? Will it offer continual
happiness? Fashion appears and surprises again and again each
season. It is on the constant horizon of being, something
Heidegger sought to find in Being itself.[492] Fashion is not the

---

[489] Nancy, Jean-Luc. *Being Singular Plural*. Trans. Robert D. Richardson and
Anne E. O'Byrne. Stanford: Stanford Univ. Press, 2000, p. 171.

[490] "It needs only that the ordinary course of things be interrupted in order to
vindicate to common things an uncommon significance, to life as such, a
religious import." Feuerbach, Ludwig. *The Essence of Christianity*. Trans.
George Eliot. New York: Harper & Brothers Publishers, 1957, p. 278.

[491] "Disturbance disturbs order without troubling it seriously." Levinas,
Emmanuel. *Basic Philosophical Writings*. Ed. Adriann Peperzak et al,
Indianapolis: Indiana University Press, 1996, p. 70.

[492] "*How is this disclosive understanding of Being at all possible for Dasein?* Can
this question be answered by going back to the primordial *constitution-of-Being*
of that Dasein by which Being is understood?...Is there a way that leads from
primordial *time* to the meaning of *Being*? Does time itself manifest itself as the
horizon of *Being*?" Heidegger, Martin. *Being and Time*. Trans. John Macquarrie
& Edward Robinson. New York: Harper & Row Publishers, 1962, p. 448.

source of surprise but the symptom of a being that is always surprising itself.[493]

143.

> 'If life is Being, than what is most "alive" is what most is. If 'what is alive is "only a very strange kind of killing" (Nietzsche), then what is strangest is also what is most alive and what most is.' (then, quoting Heidegger) 'In the rare, the abrupt, Being shows its light,' So everything mediocre is decadence, the tendency to the generality of killing.'
> - From Hannah Arendt's journal, in *Arendt-Heidegger Letters: 1925-1975*[494]

For Arendt, it was in lifeless mediocrity, that we discover decadence. However, there is also in decadence a tendency to privilege rarity. The love of the exceptional is part of the decadent tendency to fragmentation.[495] Everything is interesting on its own because everything means something different. This is the contemporary state of thought in which we refuse to rest on an absolute, we resist totality and depend on the rare surprise, we need the surprise to affirm our decadence and that we do not know this life. That rarity may be worked to death, as is often the case with decadence, to the point that we forget the rare is rare and thus, forget the truth of desire.

---

[493] Both Benjamin and Mallarmé called fashion "la souveraine de tout le monde." Fashion is "a universal model of contemporariness." Lehmann, Ulrich. *Tigersprung: Fashion in Modernity.* Cambridge, Massachusetts, 2000, p. 263.
[494] Arendt, Hannah and Martin Heidegger. *Letters: 1925-1975.* Ed. Ursula Ludz. Trans. Andrew Shields. New York: Harcourt, Inc., 2004: p. ix.
[495] There is a "decadent impulse that fragments," Bernheimer, Charles. "Unknowing Decadence," in Constable, Liz and Dennis Denisoff and Matthew Potolosky. *Perennial Decay: On the aesthetics of politics and decadence.* Philadelphia: University of Pennsylvania Press, 1998, p. 62.

144.

In contemporary decadence, we often forget the surprise of danger because we have become accustomed to the pleasurable surprise. The surprise can be a killing, the very basis for destroying being. The surprise can be a disaster. The surprise can be simply a state change or interruption. Interruption is the essential role of thought, to arrest mediocrity, to arrest sovereignty. Badiou explains that the significance of interruption:

> Philosophy must examine the possibility of a point of interruption... because thought at least must be able to extract itself from this circulation and take possession of itself once again as something other than an object of circulation. It is obvious that such a point of interruption can only be an unconditional requirement; that is something which is submitted to thought with no other condition than itself and which is neither exchangeable or capable of being put into circulation. That there be such a point of interruption, that there be at least one unconditional requirement, is, in my opinion, a condition *sine qua non* for the existence of philosophy. In the absence of such a point, *all there is* is the general circulation of knowledge, information, merchandise, money and images. In my opinion, this unconditional requirement cannot be solely supported by the proposition of the polyvalence of meaning. It also needs the reconstruction or re-emergence of the category of truth.[496]

The point is a point of vanishing and re-emergence. What Badiou notes however is that in the relationship between interruption and truth, truth breaks through.

---

[496] Badiou, Alain. *Infinite Thought*. Trans. Justin Clemens. New York: Continuum, 2003, p. 49.

> A truth thus appears, in its newness, because an
> eventual supplement interrupts repetition. Examples:
> the appearance, with Aeschylus, of theatrical Tragedy;
> the irruption, with Galileo, of mathematical physica; an
> amorous encounter which changes a whole life; the
> French Revolution of 1792.[497]

One event can break through a sequence of events, and alter the
outcome. In the gesture of pouring out the only drinking water
on a desert island, this decadent gesture interrupts survival.

Flirtation

> In the age of innocence lost, what we yearn for is
> innocence found: youth, creativity and vitality.
> - Camila Nickerson, *Vogue*[498]

145.

A surprise may often invite us into a new circumstance and may
or may not be exclusive. Flirtation is an invitation into a private
dialogue, an exclusive often completely unspoken invitation to
begin. What we want is to return to the "innocence of
becoming," which requires that we give ourselves over to the
beginning and let go of ends.[499] We take pleasure in the first
fifteen minutes of anything because this prelude is to us like the
childhood of life. Flirtation is a precursor to a possible legitimate

---

[497] Ibid. p. 62.

[498] Camilla Nickerson, *V Magazine*, V18, March / April 2002.

[499] "The absolute necessity of a total liberation from ends: otherwise we should
not be permitted to try to sacrifice ourselves and let ourselves go. Only the
innocence in becoming gives us the *greatest courage* and the *greatest freedom*!"
Nietzsche, Friedrich. *The Will to Power*. Trans. Walter Kaufmann. New York:
Random House, 1968, p. 416. See also Nietzsche, Friedrich. *Twilight of the Idols
/ The Anti Christ*. New York: Penguin Books, 1990, section 26. and Schirmacher,
Wolfgang. "Art(ificial) Perception: Nietzsche and Culture after Nihilism,"
lecture, Toronto, 1999.

union, to procreation. It is a moment of joy and anxiety. It is
when flirtation is an end in itself that it is decadent.

146.

> They were stars on this stage, each playing to an
> audience of two; the passion of the pretence created the
> actuality... for the most part their love expressed Gloria
> rather than Anthony. He felt often like a scarcely
> tolerated guest at a party she was giving.
> - F. Scott Fitzgerald, *The Beautiful and Damned*[500]

Flirtation is a decadent show, an embellished expression of
desire that alludes to the truth of a larger game between the
genders. In Žižek's description of the charade of a man and a
woman, he describes of man: "he is simultaneously aware that
only a relationship to a woman can bring him genuine
'happiness...his 'wager' is that woman will be most effectively
seduced precisely when he does not sublimate all his activity to
her-what she will be unable to resist is her fascination with his
'public' activity, her secret awareness that he is actually doing it
for her."[501] The same event happens in reverse for the woman
whose charade in the private realm is for man. This is not
flirtation, or love affair but masquerade in gender, a masquerade
that involves all traits and qualities.

147.

> From the loved being emanates a power nothing can
> stop and which will impregnate everything it comes

[500] Fitzgerald, F. Scott. *The Beautiful and Damned*. New York: The Modern Library, 2002, p. 112.
[501] Žižek, Slavoj. *The Žižek Reader*. Ed. Elizabeth and Edmund Wright. Oxford: Blackwell Publishers, 1999, p. 141.

into contact with, even if only by a glance.
- Roland Barthes, *The Lover's Discourse*[502]

Flirtation is a game between sender and receiver, and also a covert conspiracy from the world. The two who play are not necessarily trying to satisfy desire but rather to locate pleasure in the private communication and suspense of desire fulfillment. We maintain a process of continual flirtation with desire, which we try to achieve through effort or restriction. We socially refuse to allow total exposure, even though media uses the terminology. Instead we follow a practice of keeping truth at bay, never satisfying desire.

148.

The practice of concealing and revealing is evident in historically decadent periods but surely, like any era, we are fluent in fantasy and what is privately "possible in dreams, love, imagination."[503] Because of the translucence of aura, media is no longer secretive about its role as the negotiator of fantasy, and thus desire. An advertisement for peach cobbler reads: "You pretend you don't want it, we'll pretend we believe you."[504]

149.

"The orgy of modernity," wrote Baudrillard, "consisted in the exhilaration of deconstructing the object and representation. During that period, the aesthetic illusion was still very powerful, as is, for sex, the illusion of desire."[505] He continues that finally

---

[502] Barthes, Roland. *A Lover's Discourse*. Trans. Richard Howard. New York: Vintage Classics, 1977, p. 173.
[503] Maslow, Abraham. *Toward a Psychology of Being*. New York: Van Nostrand Reinhold, 1968, pp. 197-198.
[504] Steak and Shake, in store promotion, 2000.
[505] Baudrillard, Jean. *Screened Out*. Trans. Chris Turner. New York: Verso Books, 2002, p. 181.

however, "we have lost the desire for illusion. After the orgy and the liberation of all desires, we have moved into the transsexual, in the sense of transparency of sex, into signs and images which obliterate the whole secret."[506]

We have lost desire for illusion but we have not lost desire. Desire depends on fictional relations with the world that are facilitated by the media industry and our own private fantasies.[507] And while the loss of illusion has been accompanied by increasing transparency we have not obliterated the whole secret. Media involves us in the one side flirtation, revealing and concealing on our behalf. Heraclitus first explained that "the nature of things is in the habit of concealing itself."[508] Dasein is free to conceal *and* reveal itself.

150.

The flirtation of media is accomplished via a legal display of seductive media called soft-core. Soft-core is more than keeping "romance under surveillance" it is a media strategy.[509] The term is technically applied to inexplicit sexual material without intercourse or violation. Soft-core then is understood by the threshold into hard core, or extreme sexual content.[510] Soft-core is what is allowed to be openly traded. It is actually protected by US law that allows it to appear across mass media in magazine

---

[506] Ibid. p. 181.
[507] "Imagination is considered in and of itself, here in conjunction with the faculty of desire." Hölderlin, Friedrich. *Essays and Letters on Theory*. Trans. Thomas Pfau. New York: State University of New York Press, 1988, p. 33.
[508] Heraclitus, Fragment 54. http://philoctetes.free.fr/heraclitefraneng.htm
[509] Eugenides, Jeffery. *The Virgin Suicides*. New York: Warner Books, 1993, p. 117.
[510] The phrase "hard core" originated however, as a political description for a loyal faction of a group most resistant to change, the hard core of a separatist movement. We still describe hard-core sports, hard-core management, hard-core governments, or any sanction deemed extreme.

covers, and late night TV. It is cultural currency that can go anywhere. Contemporary media thrives on soft-core as a "perpetual striptease," that never goes all the way.[511] We can even perceive the production of soft-core social space–not just strip clubs and peep show businesses–but flirtation in architecture with store fronts and performance stages, partially visible cubicle office space and dressing rooms that make public the gesture of subtly making private.

151.

> An observer is a prince who is everywhere in
> possession of his incognito.
> - Charles Baudelaire[512]

Flirtation, soft-core and even pornography are decadent in that they offer a pleasure of "just looking." Looking takes pleasure in the surface without essence, without investment in consequences. Subsequently, the practices of looking attract the voyeur who is willingly spellbound by unassuming subjects and an expendable notion of sexuality. Yet are we not all voyeurs? The "voyeur's view," truly part of all visual media, rises from curiosity. We want to see something that will confirm or deny our fantasies. Despite the fact we occupy "a world that has already been disclosed"[513] we prefer to think there is more to know. "What lurks behind this falsely transparent world?"[514]

---

[511] Baudrillard, Jean. *Screened Out*. Trans. Chris Turner. New York: Verso Books, 2002, p. 182.
[512] Baudelaire, Charles. *Oeuvres*,Vol. 2. Ed. Yves-Gerard Le Dante. Paris: Bibliothèque de la Pléïade, 1931-2, p. 333.
[513] Heidegger, Martin. *Being and Time*. Trans. John Macquarrie & Edward Robinson. New York: Harper & Row Publishers, 1962, p. 254.
[514] Baudrillard, Jean. *Screened Out*. Trans. Chris Turner. New York: Verso Books, 2002, p. 182.

152.

"Society," wrote Baudrillard, "is the degree zero of seduction." Social life must be ever visible of its boring obedience. "Control," "caution," "criticism" are brakes on fantasy's enactment, intended to limit spontaneity.[515] And even with "behind the scenes" of everything in our absolutely true, "Real Hollywood Story" of everyone, including their scandalous sex lives, we rarely see the actual act of sex in mass media. It is always possible that someone is leading a hard core private life and possible for art or the black market to showcase it, but we are normally shown much less. The reason for the legalization of only "harmless" images is for the benefit of the collective. Democratic society needs to permit private liberty *and* ordain it. The legalization of soft-core images, in tandem with the prohibition of hard core, serves to reinforce our system. Mass media promotes private life as free, but *self-restrained*. The consequence is that we assume goodness to what we see and a forbidden quality to what we cannot see. This is why the unveiling of new products is so attractive, because there is potential surprise of the *unseen obscene*.[516]

153.

Mercutio:
True, I talk of dreams,
Which are the children of an idle brain,
Begot of nothing but vain fantasy
- William Shakespeare, *Romeo and Juliet* [517]

---

[515] Lefebvre, Henri. *The Production of Space*. Trans. Donald Nicholson Smith. Cambridge: Blackwell Publishers, 1991, p. 315.
[516] We operate with the false conception that "everything that appears is good: whatever is good will appear." Debord, Guy. *The Society of the Spectacle*. Trans. Donald Nicholson-Smith. New York: Zone Books, 1994, p. 15.
[517] "Romeo and Juliet," Act I, Scene IV. Shakespeare, William. *The Complete Works*. Ed. G. B. Harrison. New York: Harcourt Brace, 1952, p. 481.

Classic soft-core associated with historical periods of decadence, often involves a relationship to the abundance of nature. Contemporary subjects in soft-core fashion photos are enjoying the bounty of capitalism. Soft-core lessens our defenses to consumption. In the spectacle, we are aggressively confronted with the "sale" sign and we become familiar with the obscene tactics of the market. Consumer society prefers symbolic exchanges that replace the moment of real decision in existence. The spectacle relies on the truth that we know we cannot control our desire to buy, the fashion photograph operates on the premise that the consumer believes he can control desire, and therefore exhibits a much more controlled picture. With fashion and luxury goods photographs, everything is restrained, including the product. The world is being sold to those who already possess it, and this time the sales tactic is not aggressive but so mild it does not even seem like sales. We not only accept harmless sexual events, but we ascribe the same harmlessness to consumption. This combination of discreet sexuality with conspicuous consumption is an ideal merger for decadent capitalism, already conscious of its own decadence. The contrast is low end promotion with its hard core, always visible, always abundant excessive style where nothing is hidden. Consumer society is charged with a sort of aristocratic decadence, in its attachment to safe, game-like symbolic exchanges that imply a conservative fear of the moment of real decision. A "tryst," understood as a romantic escape, originates from the words for hunting, in pursuit. Our contemporary tryst is a pursuit of desire in the field of media.

154.

Commercial photographer Garry Gross photographed child actress Brooke Shields, standing nude in a bathroom. The photograph was taken with permission from the actress' agent-mother but the image went public because of a lawsuit. In 1983, artist Richard Prince re-photographed the image and enshrined it in a New York gallery space called "Spiritual America."[518] Prince's Spiritual America appeared at a time when the president was an ex-movie star, when American culture equaled Hollywood. And while his photograph showcases an 80's celebrity, it also has an ideal classical form and pose. The relationship between the photo's scandalous significance and its timeless nude form contributes to its effectiveness; it attracts this generation, and also any other. In this way the nude form is essential to breaking through ideology and history. The very notion of "the naked truth" disrupts ideological divisions of visual territory.

155.

In flirtation and soft-core we find that possibility is essential and nowhere more so than in youth. Youth signifies unlimited possibility.[519] But because of their age, young people are limited by "the age of consent." The paradox of soft-core is possibility and the limit, e.g., *Lolita*. The reality of a sixteen-year-old girl or boy may be utter discontent, but a soft-core photo, novel or film thrives off of the potential. Larry Clark, Terry Richardson and Richard Kern have all made careers on young subjects confident enough to overcome their awkward inhibitions. But somehow like the teenager—who can never to any extent be "understood"—soft-core evades our final interpretation.

---

[518] The name was borrowed from a 1923 Alfred Stieglitz photograph of a horse with castrated genitals, commenting on the cultural lack of the United States.

[519] "At seventeen you can do anything. You have nothing to lose. You start with nothing, so you can attempt anything." Susann, Jacqueline. *Valley of the Dolls.* New York: Grove Press, 1966, p. 367.

Really then soft-core is pure decadence as is a teenager–we ascribe complicated motivations but then find nothing of complex significance behind the surface. Unlike the concealing and revealing of being, we find that media has concealed and revealed nothing. Yet for the young person, even in its nothingness, the experience means something. Pablo Neruda wrote, in "Juventud," "Las gotas vitales resbalando en los dedos, La dulce pulpa erótica... Mirado desde arriba, desde el vidro excondido: toda la adolescencia mojándose y ardiendo, Como una lámpara derribaba en la luvia."[520]

156.
Soft-core teen films are often filled with decadent indulgence like alcohol, consumption or throw away emotions. The films however also normally endorse some social contribution of Hegelian skills, whether athletics, looks, popularity or scholarship. But the consistent element of the teen film is illumination of the threshold of sexual desire. *Kids* (1995), *Splendor in the Grass* (1961), *Sixteen Candles* (1984), *Fast Times at Ridgemont High* (1982), *Valley Girl* (1983), *The Last Picture Show* (1971), and others, have established a technique for looking at the world with a constant concern for "going too far." In the novel *The Virgin Suicides*, author Jeffrey Eugenides writes of an encounter in which the character Trip Fontaine is approached by Lux Lisbon one night in his car: "he felt himself grasped by his long lapels, pulled forward and pushed back, as a creature with a hundred mouths started sucking the marrow form his bones. She said nothing as she came on like a starved animal...after only a few minutes, with only the words 'Gotta

---

[520] "The drops of life slipping on the fingertips, the sweet sexual fruit / ... / seen from above, from the hidden window: / adolescence all wet and burning / like a lamp turned over in the rain. Bly, Roberts, ed. *Neruda and Vallejo: Selected Poems.* Trans. Robert Bly, et al. Boston: Beacon Press, 1971, pp. 90-91.

get back before bed check,' Lux left him, more dead than alive."[521] Her sexuality was asserted but restrained by an authority calling her back to bed. When the characters do cross the threshold it finds Trip stating "I got sick of her right then," and it contributes in part to Lux's suicide. The message of the teen story, is that going too far will lead to unhappiness.[522] Even when the teen film appeals to social interest over sexual, as in *Rebel Without a Cause* (1955), *Dead Poets Society* (1989), *Elephant* (2003), or even *The Breakfast Club* (1985), we still find the fear of the limit set by the adult. The teen may act like everything is possible and none of it matters anyway, but the limit–the threshold into adulthood, and hard core reality–looms over each and every scene like an invisible God.

Hoax

It happened that a fire broke out backstage in a theater. The clown came out to inform the public. They thought it was just a jest and applauded. He repeated his warning, they shouted even louder. So I think the world will come to an end amid general applause from all the wits, who believe that it is a joke.

- Søren Kierkegaard[523]

---

[521] Eugenides, Jeffery. *The Virgin Suicides*. New York: Warner Books, 1993, p. 86.

[522] There is of course always the exception, as in *Dazed & Confused* (1993) when Mitch Kramer returns home in the morning after a night of lawlessness and evades punishment. There is a testing of limits that dominates the film in a sort decadent indulgence into consequence without harm. The film is propaganda for decadence, like contemporary teen comedies, suggesting that no consequence is fatal.

[523] Kierkegaard, Søren. *Provocations: The spiritual writings of Søren Kierkegaard*, Ed. Charles E Moore, Farmington: The Plough Publishing House, 1999, pg. 404.

157.

To a young child, the entire world is constant surprise. The performance of mass media can thus be perceived by children as equivalent to the adult world.[524] But where is the end of the performance? In Goya's "Que viene el Coco,"(1797), a figure is obscured by a sheet and surprises a group of children who cry while the nanny smiles at "the ghost" as if she knows him.[525] In flirtation two are invited to play a game in which the rules are shared but a hoax is an invitation to deception. It is an empty invitation.

158.

The hoax is an effort to instill fear but it is not the hoax itself that should be feared. We socially operate on the lookout for hoaxes all of the time.[526] The culture industry, in its pure fiction, relies upon the inaccessibility of truth. It can only retain its authority by appearing as the discerner of truth. The Loch Ness Monster, Bigfoot, the Bermuda Triangle and J.T. Leroy are moments in which media reveals scandal. The larger they are made out to be the more they de-stabilize security.

---

[524] "The power of spurious realities battering us today-these deliberately manufactured fakes never penetrate the heart of true human beings. I watch the children watching TV and at first I am afraid of what they are being taught, and then I realize, they can't be corrupted or destroyed. They watch, they listen, they understand, and, then, where and when it is necessary they reject. There is something enormously powerful in a child's ability to withstand the fraudulent." Dick, Philip K. *I Hope I Shall Arrive Soon.* New York: Doubleday & Company, 1985, p. 22.

[525] Hannah Arendt describes how her mother intentionally frightened her and the moment was later brought into adult fears of love. Arendt, Hannah and Martin Heidegger. *Letters: 1925-1975.* Ed. Ursula Ludz. Trans. Andrew Shields. New York: Harcourt, Inc., 2004: p. 51.

[526] Sokal, Alan and Jean Bricmont. *Intellectual Imposters.* New York: Economist Books, 2003.

159.

Decadence is so far from truth it appreciates the art of deception as so worthy of time and attention that one is willing to pay for it. Marie Tussaud's 19th century invention of the wax figure museum is accepted hoax. The wax museum only works if one already knows the figures in media, otherwise it is just realistic sculpture. The hoax of the wax figure is not intended to be as realistic as possible, but as deceiving as possible in resemblance to the *media version* of the person. We need no taste or preferences to appreciate the wax museum, and only knowledge of the top heroes of mass media. This is the basis of entertainment in our time, which explodes in Vegas.

160.

The contemporary hoax comes forward into media as a surprise event, only to be discovered to have no event, other than its reception. Fame always arrives like an event of reception. When does fame begin? Where did the famous person come from? The hoax of fame is its lasting.

Orson Welles' *Vérités et mensonges* (1974), celebrates famous painter Elmyr de Hory and famous author Clifford Irving who have retired together to Ibiza, Spain. Their fame is from an art of fakery, false paintings bought by MoMA and false memoirs of Howard Hughes. Welles, who was also responsible for *The War of the Worlds* hoax, intentionally makes the film unstable and points in the end to the great basis of hoax–no shame. There is no shame because of the sobering point that both true and false events are forgotten: "Go on singing," says Welles in the film. Our efforts at truth and hoax equally fade away. "Everything must finally fall in war, or wear away into the ultimate and universal ash–the triumphs, the frauds, the treasures and the fakes. A fact of life: we're going to die...Maybe a man's name doesn't matter all that much."

161.

The hoax of American history is not only political but cultural. Andy Warhol suggested that Europeans could love kitsch because they lived among ruins while we Americans have to reject kitsch and love tradition. We make claims that companies were "established" in particular years, even if it was only 10 years ago. There are grand assertions like "the real" "the original" or "most loved;" it is the spirit of capitalism which has become global. Coca Cola is "The Real Thing," and "Zambia, The Real Africa."[527] "America's Most Diverse" is apparently Yamaha Motor Corporation, while "The Original Mexican Restaurant," is not in Mexico but San Antonio, Texas. The assertion of realness and originality is already understood to be part of the hoax we accept. We already know that nothing is actually original. Original has lost its meaning from "being that which is singular" to that which is simply branded.

162.

PETER: We're making a film of English life and we want to use Boltwell.
JULIA: But I understand that Boltwell is in a very decayed condition.

---

[527] Zambia Tourism, http://www.zambiatourism.com/

PETER: Exactly. It is. And that's why we're interested.
The most decayed noble mansion in England! At least,
of any that are still inhabited. We've got a team of
experts over to study the decay, so as to reproduce it.
Then we build another Boltwell in California.
- T.S. Eliot, *The Cocktail Party*[528]

The motivation in decadent Hollywood is "make it look like..."
Yet in cinema nothing ever looks authentic because none of the
props show authentic age or use. The set is not weathered and
confused like reality. There is no dust, unless it is called for in
the script. This is especially the case with sets and props where
stylists make a scene from 2001, a room of things from 2001. In
reality, time is always sliding in every direction, with items from
countless years piling up and surrounding us. In Stanley
Kubrik's *Barry Lyndon* (1975), every detail, even to the clothing
inside of drawers, was selected to be of related time to the events
in the film. Now reality TV actually has real clothes in drawers,
but the characters are still in a set, and often prefer to stay in the
reality television games than return to their reality.

163.

I must admit the existence of Disneyland (which I *know*
is real) proves that we are not living in Judea in 50 A.D.
- Philip K. Dick, *I Hope I Shall Arrive Soon*[529]

Disney really has some of the best architecture of our time
because they have managed to re-create the world, particularly at
EPCOT Center. But like any theme park or carnival of earlier
times, Disney is collective endorsement of deception. More than

[528] Eliot, T.S. *The Cocktail Party*. New York: Harcourt, Brace and Company,
1950, pp. 168-169.
[529] Dick, Philip K. *I Hope I Shall Arrive Soon*. New York: Doubleday &
Company, 1985, p. 19.

just simulacra, it is accepted hoax. We embrace the artifice as real, or at least allow it a real part of our world. The pretend world engages in commerce, it takes from commerce in order to sustain itself. Santa Claus is a coming together of masquerade and hoax for children, that also takes from commerce. The hoax prepares children for a world whose "reality" will delight them, though let them down.[530] The hoax for children suggests that the world will carry on a charade for your behalf. Is this an offer to imagination?[531] This is the area of the hoax that seduces us and reminds us of the capacity of the mind. Delusion is an essential faculty of decadence, that fantasy is a valuable skill and can sustain us even without addressing truth.[532]

164.

> Heidegger says quite proudly, "People say Heidegger is a fox." He arrived at an idea entirely new and unheard of among foxes: he built himself a trap as a fox den...our fox hit upon the idea of decking out his trap as beautifully as possible... The fox living in the trap said proudly: "So many fall into my trap; I have become the best of all foxes."
> - Hannah Arendt, in *Arendt-Heidegger Letters: 1925-1975*[533]

---

[530] From conversation with William Rauscher.

[531] "Childhood tells them that the mind is not given. But that it is possible." Lyotard, Jean-François. *The Postmodern Explained to Children: Correspondence 1982-1985*. Trans. Thomas Pefanis. London: Turnaround, 1992, p. 115.

[532] We are not allowed to yell fire in a theater as a jest. It is a crime to lie about this because it disrupts both pleasure and fictive communication with a question of action and real truth.

[533] Arendt tells a story about a Heidegger the fox who builds a trap for himself. "Of course everybody could walk right out of it except him." Arendt, Hannah and Martin Heidegger. *Letters: 1925-1975*. Ed. Ursula Ludz. Trans. Andrew Shields. New York: Harcourt, Inc., 2004: p. 305.

In order for a hoax to truly be a success it must be the best, or appear to be the best. The great hoax is not merely convincing like a wax museum, but passes the test as truth to a discriminating few. The creator of the hoax knows it is a trap, a bait and switch, a con, a trick to evoke interest or fame. But the creator of a great hoax also points to a lack in the social fabric that we fail to find life rich enough as it is and that we have lost the ability to recognize truth. The grand hoax then is philosophy, which has in every era succeeded at convincing us that the truth cannot be known.

VII. Desire

Only since this morning I have met myself as a middle-aged man beginning to know what it is to feel old. That is the worst moment, when you feel you have lost the desire for all that was most desirable, and before you are contented with what you can desire; before you know what is left to be desired; and you go on wishing that you could desire what desire has left behind.
- T.S. Eliot, *The Cocktail Party*[534]

---

[534] Eliot, T.S. *The Cocktail Party*. New York: Harcourt, Brace and Company, 1950, p. 65.

Lips of Blood

> Like the thickets of paradise wherein after sinning
> Adam hid, hearing the voice of God "moving through
> the garden from the way whence comes the day." Glory
> is the response to the summons without any possible
> evasion, a surprise to the response to the summons
> without any possible evasion, a surprise to the
> respondent himself, but by which, driven out, he
> develops sincerity or Saying.
> - Levinas, *Basic Philosophical Writings*[535]

165.

What is the surprise in the fall? God approaches Adam and Eve
and they admit to Him that they have hidden because they were
naked. But God asks, "Who told you that you were naked?" The
surprise is their confession of guilt before they even admit to
having eaten the fruit. In this way, speaking is the surprise of the
being. This is also how we regard the revelation of truth.

In thought, we are constantly engaged with the unveiling of
being, a process the keeps desire alive. For Kant, being was
defined by desire, with recurring desire called inclination.
Recurring desires seem logical to an individual, even if it is
unreasonable to others. Recurring desires seem more stable to a
person than unpredictable singular emotions about particular
things.[536] Desire rises forward again and again in pursuit of
resolution and therefore, as Kant expressed, "all desire contains
(doubtful or certain) anticipation of what is possible."[537]

---

[535] Levinas, Emmanuel. *Basic Philosophical Writings*. Ed. Adriann Peperzak et
al, Indianapolis: Indiana University Press, 2296, p. 103.
[536] Kant, Immanuel. *Anthropology from a Pragmatic Point of View*. Trans. by
Victor Lyle Dowdel. *Carbondale, IL:* Southern Illinois University Press, 1978,
pp. 155-6.
[537] Ibid. p. 77.

166.

Desire frequently comes up against truth, or collides with a moment of truth. The revolutionary is always full of desire and driven by what is possible. Badiou writes:

> the desire of philosophy implies a dimension of revolt: there is no philosophy without the discontent in thinking in its confrontation with the world as it is. Yet the desire of philosophy also includes *logic*; that is, a belief in the power of argument and reason. Furthermore, the desire of philosophy involves universality: philosophy addresses all humans as thinking beings since it supposes that all humans think. Finally, philosophy takes *risks*: thinking is always a decision which supports independent points of view. The desire of philosophy thus has four dimensions: revolt, logic, universality and risk.[538]

The desire for revolt is like a backward-working away from truth. We also know that ontological truth can appear at times to be the inverse of Badiou's proposal–illogical, local and safe-meaning that what has been proposed for an agenda of contemporary thought is a call to revolution that will return to exactly the same position where we currently reside. The call for revolution rises from a blood of desire and our lips speak the ideology.

167.

The ongoing disruption in decadence is the unrelenting challenge from desire that throws down the gauntlet each moment and ruptures the state of contentment. This is why political rebellions hardly disturb decadence because it is not a

---

[538] Badiou, Alain. *Infinite Thought*. Trans. Justin Clemens. New York: Continuum, 2003, pp. 39-40.

king that reigns but desire.[539] In democratic capitalism, we no longer need to talk about power because we can recognize the reign of desire, of which no one is master. The woman, because she has been owned and controlled and is always seduced, has known for sometime that power cannot control desire, thus her indifference to power.

168.

> They did not want a revolution they wanted only its spectacle.
> - Jean Baudrillard, *Seduction*[540]

Decadence is too indulgent for outward effort and thus negates others not through assassination but by slander.[541] Thus in the contemporary era, we no longer have blood on our hands but on our lips where we destroy whatever stands in the way of desire. "Yes" and "no" have become weapons in a world of many truths but are used to speak for or against whatever we most want.

What then is courage in decadence? The hero of decadence is the one who does not change the style but the substance. Not a no, or a yes but a why. A revolution always surprises and confuses the establishment because it rejects the existing value system and negates structural binaries. The revolution then makes it

---

[539] "Let us see if he can make it out of his matters any better than before," Edwards concludes. Edwards, The Rev. Jonathan. *Freedom of the Will*. Morgan, Pennsylvania: Soli Deo Gloria Publications, 1996, p. 78.

[540] Baudrillard, Jean. *Seduction*. Trans. Brain Singer. New York: St. Martin's Press, 1990, p. 59.

[541] "This subversion of values that philosophers, artists and writers, and then psychoanalysis and young people have carried out in public is a radical mutation in the very essence of Humans…we still haven't measured the extent of these advances nor what that rupture means for our usual behavior, for our need for security and identity. A cruelty has come to light: it's the black-cloth of freedom, jouissance, creativity itself." Kristeva, Julia. *Revolt, She Said*. Trans. Brian O'Keefe. New York: Semiotext(e), 2002, p. 88.

impossible for the reigning power to defend itself because it is unprepared to fight for values it does not know or aesthetics it does not utilize. The revolutionary often confronts decadence and is willing to risk everything to produce "lasting change." Christ was such a problem for the Romans because he did not call for a new style but for admission of the absolute value of truth. But we normally find that if we slash the establishment for a new republic we eventually get Emperor Bonaparte.[542] Revolution can disrupt decadence, but in time it too surrenders to desire. The more contemporary situation, especially in the U.S. has been described as "a crisis once a generation," because economic or social we are now most comfortable with the cycle of revolution.[543]

169.

Restrictions may create differences between age, gender and social groups. Wherever a contemporary social restriction is crossed, it no longer results in death but arbitration, and thus we now have the decadent era of negotiation. The same situation is evident in thought where we no longer cross a threshold of truth or power but allow that all meaning is negotiable.

---

[542] "Men make their own history, but they do not make it just as they please, they do not make it under circumstances chosen by themselves, but under circumstances directly encountered, given and transmitted from the past." Marx specifically addresses the Revolution of 1848. "The Eighteenth Brumaire of Louis Bonaprate," in Marx, Karl and Friedrich Engels. *Collected Works*, vol. 11. London: Lawrence & Wishart, 1979, pp. 103-104.

[543] Comment by John Williamson from a conference by the Swiss Foundation of World Affairs on the topic of Globalization of the International Market, Swiss American Chamber of Commerce, Club 101, New York, December 9, 2004.

Decadence then appears to be an *age of consent*–yes to everything.[544] The yes is a continual affirmation. It is the basis of passion and acceptance. But what then of no?[545] Is no another means of fidelity? Of other passion? In the same manner that a decadent invests in the integrity of a surface, the decadent speaks with elaboration. If it is a "yes," it is a "yes" to the extreme, and a "no" is a "no" without possibility. Decadence is more than one word, a saying, a poem, an opus of elaboration, alliteration, fiction. It is also the decay of the word, of words, of the word into txt msgs & communication that is w/o the rules of grammar. Finally we have let go of the restriction of language itself.

170.

Rebellion is, unlike revolution, simply acting out, often re-acting to some frustration. Whenever something that we desire is unavailable, we find that it "frustrates endeavor or desire."[546] No matter how strong or weak the desire, the idea of "impossibility" transforms desire to necessity. Rebels already have basic needs met and though they may fight to denounce the mystification of authority, they are too comfortable to risk their lives. Rebellion frequently occurs because individuals suspect that some information or resource is being kept from them, as in stratified societies or children among adults. And in fact, some information and resources are probably kept from them and therefore most of rebellious demands are legitimate. But the keeping of information or resources is normally just authoritarian resource management and typically not the

---

[544] The yes, is the word of God (the great initiation of life), the word of memory, to agree. Derrida, Jacques. "A Number of Yes," *Deconstruction, A Reader*. Ed. Martin McQuillan. New York: Routledge, 2000, pp. 97-106.

[545] Regarding the "not" of sexuality, Butler, Judith. *The Psychic Life of Power*. Stanford: Stanford University Press, 1997, p. 135.

[546] Edwards, The Rev. Jonathan. *Freedom of the Will*. Morgan, Pennsylvania: Soli Deo Gloria Publications, 1996, p. 16.

elaborate deception they speculate because humankind has lost the faculty of elaborate deception. Deception was once a strategic means for survival that has denigrated into a mild manipulation for the most pleasure.

171.

While Kristeva suggests "the individual rebels precisely in order to occupy the position of authority,"[547] rather the rebel often just wants acknowledgement, influence and pleasure, which he may confuse as power.[548] Thus countless rebellions have only been demands for the information and resources of pleasure. Today we tolerate rebellion as if it were normal behavior, in part because we know there is no satisfaction for the demand of unquenchable desire. We now accept a "libertine ideology of salvation through desire."[549] This realization is the double bind of decadence to avoid truth but to want to resolve desire, which is as dogmatic and demanding as truth.[550]

Kristeva posed, "the truth proclaimed by Judaism and Christianity makes them indispensable at this current stage of human history. The genius of psychoanalysis will have been to take the power of desire seriously, as well as the truths of monotheism, and to show that they are the inevitable–though variable–conditions for questioning values, and giving human desire its meaning."[551] We are at a point of decadence where we

---

[547] Kristeva, Julia. *Revolt, She Said*. Trans. Brian O'Keefe. New York: Semiotext(e), 2002, p. 82.

[548] "Pleasure is a feeling of power." Nietzsche, Friedrich. *The Will to Power*. Trans. Walter Kaufmann. New York: Random House, 1968, p. 238.

[549] Kristeva, Julia. *Revolt, She Said*. Trans. Brian O'Keefe. New York: Semiotext(e), 2002, p. 22.

[550] But the desire is, as Kristeva described "unalterable, infinite, absolute and destructive." Ibid. p. 23.

[551] Ibid. p. 27.

can question the role of desire and have an assertion of truth. But psychoanalysis has not taken desire or monotheism seriously; it has taken the human seriously and thus our answers have been self-reflexive and anthropocentric.

172.

We have such a contemporary state of constant rebellion there is no more social surprise, as they are officially planned in France for example. The demands of the rebel, which are often the demands of the powerless, are nothing more than amusement to the establishment. In some instances a small rebellion, like the charade of an avant garde, can even quiet desire for total revolution. May 1968 announced a demand with what results? It was a student riot with academic consequences until the attractive spokesmen, Jean-Luc Godard and François Truffaut, formed the Cinemateque Defense Committee and withdrew from the 21st International Festival du Cannes, therefore taking an amusing student rebellion to real consequence in the culture industry. Partial power thus gained an influence because it's showmen withheld novelty from the legitimate power.

There is also always a capacity for the rebel to simply laugh at the true impotence of power. The 1968 Swiss demand for an "Unobstructed view of the Mediterranean," signified the futility of both the rebel's demand and the political power, a power with reach only as far as a border, and a border always just before paradise.

173.

Rebellion is equal in strength to prohibition.[552] They mediate the access to pleasure. What is power now but access to pleasure? If we think of children sharing a particular toy and the children fight to have the particular toy, they fight to have the toy because they really want dominion over their own contentedness. When we rebel or restrict others we are merely proving the need to control desire, allowing desire to control us and thus destroying the natural effortlessness to action we really want. We are willing to risk everything for what we desire, which makes a suggestion like "life is devoted to calculating security," seem like it should be "life is devoted to calculating pleasure."[553]

174.

Resistance is frequently unproductive because reality is not resistance.[554] Reality relies upon submission. Resistance is not necessarily a "no" with consequence, but often an effort to suspend destiny. The resistance movement is built on desire to post-pone the inevitable and gains nothing but waiting time. The only successful resistances are separation and death. Suicide is resistance by separation from the world through death; it is not total surrender but total refusal.[555] Jeffrey Eugenides wrote of the virgin suicides, "They had killed themselves over the failure to find a love none of us could ever be. In the end, the tortures tearing the Lisbon girls pointed to a simple reasoned *refusal* to

---

[552] Prohibition, explains Judith Butler is "the very operation of desire as it turns on its own possibility." Butler, Judith. *The Psychic Life of Power.* Stanford: Stanford University Press, 1997, p. 63.

[553] Badiou, Alain. *Infinite Thought.* Trans. Justin Clemens. New York: Continuum, 2003, p. 41.

[554] Heidegger, Martin. *Being and Time.* Trans. John Macquarrie & Edward Robinson. New York: Harper & Row Publishers, 1962, p. 252.

[555] "Not nothing is worth anything but life is no longer worth anything," Nietzsche, Friedrich. *Twilight of the Idols / The Anti Christ.* New York: Penguin Books, 1990, p. 98.

accept the world as it was handed down to them, so full of flaws."[556]

Ennui

> Now whenever we are not striving for something, or are not intellectually occupied but are thrown back on existence itself, its worthlessness and vanity are brought home to us; and this is what is meant by boredom. Even our inherent and *ineradicable* tendency to run after what is strange and extraordinary shows how glad we are to see an interruption in the natural course of things, which is so tedious. Even the pomp and splendor of the great are nothing but a vain attempt to get beyond the essential wretchedness of our existence. For after all, what are precious stone, pearls, feathers, red velvet, many candles, dancers, the putting on and off of masks, and so on? No man has ever yet felt entirely happy in the present, for he would have been intoxicated.
> - Arthur Schopenhauer [557]

175.

Desire and decadence can be braided together but are unbound to the situation, meaning whatever is available is ultimately futile. If desire is by chance resolved by some available resource, then for the decadent, that resource must be modified so to satisfy.[558] But most often in decadence, desire is without aim or resolution.

---

[556] Eugenides, Jeffrey. *The Virgin Suicides*. New York, Warner Books, 1993, p. 245.
[557] Schopenhauer, Arthur. *Philosophical Writings*. Ed. Wolfgang Schirmacher. New York: The Continuum Publishing Company, 2002, p. 24.
[558] "Desire is to lack what one has." Barthes, Roland. *A Lover's Discourse*. Trans. Richard Howard. New York: Vintage Classics, 1977, p. 226.

176.

All day long I think of things but nothing seems to satisfy
Think I'll lose my mind if I don't find something to pacify
Can you help me occupy my brain?
Oh yeah
I need someone to show me the things in life that I can't find
I can't see the things that make true happiness, I must be blind
Make a joke and I will sigh and you will laugh and I will cry
Happiness I cannot feel and love to me is so unreal
And so as you hear these words telling you now of my state
I tell you to enjoy life I wish I could but it's too late
- Ozzy Osbourne, "Paranoid," 1970

Ennui is a state of weariness, with desire that cannot be satisfied. In ennui, desire is "wandering and uncertain of its object."[559] It is a fullness of indiscriminate desire.[560] Desire comes from the phrase "*de sidere*" meaning "from the stars," implying "await what the stars will bring."[561] Ennui has also some feeling of

---

[559] The question is if human desire corresponds to something that exists or must exist somewhere. "We remain conscious of a desire which no natural happiness will satisfy. But is there any reason to suppose that reality offers a satisfaction to it?...A man's physical hunger does not prove that the man will get any bread...But surely a man's hunger does prove that he comes of a race which repairs its body by eating...I do not believe that my desire for paradise proves that I will enjoy it, I think it a pretty good indication that such a thing exists." Lewis, C.S. *The Essential C.S. Lewis.* Ed. Lyle W. Dorsett. New York: Simon & Schuster, 1988, p. 364. Lewis also asks if our desire "not too strong but too weak. We are half-hearted creatures, fooling about with drink and sex and ambition when infinite joy is offered us, like an ignorant child who wants to go on making mud pies in a slum because he cannot imagine what is meant by the offer of a holiday at sea. We are far too easily pleased." Ibid. p. 362. We can also think of Heidegger's "ability to be astonished by the simple." Arendt, Hannah and Martin Heidegger. *Letters: 1925-1975.* Ed. Ursula Ludz. Trans. Andrew Shields. New York: Harcourt, Inc., 2004: p. 156.
[560] Boredom is not the same as ennui and implies usually a "lack of want." "Want and boredom are the two poles of human life," Schopenhauer, Arthur. *Philosophical Writings.* Ed. Wolfgang Schirmacher. New York: The Continuum Publishing Company, 2002, p. 31.
[561] Online Etymology Dictionary, http://www.etymonline.com/

waiting in vain, that one is always waiting for pleasure's timing and that it will not satisfy anyway. It is a feeling that nothing can be done, but something *must* be done.

177.

> Travel, which had once charmed him, seemed, at length, unendurable, a business of color without substance, a phantom chase after his own dream's shadows…It seemed a tragedy to want nothing—and yet he wanted something, something. He knew in flashes what it was –some pather of hope to lead him toward what he thought was an imminent and ominous old age.
> - F. Scott Fitzgerald, *The Beautiful and Damned*[562]

Ennui is not an early state of development. Ennui arises after everything "worthy" has already been tasted.[563] The critic is a prime example of decadent ennui; one who always evaluates but never acts for himself, he finds all things already familiar and yet not the great answer we allegedly need.

---

[562] Fitzgerald, F. Scott. *The Beautiful and Damned*, F. Scott Fitzgerald, New York: The Modern Library, 2002, p. 46.

[563] After much experience one can develop extreme taste, but there is also lack of action. In "Unknowing Decadence," Charles Bernheimer writes, "Decadence is antiteleological and antimetaphysical–yet cannot do without illusions of metaphysics. In this sense, it cannot not judge its own value negatively from the point of view of history, nature or ethics. But this judgment is not final, as it becomes an allegory after the Umschwung. Decadence holds judgment in suspension. It fights against betraying the materiality of signs and objects and tries to adhere to surfaces and sensations. It wants to claim autonomy in its own realm, commandeering death to undertake its own work rather than serve the interests of life. Thus diverted from its natural function, this agency promotes unnatural practices and generates perverse pleasures." "Unknowing Decadence," by Charles Bernheimer in Constable, Liz and Dennis Denisoff and Matthew Potolosky. *Perennial Decay: On the aesthetics of politics and decadence.* Philadelphia: University of Pennsylvania Press, 1998, p. 62.

178.
In *A Rebours,* Des Esseintes' pursued every pleasure of beauty, luxury and cuisine. "'They don't divert *me,* the pleasures other people enjoy,' protested Des Esseintes."[564] He was haunted by desire because he did not want *anything but* rest from desire. One with ennui knows that wonderful things happen every day yet finds these wonderful things to be ordinary. The condition of ennui is to have seen it all before, in five different languages, and then complain that this world of excess is still not interesting enough. It can become a personal crisis of meaning, arising from the desire that life should continue to exceed expectations, to surpass the endless call of desire.

179.
New York City thrives by a "keep your options open" attitude, driven by desire to excess and decadence. But because such a great number of things can be done, there is accompanying ennui. If anything is done, none of it is interesting because of a shadow of abundance, that something else is always possible, and thus possibly more interesting. The potential of reality is discredited and overdetermined as a waste of time because even all of it together would not satiate. This is the basis of capitalism.

180.
Decadence is accompanied by a dismissal of possibility, especially today where so much of life has already been explained and is thus uninteresting. Now there is no place for anything radical, because it has all been seen before and will be deconstructed in time anyway. Though we may still act as

[564] Huysmans, J.K. *A Rebours.* Trans. Havelock Ellis. New York: Dover, 1969, p. 198.

though thought could wake us up from our sleep, expecting the next contribution to be valuable, we find in a matter of years that the new perspective has grown familiar and is not so interesting anymore. So while we reject old solutions because we claim that we have evolved for the better we find the new is no move forward and the return of dissatisfaction and ennui dominates. This is the inability to be content that is necessary for the success of capitalism.

181.

The opposite of ennui is to be charmed, especially by the past. Theodor Adorno explained that, "the disinterested pleasure that according to Kant is aroused by works of art, can only be understood by virtue of historical antithesis still at work in each aesthetic object. The thing disinterestedly contemplated pleases because it once claimed the utmost interest and thus precluded contemplation."[565] To be charmed, to have a sort of attraction without particular interest, is according to Adorno a product of a historical element at work. With ennui, the disinterest is the result of historical element that no longer works. When we are bored, the past is nothing but the dead world that will be forgotten and the future is seen to face the same destiny. Thus the crux of boredom is the paralyzing consciousness of mortality.

182.

Ennui is surely not possible in the state of emergency. If anything goes wrong, then "disinterest" must be put aside in order to pay attention to life. But ennui is also such a lack of

---

[565] Adorno, Theodor. *Minima Moralia.* Trans. E.N. Jephcott. New York: Verso Books, 1997, p. 224.

observance that it does not realize that *it is* the state of emergency; it is the catastrophe of the human spirit:

> Hell–golden age
> Key words for this hell: ennui, gambling, pauperism
> One canon for these dialectics: fashion
> The golden age as catastrophe.
> - Walter Benjamin[566]

183.

Ennui is not limited to the asset class, rather it is common to any people who have allowed leisure and pleasure to dominate and result in sloth. In many ways, it results simply from the judgment of having nothing *better* to do. "The lax allegiance of the lower middle class" has not only been used to account for their lack of organization to revolution but is the basis for ambivalence that maintains average comfort.[567]

184.

Jacques Barzun, who invested over a decade studying decadence, concluded that, "a failure of will, which is to say the wish without act, is characteristic of institutions in decadence."[568] This is similar to Nietzsche's emphasis of a weakness in will in decadence. Ennui is the state of desire that does not appear to end and instead exhausts the individual.[569]

---

[566] Benjamin, Walter. "Das Passagen-Werk," p. 1213, This partial citation as appears in Lehmann, Ulrich. *Tigersprung: Fashion in Modernity.* Cambridge, Massachusetts, 2000, p. 263.

[567] Veblen, Thorstein. *The Theory of the Leisure Class.* New York: Dover Publications, 1994, p. 200.

[568] Barzun, Jacques. *From Dawn to Decadence.* New York: Harper Collins, 2000, p. 781.

[569] *"This can't go on!* Yet it goes on, it lasts, if not forever, at least a long time." Barthes, Roland. *A Lover's Discourse.* Trans. Richard Howard. New York: Vintage Classics, 1977, p. 140. "Your striving and struggling renders your spirit increasingly strong and flexible," in a letter to his brother. Hölderlin, Friedrich.

Desire constantly begs for recognition and satisfaction. The easiest response of which is permission by the path of least resistance.

In *The Beautiful and Damned*, Fitzgerald describes the protagonist's ennui: "Anthony's affair with Dorothy Raycroft was an inevitable result of his increasing carelessness about himself. He did not go to her desiring to possess the desirable, nor did he fall before a personality more vital, more compelling than his own...He merely slid into the matter through his inability to make definite judgments."[570]

185.
Ennui, already in the stride of ease calls for an easy next step, an even slower pace, a coma. For this reason, the comfort of drink is pleasing. The comfort of media, from the couch, is pleasing. The comfort of anything near sleep is desired.

Intoxication

I AM joy before death.
Joy before death carries me.
Joy before death hurls me down.
Joy before death annihilates me.
- Georges Bataille, *Visions of Excess*[571]

Essays and Letters on Theory. Trans. Thomas Pfau. New York: State University of New York Press, 1988, p. 133.

[570] Fitzgerald, F. Scott. *The Beautiful and Damned*. New York: The Modern Library, 2002, p. 273

[571] Bataille, Georges. *Visions of Excess: Selected Writings 1927-1939*. Minneapolis: University of Minnesota Press, 1985, p. 237.

186.

"The economy of jouissance is something we can't yet put our fingertips on," explains Lacan. We certainly exhibit desire for pleasure as end without end, and intoxication serves as a plateau, giving us a rush of pleasure and yet not completely resolving the persistence of desire. Decadence has such an engagement with desire and excess that it is ripe with intoxication from beauty, drink, cuisine and materialism.[572] Intoxication is the result of too much of something that in certain quantities is pleasurable. Intoxication is unique in that it relies on pre-existing familiarity, that is knowing a substance as pleasurable in small quantities, but it then gives a surprise attack of too much intensity.

187.

We assume that something has intoxicated us, but not the reverse. Even when we resist intoxication by substances, we find a wave of passion can overcome reason. "No thank you," becomes "please." Intoxication then hovers in a limbo in which we may return to a sober state or cross over to unconsciousness. Because decadents always seek to resolve desire, intoxication becomes unconsciousness which then allows desire to be put to sleep for a time.

---

[572] There is "intoxication as music; intoxication as cruelty in the tragic enjoyment of the destruction of the noblest; intoxication as blind enthusiasm for single human beings or ages." Ibid. p. 20.The intoxication caused by mass production was apparent to Benjamin: "the intoxication to which the flâneur surrenders is the intoxication of the commodity around which surges the stream of customers." Benjamin, Walter. *Charles Baudelaire: A Lyric Poet in the Era of High Capitalism.* Trans. Harry Zohn. London: NLB, 1969, p. 55.

188.

'Zeus made all things,' says an Orphic line, 'and Bacchus perfected them.'
- Simone Weil, *Waiting for God*[573]

Intoxication is inclined to fantasy.[574] But that is often a fantasy addressing being limited and bound to this world.[575] It can be an impetus to take over the world or to simply be enveloped by it.[576] It is normally understood as a numb but pleasing experience that simulates authentic contentment.

189.

The idea in pharmaceutical psychiatry is that a subject is intoxicated with a particular emphasis. A doctor can step in and flood an individual with an element that will alter the patient's expression to meet "real world" expectations. An individual may try to self-medicate for the same aim. Yet as one who both administered and self-medicated, Freud was ultimately suspect of intoxication's effectiveness. He explained that "I do not think anyone completely understands its mechanism."[577] What he did

[573] Weil, Simone. *Waiting for God*. Trans. Emma Craufurd. New York: G.P. Putnam's Sons, 1951, p. 164.
[574] "Themes of 'wonder' and 'marvel of Being' are suspect if they refer to an ecstatic mysticism that pretends to escape the world," explained Nancy. Nancy, Jean-Luc. *Being Singular Plural*. Trans. Robert D. Richardson and Anne E. O'Byrne. Stanford: Stanford Univ. Press, 2000, p. 10.
[575] "No man has ever yet felt entirely happy in the present, for he would have been intoxicated." Schopenhauer, Arthur. *Philosophical Writings*. Ed. Wolfgang Schirmacher. New York: The Continuum Publishing Company, 2002, p. 24.
[576] In Nietzsche's discussion of intoxication he describes the Dionysian and Apollonian styles. Intoxication is usually associated with the Dionysian drive toward excess and destruction but it is also relevant to extreme calm of the Apollonian. Nietzsche, Friedrich. *The Will to Power*. Trans. Walter Kaufmann. New York: Random House, 1968, p. 420.
[577] Freud, Sigmund. *The Freud Reader*. Ed. Peter Gay. New York: Norton & Company, 1989, p. 730.

believe was that intoxication creates a semblance of meaning because it simulates happiness. Freud writes:

> Nobody talks about the purpose of the life of animals, unless, perhaps, it may be supposed to lie in being of service to man…only religion can answer the question of the purpose of life…we will therefore turn to the less ambitious question of what men themselves show by their behavior to be the purpose and intention of their lives. What do they demand of life and wish to achieve in it? The answer to this can hardly be in doubt. They strive after happiness; they want to become happy and remain so.[578]

Barthes expressed a similar attitude. "Joy has no need of heirs or of children. Joy wants itself, wants eternity, the repetition of the same things, wants everything to remain eternally the same."[579] We could consider that intoxication is not a potential state but instead an ultimate state toward which we are all always contributing with different substances and means.[580] It is a favored ongoing state in decadence, to surrender to a "mere feeling," instead of truth.

190.

> Have you ever said Yes to a single joy? O my friends, then you said Yes to *all* woe. All things are entangled, ensnared, enamored; if you ever wanted one thing twice, if you ever said, "You please me, happiness!

---

[578] Ibid. p. 729.

[579] Barthes, Roland. *A Lover's Discourse*. Trans. Richard Howard. New York: Vintage Classics, 1977, p.56.

[580] Freud further explained that "there is no golden rule which applies to everyone; every man must find out for himself in what particular fashion he can be saved. All kinds of different factors will operate to direct his choice." Freud, Sigmund. *The Freud Reader*. Ed. Peter Gay. New York: Norton & Company, 1989, p. 734.

Abide, moment!" then you wanted *all* back. All anew, all eternally, all entangled, ensnared, enamored—oh then you *loved* the world. Eternal ones, love it eternally and evermore; and to woe too, you say: go, but return! *For all joy wants—eternity.*
- Friedrich Nietzsche, *Thus Spoke Zarathustra* [581]

In intoxication we eventually lose resistance and become unable to discern, not only between need and desire but also between action and consequence. Believing in our own subjectively deluded remedies hastens inevitable exhaustion.[582] Consistent exhaustion overtime is will to tragedy.[583] Then, one longs for the sleep, the end of suffering.[584]

For Nietzsche, "whenever the will to power declines in any form there is every time also a physiological regression a décadence...the divinity of décadence...becomes the God of the physiologically retarded, the weak...they call themselves 'the good.'"[585] Does anyone in the 21st century dare to claim goodness? Brian Ingraffia writes that "Derrida has deconstructed the metaphysical belief in truth proceeding from and present in our own consciousness," that we cannot even judge our own goodness.[586] What then is left? What we most fear is that all of

---

[581] Nietzsche, Friedrich. *Thus Spoke Zarathustra: A Book for All and None.* Trans. Walter Kaufman. New York: The Modern Library. 1992, p. 323.

[582] "Nietzsche considered the exhausted "harmful," and warned of their potential to create problems for humankind." Nietzsche, Friedrich. *The Will to Power.* Trans. Walter Kaufmann. New York: Random House, 1968, p. 30.

[583] "The advent of myth," explained Jacques Barzun in From Dawn to Decadence, "joined to the earthly twins, fatigue and boredom, contributed to the outbreak of Wagnerism." Barzun, Jacques. *From Dawn to Decadence.* New York: Harper Collins, 2000, p. 637.

[584] "Most general types of decadence," Nietzsche, Friedrich. *The Will to Power.* Trans. Walter Kaufmann. New York: Random House, 1968, p. 26.

[585] Nietzsche, Friedrich. *Twilight of the Idols / The Anti Christ.* New York: Penguin Books, 1990, p. 139.

[586] Ingraffia, Brian. *Postmodern Theory and Biblical Theology.* Cambridge: Cambridge University Press, 1995, p. 224.

the attitudes of decadence will exist together in a willing intoxication: "They have become ungovernable, this 'waste land' where new sufferings are disguised with the name of former pleasures; and where people are so afraid. They go round and round in the night and are consumed by fire. They wake up startled, and, fumbling, search for life. Rumor has it that those who were expropriating it have, to crown it all, mislaid it."[587]

191.
Intoxication from potentially threatening substances is governed and often illegal. In this regard we have come to associate habitual intoxication with depravity, that it is unfortunate for a subject to "prefer what is harmful to it."[588] But what of a momentary intoxication as a state of bliss that may prompt change? What results from intoxication is not always debauchery. Masterpieces rise from intoxication of the spirit. "What a tremendous amount can be accomplished by that intoxication which is called 'love'," writes Nietzsche.[589]

192.

> Intoxication as virtue! Intoxication as vehicle to a "lost world!"
> - Georges Bataille, *Visions of Excess*[590]

In *Valley of the Dolls*, Neely explains her addiction to barbiturates: "I am not self-destructive. Everything just went

[587] Debord, Guy. *In Girum Imus Nocte Et Consummimur Igni*. London: Pelagian Press, 1990, p. 74.
[588] Nietzsche, Friedrich. *Twilight of the Idols / The AntiChrist*. New York: Penguin Books, 1990, p. 129.
[589] Ibid. p. 425.
[590] Bataille, Georges. *Visions of Excess: Selected Writings 1927-1939*. 1985. Minneapolis: University of Minnesota Press, 1985, p. 205.

wrong."[591] When does intoxication happen? Was the drunk vagrant already a drunk and thus became a vagrant or did his vagrancy lead to drunkenness? This is why in thought we prefer reason and doubt passion because it is assumed that the consistency of reason is closer to truth while unpredictable passion leads to intoxication and thus lack of truth.[592] Yet we have also become accustomed to the reverse, of a century of lips of blood, expressions of passion that claim to get at the truth. Philosophy rejects both reason and passion as the basis for the existence of God. We cannot trust reason because it has failed in the past, and we cannot trust passion because it is prone to intoxication.[593] But what of intoxication as source of truth? Intoxication can be like an unfolding mystery, exposing meaning that did not seem to exist. The great hope placed in intoxication, among artists and creators is that intoxication is the gateway to discovery of all meaning.[594] "Lewis Carol was the father of surrealism…It's all about opening different doors, like Alice," explained Jean-Charles de Castelbajac.[595] The internet is intoxication by information, where all things lead to something else. The meaning is related but often like a series of doors onto

---

[591] Susann, Jacqueline. *Valley of the Dolls*. New York: Grove Press, 1966, p. 366.

[592] "We are so accustomed to the old oppositions of reason and passion, of mind and life, that the idea of passionate thinking, in which thinking and being alive become one, can be a bit startling." Arendt, Hannah and Martin Heidegger. *Letters: 1925-1975*. Ed. Ursula Ludz. Trans. Andrew Shields. New York: Harcourt, Inc., 2004: p. 153.

[593] The Christian Bible warns against both intoxication and human reason but also philosophy. See to it that no one takes you captive through hollow and deceptive philosophy, which depends on human tradition and the basic principles of this world rather than on Christ. Colossians 2: 8. *The Holy Bible*. New International Version. Grand Rapids, Michigan: Zondervan Publishing House, 1996, p. 995.

[594] Like the state of love, in intoxication everything has meaning, absolutely "everything signifies." Barthes, Roland. *A Lover's Discourse*. Trans. Richard Howard. New York: Vintage Classics, 1977, p. 63.

[595] Speyer, Ariana, Ed. *The Real Thing: Fashion Interviews from Index Magazine*. New York: Index Books, 2003, p. 80.

empty rooms the only meaning is in the one who connects them and can remember where he has already been.

193.

Both types of intoxication, chemical or fullness of life, can generate a "feeling of *power*."[596] Intoxication gives energy, a feeling of infallibility but it also produces a lack of command. In some ways this is the reality of power, a mere fantasy which never really has full command, but believes that it does. Power can also be a form of intoxication.[597]

194.

In T.S. Eliot's *The Cocktail Party* there is "nothing in the place fit to eat," until the character Julie finds champagne for lunch.[598] Intoxication seeks continuing pleasure in whatever way may be available. But the desire for continued pleasure may only mean decline. This is especially the case if we have already felt a great height of intoxication.[599] When we realize the height are we already descending?

195.

Nietzsche describes that one who is intoxicated has an "indifference to life or death." Yet I would suggest the indifference is really simply that something else holds greater

---

[596] Nietzsche, Friedrich. *The Will to Power*. Trans. Walter Kaufmann. New York: Random House, 1968, p. 424. "There are two sources of intoxication: the over-great fullness of life and a state of pathological nourishment of the brain." Nietzsche, Friedrich. *The Will to Power*. Trans. Walter Kaufmann. New York: Random House, 1968, p. 31.
[597] Ibid. p. 424.
[598] Eliot., T.S. *The Cocktail Party*. New York: Harcourt, Brace and Company, 1950, p. 58.
[599] "It's different when you reach the summit ...The elements have left you battered, deafened, sightless-and too weary to enjoy your victory." Susann, Jacqueline. *Valley of the Dolls*. New York: Grove Press, 1966, p. 3.

importance in the moment. One who is intoxicated often finds something so valuable, which is usually the value of being intoxicated, that they do not think about life or death. Even spiritual intoxication reaches above life and death. The very idea that "for God everything is possible," also allows one "to believe his downfall is impossible."[600] This is why intoxication is so essential to decadence, because it is inclined to feelings above reality. But the feeling is also of continuation, of continuing in passion, without discretion for life or death, or for resources, or for anything. And thus it is also why intoxication is an altered state; one is always haunted in intoxication of the memory of prior clarity.

196.

> Scenes of wild religious enthusiasm...reminiscent of a negro camp-meeting in Southern America...broke out in the heart of Mayfair yesterday evening at a party given for the famous American revivalist Mrs. Ape by the Viscountess Metroland....Countess of Throbbing rose to confess her sins...the Duchess of Stayle next threw down her emerald and diamond tiara, crying "a Guilt Offering" an example which was quickly followed by the Countess of Circumference and Lady Brown, until a veritable rain of precious stones fell on to the parquet flooring, heirlooms of priceless value rolling among Tecla pearls and Chanel diamonds. A blank cheque fluttered from the lands of Maharajah of Pukkapore.
> - Evelyn Waugh, *Vile Bodies*[601]

---

[600] Kierkegaard, Søren. *The Sickness Unto Death*. Trans. Howard Hong and Edna Hong. Princeton: Princeton University Press, 1980, p. 39.
[601] Waugh, Evelyn. *Vile Bodies*. New York: Little, Brown and Company, 1958, p. 145.

Intoxication often leads to the overflowing of excess, to a total freedom of resources, to liberated expenditure. We witness a freedom that we had at first, a freedom to fulfill desire replaced by the letting go of desire for something better.

Love

> I'd stay forever on my knees for you...What is it you're giving up here? What are you putting in bondage? It's your soul...you give your love to be profaned...Love!– this is everything, it's a diamond, a maiden's treasure, this love! To deserve this love a man would be ready to lay down his life, to face death.
> - Fyodor Dostoevsky, *Notes from Underground*[602]

197.

The woman has historically been less powerful than man, thus more often controlled, and thus always already seduced. Yet in her captivity the woman's desire is not subdued. She thus knows that power cannot stop desire, thus power has limits, a possible basis for her traditional indifference to leadership. And now, after power has been openly debased through postmodernism, there is acknowledgement of the great power of desire.

198.

For Kant, being is guided by desire for a particular end. Recurrent desire is called inclination to an end. Emotions may come and go and are considered unreasonable, but it is desire that re-affirms its presence. Because of its constant re-

---

[602] Dostoevsky, Fyodor. *Notes from Underground.* New York: Vintage Books Random House, 1993, p. 99.

appearance, desire seems consistent and thus logical to an individual, even if out of control and unreasonable to others.[603]

199.

Ennui may persist for entire lives, but we witness the reappearance of desire whenever there is new hope *in* some thing. And even though decadence involves consciousness of the futility of everything, the object of desire is held in a state of exception to limit, that is until the next point of desire arises. Madame Emma Bovary suffered from ennui and her husband encouraged her to get a passion for riding and so "it was the riding habit that decided her."[604] Eventually however Madame Bovary locates her desire in Rodolphe, then in Leon, then God. Flaubert described Madame Bovary:

> She came to share Rodolphe's fears, love had intoxicated her at first, and she had no thought beyond it. But now life was inconceivable without it... As time went on he stopped making any effort, secure in the knowledge that he was loved ....It was not an attachment; it was a kind of permanent seduction. She was in bondage... Her depravity was so deep and so dissembled as to be almost intangible: where could she have learned it?"... She wasn't happy and never had been. Why was life so unsatisfactory? Why did everything she leaned on crumble instantly to dust?[605]

---

[603] Kant, Immanuel. *Anthropology from a Pragmatic Point of View.* Trans. by Victor Lyle Dowdel. *Carbondale, IL:* Southern Illinois University Press, 1978, pp. 155-6.
[604] Flaubert. Gustave. *Madame Bovary.* Trans. Francis Steegmuller. New York: The Modern Library, 1982, p. 177.
[605] Ibid. p. 186, p. 192, p. 316, p. 322.

Madame Bovary's desires fail her, though she does not fail to continue desiring.[606] Desire never rests and to make matters worse "the dice love plays are madness and confusion."[607]

200.

> The poets fool us; they are the only ones to whom love
> is not only a crucial, but an indispensable experience,
> which entitles them to mistake it for a universal one.
> - Hannah Arendt, *The Human Condition*.[608]

We could argue that decadent love is distinguished from pathos. Decadent love is a self-fulfilling wandering, a fragmented love that can be satisfied here or there. The poets and philosophers have created the theoretical fragmentation of love. We have broken it apart like ideology. Now there are many love affairs.[609] We speak of "brotherly love," "Platonic love," "Christian love," "romantic love." We are only describing styles. The moving target of desire is part of our fragmentation of love, that we think love could be fulfilled partially in different places. We continue to want but do not know where or how to resolve it in full. We believe we find *it* again, each time in a new more interesting style, failing to see *it* at all times.

---

[606] After her lovers, Madame Bovary locates her desire in God and "she was filled with wonderment at the discovery that there was a bliss greater than happiness–a love different from an transcending all others…a love that increased throughout eternity! Among the illusions born of her hope she glimpsed a realm of purity in which she aspired to dwell: it hovered above earth." Ibid. p. 241.

[607] Plato. *Phaedrus*. Trans. Alexander Nehamas and Paul Woodward. Cambridge: Hackett Publishing Company, 1995, p. 91.

[608] Arendt, Hannah. *The Human Condition*. Chicago: The University of Chicago Press, 1958, p. 242, note 81.

[609] There is in love a suspension, a constant anticipation. "Being allowed to wait for the beloved–that is what is most wonderful–for it is in that waiting that the beloved is 'present.'" Arendt, Hannah and Martin Heidegger. *Letters: 1925-1975*. Ed. Ursula Ludz. Trans. Andrew Shields. New York: Harcourt, Inc., 2004, p. 18.

201.

It is as if every love begins the same: "I knew no end of desiring
you."[610] But then confusion arises, is it desire or you of which I
know no end? The Hebrew Proverb, "what a man desires is
unfailing love," is evidenced by all men trying to locate an
earthly love that will not fail.[611] In an overwhelming state of
desire, we are consumed by an invisible relation to the world, a
longing that has no match. An individual then finds something
worthy that seems obscured to others and to exclusively satisfy
and to resolve placeless longing. The love of this particular thing
brings rest from searching and the world is light and effortless
again.

202.

> Everything that is taxed with being exaggerated, you
> have made me feel.
> - Gustave Flaubert, *Sentimental Education*[612]

In decadence there is an object of obsession that becomes a site
for total investment of desire, and thus a site of indulgence. "The
other," describes Roland Barthes, "with whom I am in love
designates for me the specialty of my desire."[613] This is why the
sense of "true" love offers relief to decadence because there is a
sense that *truth has been located*. This can sometimes be a
strong inclination for addiction, of sacrificing at most an entire

---

[610] Derrida, Jacques. *Spurs*. Chicago: The University of Chicago Press, 1978, p.
155.
[611] Proverbs 19:22. *The Holy Bible*. New International Version. Grand Rapids,
Michigan: Zondervan Publishing House, 1996, p. 552. In Psalms 130:7 it is
written: "For with the Lord is unfailing love." Ibid. 527.
[612] Flaubert, Gustave as cited in Barthes, Roland. *A Lover's Discourse*. Trans.
Richard Howard. New York: Vintage Classics, 1977, p. 191.
[613] Barthes, Roland. *A Lover's Discourse*. Trans. Richard Howard. New York:
Vintage Classics, 1977, p. 19.

lifetime to a single purpose, place or thing, to the point of death. The obsession is a deception that is considered perverse to outsiders. Des Esseintes calls this tendency in himself, "the demon of perversity."[614] Such devotion is of course also the fuel of ordinary, everyday "life's work," returning again to the plow, or the computer. This is visible in Gaudi who lived in squalor for stylizing his buildings. And filmmaker Pier Paolo Pasolini explained about his work, "the mark which has dominated all my work, is this longing for life, this sense of exclusion, which doesn't lessen but augments this love of life."[615] It is not the medium of film that motivated him, but love fulfilled.

203.
Camus describes Don Juan moving with desire. "If he leaves a woman," writes Camus, "it is not because he ceased to desire her... but he desires another and no that is not the same thing."[616] If desire is a moving target, and we are especially decadent, we will move with it. Certainly, some live by pleasure ethics, always pursuing whatever they desire. But rather than the

---

[614] Huysmans, J.K. *A Rebours*. Trans. Havelock Ellis. New York: Dover, 1969, p. 178.
[615] Attributed to Pasolini from a private interview in the 1960's. http://en.wikipedia.org/wiki/Pier_Paolo_Pasolini#Quotes. There is risk involved in basing all of one's pleasure in one area of life. Simone de Beauvoir writes that "It is in a state of fear that the serious man feels this dependence upon the object....he escapes the anguish of freedom only to fall into a state of preoccupation, of worry. Everything is a threat to him, since the thing which he has set up as an idol is an externality and is thus in relationship with the whole universe and consequently threatened by the whole universe, and since, despite all precautions, he will never be the master of this exterior world to which he has consented to submit, he will constantly be upset by the uncontrollable course of events. He will always be saying that he is disappointed, for his wish is to have the world harden into a thing that is belied by the very movement of life." de Beauvoir, Simone. *The Ethics of Ambiguity*. Trans. Bernard Frechtman. New York: Citadel Press, 1996, p. 51-52.
[616] Camus, Albert. *The Myth of Sisyphus*. Trans. Justin O'Brien. New York: Vintage International, 1955, p. 71.

desired object, weather a delicious meal or a seductive woman, "it is love the subject loves, not the object" writes Barthes. The love is the experience where desire meets resolution, where desire is surprised by return. And then begins the chase for this encounter, so much so "the being I am waiting for is not real, I create and re-create it over and over."[617]

204.

>Alas, our young affections run to waste...
>Love, fame, ambition, avarice–t'is the same
>- Lord Byron, *Childe Harold's Pilgrimage: Canto IV*[618]

The obsession of love is a performance. Now, with a force of love, "I am my own theatre."[619] Young love in particular is motivated by self-expression and affirmation. I found a sign that read "Christopher loves Audra forever." Christopher loves Audra with a fantasy of limitless love. Their love is likely highly decorated with notes and gifts and tattoos that promise fidelity. They believe that their love will always be, even though next week it could be with someone else. Adolescent love is the elaboration of the present, in denial of immanent decline. It thrives on a fantasy of forever but is subject to the situation of expiring at any moment. It is decadence par excellence because it is not just a squandering of resources but putting everything at stake, all of my life and all of its time, forever. This is the declaration of marriage, without end. The contract requires that all that one has be sacrificed in the name of a partnership. This is why a wedding is such a decadent site because it is an effort to

---

[617] Barthes, Roland. *A Lover's Discourse*. Trans. Richard Howard. New York: Vintage Classics, 1977, p. 41 and p. 39.
[618] Bernbaum, Ernest, Ed. *Anthology of Romanticism*. New York, The Ronald Press Company, 1933, p. 577.
[619] Ibid. p. 161.

embellish the already overdetermined present in deterrence from the threat of mortality, also the basis for the birthday cake.

205.

You see, if you make believe hard enough that something is true, then it is true for you.
- Ned Merrill, *The Swimmer* (1968)

To a lover, especially a decadent one, love justifies any action. Instead of love without end it is love as end, as noble end.[620] Barthes extended the concept by writing that in love it means "all or nothing."[621] When we submit to love we submit to it because we hope it will satisfy all.[622] "Wouldn't I be justified in abandoning myself ... Are not excess and madness my truth and strength?," continued Barthes.[623] We continually re-invest in desire in order to give it the appearance of an endless love. But love like being, is mutable. It is in fact in an exclusive love affair that we discover this agency. Even a consistent love is unpredictable and may be potent one day, while faded the next. In the eventual return, when we re-discover it again, we understand no more of the other being with whom we have

---

[620] De Beauvoir explains that "I cannot genuinely desire an end today without desiring it through my whole existence." De Beauvoir, Simone. *The Ethics of Ambiguity*. Trans. Bernard Frechtman. New York: Citadel Press, 1996, p. 27.

[621] Barthes, Roland. *A Lover's Discourse*. Trans. Richard Howard. New York: Vintage Classics, 1977, p. 163.

[622] We can ask what of love is a shared delusion in a hope for the future? "When I say my joy in you is great and growing," writes Heidegger, "that means I also have faith in everything that is your story I am not erecting an ideal...only then is love strong for the future, and not just a moments fleeting pleasure...But such faith is also kept from misusing that other's trust in love. Love that can be happy into the future has taken root." Arendt, Hannah and Martin Heidegger. *Letters: 1925-1975*. Ed. Ursula Ludz. Trans. Andrew Shields. New York: Harcourt, Inc., 2004: p. 25.

[623] Ibid. p. 42.

exclusive love, but we instead we grow in understanding of love itself, as that which always returns.

206.

> Love is not holy because it is a predicate of God, but it is a predicate of God because it is in itself divine.
> - Ludwig Feuerbach, *The Essence of Christianity* [624]

Badiou explains: "Lacan distinguishes love and desire in philosophical terms because he says that love is connected with being, and desire is connected with the object." [625] Lacan states:

> I shall have to articulate what serves as the linchpin of everything that has been instituted on the basis of the analytic experience: love. People have been talking about nothing else for a long time. Need I emphasize the fact that it is at the very heart of philosophical discourse?... Love aims at being, namely, at what slips away most in language–being that, a moment later, was going to be, or being that, due precisely to having been, gave rise to surprise. [626]

The object of love becomes associated with the original surprise encounter and is confused as the source of pleasure or at most, the source of being. Lacan explained, "in love it is not the meaning that counts, but rather the sign, as in everything else. In fact, therein lies the whole catastrophe. And you can't say, in

[624] Feuerbach, Ludwig. *The Essence of Christianity*. Trans. George Eliot. New York: Harper & Brothers Publishers, 1957, p. 273.
[625] Badiou, Alain. *Infinite Thought*. Trans. Justin Clemens. New York: Continuum, 2003, p. 191.
[626] Lacan, Jacques. *The Seminar of Jacques Lacan: On Feminine Sexuality, The Limits of Love and Knowledge* (Book XX, Encore 1972-1973), Ed. Jacques-Alain Miller, Trans. Bruce Fink, New York: W. W. Norton & Company, 1998, p. 39.

translation through analytic discourse, love slips away as it does elsewhere."[627] It is not that an object or individual continually delivers, either on love, or promises, but rather it is being itself that always already delivers love.

207.

Love is continually asserted. We love others, as almost a violent action upon them. "I once spoke of a language," explained Lacan "in which one would say, 'I love to you,' that language modeling itself better than others on the indirect character of that attack called love."[628] Whenever we love we assert it, give it, bestow it, and even in the instances of great charity (e.g. Mother Teresa) we insist what we are giving must be given, at times against the will of the recipient. C.S. Lewis explained how impoverished children playing in dirt might refuse the loving invitation of a holiday at sea, because they cannot conceive of something so great.[629] It is not that we do not long for love but that we are suspect of the invitation to change all with which we are comfortable, which is sadly believed to be best.

---

[627] Lacan, Jacques. *Television*. Trans. By Denis Hollier, Rosalind Krauss and Annette Michelson. Ed. Joan Copjec. New York: W. W. Norton & Company, 1990, p. 41.

[628] Lacan, Jacques. *The Seminar of Jacques Lacan: On Feminine Sexuality, The Limits of Love and Knowledge* (Book XX, Encore 1972-1973), Ed. Jacques-Alain Miller, Trans. Bruce Fink, New York: W. W. Norton & Company, 1998, p. 104.

[629] "Indeed, if we consider the unblushing promises of reward and the staggering nature of the rewards promised in the Gospels, it would seem that Our Lord finds our desires, not too strong, but too weak. We are half-hearted creatures, fooling about with drink and sex and ambition when infinite joy is offered us, like an ignorant child who wants to go on making mud pies in a slum because he cannot imagine what is meant by the offer of a holiday at the sea. We are far too easily pleased." Lewis, C.S. "The Weight of Glory," Preached originally as a sermon in the Church of St Mary the Virgin, Oxford, on June 8, 1942. *The Essential C.S. Lewis*. Ed. Lyle W. Dorsett. New York: Simon & Schuster, 1988, p. 362.

208.

"Can love survive a relationship?," asked Jean-Luc Godard.[630] Love is often understood as momentary, and like beauty continually appears and transforms. Even love in the best intentions can be interrupted by an unexpected circumstance. But the answer to Godard is yes, people continue to love after the relation ends. But then we can also ask, what is the relationship? Is it with an object, a person, to reality or to truth? Is love an ongoing dialogue with the universe that is not located in a particular end, nor has an end? The understanding of a perfect and holy God is one that includes eternal love. Whether we have developed this concept from our mortal lack, or it is the real truth of the unknown divine, this is the ultimate form of truth. The eternal embrace—there is nothing that holds this promise on earth and while we can recognize desire rising from within, it is love that happens to us.

209.

While Heidegger called love a "burden," in a love letter to Hannah Arendt, he asked "Why is love rich beyond all other possible human experiences…Because we become what we love and yet remain ourselves."[631] Unlike obsession or love of an object, there is love in being, a dialogue between singular and collective, between need and possibility that is always already emerging and vanishing.[632]

Lacan wrote:

---

[630] *Tout Va Bien* (1972).
[631] Arendt, Hannah and Martin Heidegger. *Letters: 1925-1975*. Ed. Ursula Ludz. Trans. Andrew Shields. New York: Harcourt, Inc., 2004, p. 4.
[632] Nancy, Jean-Luc. *Being Singular Plural*. Trans. Robert D. Richardson and Anne E. O'Byrne. Stanford: Stanford Univ. Press, 2000, p. 4.

It is clear that, in everything that approaches it, language merely manifests its inadequacy. What makes up for the sexual relationship is, quite precisely, love. The Other, the Other as the locus of truth, is the only place, albeit an irreducible place, that we can give to the term "divine being," God, to call him by his name.[633]

When we approach the topic of love, especially the dialogue of love and being, we must consider ourselves as part of something greater than ourselves. We believe we know greatness, in front of us. But knowing only local greatness is the very crux of decadence, rather than to believe in the "other," existence beyond you. What we know of love, what we manage to speak of it, is a combination of what we are capable of in our finitude and everything that we are incapable of alone, such as eternal patience, or ubiquity. We speculate love as divine, as other, and then realize we are the subject of a great love affair, of an unrequited love eternally thrust upon us. We discover a love that will wait for us.

---

[633] Lacan, Jacques. *The Seminar of Jacques Lacan: On Feminine Sexuality, The Limits of Love and Knowledge* (Book XX, Encore 1972-1973), Ed. Jacques-Alain Miller, Trans. Bruce Fink, New York: W. W. Norton & Company, 1998, p. 45.

VIII. Truth

If we are able to understand sufficiently well the order
of the universe, we should find that it goes beyond all
desires of the wisest of us, and that it is impossible to
have it better than it is, not only for all in general, but
also for each one in particular.
- Leibniz, *Mondaology*[634]

[634] Leibniz, G. W. *Discourse on Metaphysics / Correspondence with Arnaud / Monadology.* Trans. George Montgomery. La Salle, Illinois: Open Court Publishing, 1988.

Grace

If there is any happiness,
Only the happiness of knowing.
That the misery does not feed on the ruin of loveliness,
That the tedium is not the residue of ecstasy
I see that my life was determined long ago
And that the struggle to escape from it
Is only make-believe, a pretence
That what is, is not, or could be changed.
The self that can say "I want this-or I want that"-
The self that wills--he is a feeble creature;
He has to come to terms in the end
With the obstinate, the tougher self; who does not speak,
Who never talks, who cannot argue;
And who in some men may be the guardian-
But in men like me, the dull, the implacable,
The indomitable spirit of mediocrity.
The willing self can contrive the disaster
Of this unwilling partnership–but can only flourish
In submission to the rule of the stronger partner.
- T.S. Eliot, *The Cocktail Party*[635]

210.

The coup de grâce is the necessary release in decadence, and thus the moment of truth. This is because a coup de grâce is not what someone does, but what is done to them, from the outside, and thus brings the endlessly postponed end.

"Coup de grâce" is normally used to describe the death blow to an ailing animal or dying solider. The coup de grâce could be compared to mercy, and is often translated as "mercy blow." But the specific word "grace," especially divine grace, is

---

[635] Eliot, T.S. *The Cocktail Party.* New York: Harcourt, Brace and Company, 1950, pp. 65-66.

distinguished from "mercy." "Mercy" is to defer punishment, but "grace" is to provide a positive gift that one does not expect or deserve. In decadence, with the force of desire toward decline, there is no positive benefit expected, as even pleasure declines in time. But the coup de grâce is an opening for salvation. Being stranded on a desert island and pouring out the only drinking water is a decadent expenditure. Pouring out the drinking water is an end to the situation, but a literal blow of grace would be something like the downfall of rain or rescue.

211.
Children play a game in which they fight until someone cries "mercy." When the weaker opponent is at his end, he surrenders with the call of "mercy." The stronger opponent then *relents* and the match ends.

The term "coup de grâce" is commonly associated with duels. When a weak opponent is at his end, he is unfortunately subject to the greater power of the stronger one. It is in this moment, that the strong one *attacks* with a coup de grâce ends the match.

With mercy is compassion and relent; with grace is passion and assertion. In mercy, the stronger one relinquishes his grasp. In grace, the weaker relinquishes to death.

In decadence there is a desire to control and a resistance to relinquish. Somehow in our contemporary celebrations of freedom we have lost the ability to surrender, even to one another, even when it is in our own best interest.[636] We

---

[636] Do we think that the divine is what happens to us? Do we take credit for what happens to us by calling it our own good luck? Or do we become divine? "God represented the only obstacle to the human will, and freed from God this will surrenders, nude, to the passion of giving the world an intoxicating meaning.

collectively regard resignation as weak, and quitting as the easy way out. At the same time, we are unwilling to see that we continually surrender to our own desires. We lie on our backs, like dogs waiting to be stroked by self-appointed pleasures. But these pleasures give no end, no rest and instead create a want of conclusion. The effects of pleasure result in the unwanted coup de grâce; i.e. sickness, death, salvation

212.

> "But perfect love drives out fear, because fear has to do with punishment. The one who fears is not made perfect in love. We love because he first loved us."
> - 1 John 4:18-19[637]

The way we learn of love is by the first blow of grace, being born and being an undeserving recipient of care. *This is coup de grâce, a collision with love stronger than we are.* We live with the memory of this original collision, and then we give because we have first received.[638]

Whoever creates, whoever paints or writes, can no longer concede any limitations on painting or writing...he cannot flee from this heritage of divine power–which belongs to him." Bataille, Georges. *Visions of Excess: Selected Writings 1927-1939.* 1985. Minneapolis: University of Minnesota Press, 1985, p. 245.
[637] *The Holy Bible.* New International Version. Grand Rapids, Michigan: Zondervan Publishing House, 1996, p. 1014.
[638] "It was the will to purify love of all preconditions that posed the unconditional existence of God as the supreme object of rapturous escape from the self." Bataille, Georges. *Visions of Excess: Selected Writings 1927-1939.* 1985. Minneapolis: University of Minnesota Press, 1985, p. 133.

213.

In 1936, the Prince of Wales sacrificed his empire for his love with a divorced commoner.[639] Decadence have many little ends but a coup de grâce is a complete swipe, for total consequence.[640] It means *not* giving what is desired, but rather giving what is believed to be best. "We have an effect only insofar as we are capable of giving,"[641] explains Arendt. More so, we have an effect only insofar as we are capable of giving what we know is best.

214.

The coup de grâce is the pill you do not take, because you do not know it is the remedy.

The coup de grâce is not a solution, it is the answer.

There is no way to earn the coup de grâce. The coup de grâce comes to you, in love, to save you from yourself.

215.

The French word "coup" means blow or punch but also translates as a successful action. A "coup" is to win. But then

---

[639] "You can imagine what a dramatic moment it was when the Prince of Wales looked his father, the King, straight in the eye and told him that never, under any circumstances, would he ever succeed him." Vreeland, Diana. *D.V.* New York: De Capo Press, 1984, p. 71.

[640] "Whereas love likes to discover with tenderness and will not overlook anything, and where it discovers so-called errors or mistakes (parts which in what they are or through their position and movement momentarily diverge from the tone of the whole), feels and intuits the whole only more intrinsically." Hölderlin, Friedrich. *Essays and Letters on Theory*. Trans. Thomas Pfau. New York: State University of New York Press, 1988, p. 47. "Love recognizes virtue even in sin, truth in error." Feuerbach, Ludwig. *The Essence of Christianity*. Trans. George Eliot. New York: Harper & Brothers Publishers, 1957, p. 257.

[641] Arendt, Hannah and Martin Heidegger. *Letters: 1925-1975*. Ed. Ursula Ludz. Trans. Andrew Shields. New York: Harcourt, Inc., 2004: p. 25.

does decadence always lose? Can't we see great moments of decadence as the years of glory? We must also ask if in each and every instance decadence encounters the coup de grâce? Perhaps decadence may come after a coup de grâce, in further decline and refusal. But the coup de grâce is perhaps the only intersection with decadence from the outside that does not yield to it but destroys it.

216.

In *Faust* we find that at the time of death, the spirits of "Want," "Guilt," and "Necessity," cannot enter Faust's house. The only force that can reach him is "Care":

SORGE:
Wen ich einmal besitze,
Dem ist alle Welt nichts nuetze;
Ewiges Duestre steigt herunter,
Sonne geht nicht auf noch unter,
Bei vollkommnen aeussern Sinnen
Wohnen Finsternisse drinnen,
Und er weiss von allen Schaetzen
Sich nicht in Besitz zu setzen.
Glueck und Unglueck wird zur Grille,
Er verhungert in der Fuelle;
Sei es Wonne, sei es Plage,
Schieb er's zu dem andern Tage,
Ist der Zukunft nur gewaertig,
Und so wird er niemals fertig.[642]

---

[642] http://www.gutenberg.org/dirs/etext00/7fau210.txt; CARE: Whom I once possess, shall never / Find the world with his endeavor: / Endless / gloom around him folding / Rise nor set of sun beholding, / Perfect in external senses, / Inwardly his darkness dense is; / And he knows not how to measure / True possession of his treasure. / Luck and I'll become caprices; / Still he starves in all increases; / Be it happiness or sorrow, / He postpones it till the morrow; / To the Future only cleaveth: / Nothing, therefore he achieveth. Von Goethe, Johann Wolfgang. *Faust.* New York: Anchor, 1962, p. 237.

"Care" finds Faust "between despair and striving." The same line can be read that he shows resistance to surrender. What is all this effort in this life, of striving, making, succeeding, building and changing when we each find at the end–giving in and giving up is all that is possible? At the end of life, an aged and dying body is like that of a child, when the only role to play is "recipient of care." And it is then, in the face of death we discover the great coup de grâce. Paul Tillich writes: "But who can bear to look at this picture? Only he who can look at another picture behind and beyond it–the picture of Love. For love is stronger than death. Every death means parting, separation, isolation, opposition and not participation....Love is the infinite which is given to the finite."[643]

217.

> The future is now that to which care clings–not the
> authentic, futural being of the past, but the future that
> the present itself cultivates for itself as its own, because
> the past as the authentic future can never become
> present.
> - Martin Heidegger, *The Concept of Time*[644]

The Violet Hour (1993) is a play by Richard Greenberg in which a book publisher must decide whether to publish the writing of a friend or that of a lover. He has "special" access to a the future that informs him how the book he chooses to publish will be received historically. The play is like Schrödinger's cat. Can we ever assess anything in the present without a "what if" scenario,

[643] "For love is as strong as death," Song of Solomon 8:6, *The Holy Bible*; Tillich, Paul. *The Essential Tillich*. Ed. F. Forrester Church. New York: Macmillan Publishing Company, 1987, pp. 159-160.
[644] Heidegger, Martin. *Der Begriff der Zeit / The Concept of Time*. (German-English edition) Trans. William McNeill. Oxford: Blackwell, 1992, p. 16.

looking backward at now from a future point of view, making now into history?[645] This is why deconstruction has been a coup de grâce, a necessary separation from the historic view. We were not willing to surrender, to step away from anthropocentric glory into a realm of uncertainty. We have learned that we can only control what will submit to us and that we are controlled by desires (yet we fear submission to the truth).[646] The truth is the grace we do not deserve. While we may suspend full knowledge of truth–fatal sickness, loss of money, full implications of choices–the truth remains true and it is our resistance to it that must end, in time.

Vanishing

Why should I mourn
the vanished power of the usual reign?
- T.S. Eliot, "Ash-Wednesday"[647]

218.

The expectation of loss seems to make having much better– enjoy today because you and/or this world will disappear. This is the memento mori of decadence. But we have not seen the world's end. Every ending gives way to another incarnation. The idea of an absolute disappearance satisfies our anthropocentric

---

[645] "I do not find that pictures of physical catastrophe...help one so much...we cannot always be excited. We can perhaps train ourselves to ask more and more often how the thing we are saying or doing (or failing to do) at each moment will look when the irresistible light streams in upon it." Lewis, C.S. *The Essential C.S. Lewis*. Ed. Lyle W. Dorsett. New York: Simon & Schuster, 1988, p. 392.

[646] For Freud a believer "is admitting that all that is left to him as a last possible consolation and source of pleasure in his suffering is an unconditional submission." Freud, Sigmund. *The Freud Reader*. Ed. Peter Gay. New York: Norton & Company, 1989, p. 735.

[647] Eliot, T.S. "Ash-Wednesday." *The Complete Poems and Plays 1909-1950*. New York: Harcourt, Brace and Co., 1980, pp.60-67.

hope that we are so significant only nothing could follow us. "Nos hemos repartido como ladrones el caudal de las noches y de los días."[648]

219.

Thought is engaged in the vanishing of the world.

- Jean Baudrillard[649]

We do not witness the end but rather decay, fading, falling out of fashion and continual disappearance. In language, the disappearance of a word can be the result of its association with an obsolete object or practice. Politics and power players can intentionally eliminate certain words. Fashion as a system is always forgetting and then remembering. Technology has the same character, always erasing the tools of yesterday and attempting to take new root. We are however becoming increasingly unable to bring anything from yesterday into the present. In the 20th century, we witnessed the disappearance of objects in exchange for digital versions of them. The disappearance of the art object began earlier, with the onset of photography and then minimalism.[650] What then will remain from this post-media era? Nothing? Will we be uncovered by future archeologists as the civilization without objects, as a dark age that produced only small traces? Or will all our films

---

[648] We have divided among us, like thieves / the treasure of nights and days. "Remordimiento por cualquier muerte / Remorse for any death," Borges, Jorge Luis. *Selected Poems*. Ed. Alexander Coleman. New York: Viking Penguin Collective, 1999, p. 134-135.

[649] Comments from lectures at The European Graduate School, June 12, 2004.

[650] "Art playing on its own disappearance and the disappearance of its object was still an art of great works." Baudrillard, Jean. *Screened Out*. Trans. Chris Turner. New York: Verso Books, 2002, p. 183.

survive, and they will watch our era with adoration, for the innocence in its vanishing?

220.

> I think what has triumphed isn't capitalism but the global, so to speak, and the price paid has been the disappearance of the universal in terms of a value system.
> - Jean Baudrillard, *Paroxysm* [651]

Contemporary social space is not only a manifestation of capitalist value systems but it reveals in its already abandoned vacancy, that we have been decadent and quickly overproduced social space. What was speculation in *Dawn of the Dead* (1978) is confirmed by Walead Beshty's and Brian Ulrich's photographs of decaying American shopping malls. As we watch our world vanish before our eyes, we are watching a decline of an empire. This was the cult of the eagle, an empire of freedom, freedom to buy, freedom to own, freedom to rebel. War in our territory is not common because here freedom is so seductive to everyone including the enemy. Will freedom vanish? Will it one day be impossible to explain the American republic and democratic dream without first having explain the ideology of freedom?

221.

Our desire to elaborate existence is obvious but so is our desire to relinquish. When Philip K. Dick wrote, "I like to build universes which do fall apart," [652] he was describing reality.

---

[651] Baudrillard, Jean. *Paroxysm*. Trans. Chris Turner. New York: Verso Books, 1998, p. 10.
[652] Dick, Philip K.. *I Hope I Shall Arrive Soon*. New York: Doubleday & Company, 1985, p. 5.

Humanity builds and it disappears.[653] We live and accumulate and give it up at death. Death is like a vanishing point but not all vanishings are deaths. In this life everything is in the process of vanishing. There can be a vanishing of a person, a trend, a scene, an idea, a thing, a place. Usually a moment before or during the end, when the event is broken down and torn apart, there is a vanishing point.

222.

Then their eyes were opened and they recognized him, and he disappeared from their sight.
- Luke 24:31[654]

We associate disappearance with crime. A vanishing is often considered to have been unwilling, that foul play has taken something from this world. Our fascination with lost civilizations suggests that something poisonous, sickly or savage must have prompted the disappearance. Vanishing can also be a strategic tactic to maintain resources, or it can be a performance in itself as with Patty Hearst or Skyjacker D.B. Cooper. Vanishing is not only tragedy but illusion, transformation, or solution.

---

[653] Lyotard suggested that "we could say there exists a sort of destiny, or involuntary destination towards a condition that is increasingly complex," that we want to "complexify, mediatise, numerise, synthesise and modify the size of each and every object." This opposes the opposite nature to reduce, simplify and make more efficient. Lyotard, Jean-François. *The Postmodern Explained to Children: Correspondence 1982-1985.* Trans. Thomas Pefanis. London: Turnaround, 1992, p. 92.

[654] *The Holy Bible.* New International Version. Grand Rapids, Michigan: Zondervan Publishing House, 1996, p. 880.

223.

> Death is no longer anything but a virtual imaginary
> element.
> - Jean Baudrillard, *Screened Out* [655]

"We seduce with our death," wrote Baudrillard, "with our vulnerability, and the void that haunts us."[656] Death is an unsolved disappearance. In reference to filmic story of Michelangelo Antonioni's *L'Avventura* (1959), John Milbank writes that "death itself functions only as disappearance. For we can only register the dead one as 'missing,' not in a state of death since death is not a state."[657] Death is an event with a motionless body and a ritual of mourning. The one that has died is vanished and the memory is what is worshipped.

224.

Sharon Tate is an enactment of beauty as vanishing. Tate was a beauty pageant contestant originally from Texas who married director Roman Polanski. Tate, 26 and 8 months pregnant with Polanski's child, was murdered by the Manson Family who was searching for music producer Terry Melcher. The martyr like tragedy made one of Tate's final films *Valley of the Dolls* (1967), a site of re-consideration. As viewers of the film we are voyeurs of beauty in its possibility, of the promise of genetic vitality, of the expectation for the career of Tate, but we know of her demise. The image of her thus contains the two antithetical

---

[655] Baudrillard, Jean. *Screened Out*. Trans. Chris Turner. New York: Verso Books, 2002, p. 168.

[656] "The secret is to know how to play with death in the absence of a gaze a gesture, in the absence of knowledge or meaning." Baudrillard, Jean. *Seduction*. Trans. Brain Singer. New York: St. Martin's Press, 1990, p. 83.

[657] Milbank, John. *Being Reconciled: Ontology and Pardon*. New York: Routledge, 2003, p. 145.

components at work in beauty: its pure existence for itself beyond justifications, and simultaneously its impossibility of coming to being by itself without the expectation of its loss–its ultimate vanishing. When we witness Tate on film we witness beauty we know only lasted a moment, we witness fame, an overdetermined view informed by its inevitable disappearance.

225.

"High Estate," said Pangloss, "is always dangerous, as every philosopher knows. For Eglon, King of Moab, was assassinated by Ehud, and Absalom was hanged by his hair and stabbed with three spears; King Nahab, the son of Jeroboam, was killed by Baasha; King Elah by Zimri...You know the miserable fate of Croesus, Astyages, Darius..."
- Voltaire, Candide[658]

The most powerful are the most guarded, the most inaccessible, with the most private private-life but often a public death.[659] In an effort to evade a public decline, many individuals have created their own calculated removal from society. In À Rebours, Des Esseintes' aristocratic ancestors escaped the French Revolution. His method of finally destroying his family fortune was twofold: to not reproduce and to liquidate the estate. After he decides to erase the family line he disappears to a home in the forest. It was "a remote spot, far from all neighbors," and "secure against harassment."[660] "He was really guarding

---

[658] Voltaire. Candide. Trans. John Butt. New York: Penguin, 1947, p. 143.

[659] Debord proclaimed that "The stronger the class, the more forcefully it proclaims that it does not exist, and its strength serves first and foremost to assert its nonexistence." Debord, Guy. The Society of the Spectacle. Donald Nicholson-Smith. New York: Zone Books, 1994, p. 74.

[660] Huysmans, J.K. À Rebours. Trans. Havelock Ellis. New York: Dover, 1969, p. 8.

himself," writes Huysmans and the intent was for a lifetime. The intentional vanishing from public life is also noted in the Russian Royals in 1918, Howard Hughes at the Desert Inn, Factory actor Paul America, or Bas Jan Ader's performance at sea. Fame survives disappearance.

226.

Gaius Petronius was the advisor to the Roman Nero in the matters of luxury, extravagance and leisure. In about 61 A.D, he authored *Satyricon* set in a Mediterranean town.[661] A ruler fakes his death and hosts at a banquet for himself while the guests display mourning and wailing. The wife, a new widow, finds another man and when her husband questions her adultery she is surprised. "You are dead," she explains. We cannot enact our vanishing and be pleased by the result because the world continues without us. The dream is that we are each a Persephone, that when we succumb to the underworld, all of the earth will turn bleak in despair.

227.

> I am the one that dusk defends.
> - Hannah Arendt[662]

Heidegger described that "death's own most character as a possibility gets veiled–a possibility which is certain and at the same time indefinite–that is to say, possible at any moment."[663]

---

[661] In 1969 Federico Fellini's film by the same name presented parts of the story.

[662] From a poem in her journal. Arendt, Hannah and Martin Heidegger. *Letters: 1925-1975.* Ed. Ursula Ludz. Trans. Andrew Shields. New York: Harcourt, Inc., 2004: p. 301.

[663] As Heidegger described, "One says, 'Death certainly comes, but not right away.' But with this 'but...,' the 'they' denies that death is certain. 'Not right away' is not a purely negative assertion, but a way in which 'they' interprets

And it is in thinking that death is possible in any moment that we prefer to create immediate endings and conclusions in defense of the real potential of death. We fill our lives with countless vanishing points, the disappearance of resources, the end of a book. The calendar we have inherited from the Romans gives us a constant conclusion and renewal of time. How can we ever define "being-towards-the-end"?[664] Since Heidegger we have positioned thought at an end. If we consider the concept of the "vanishing point" we find that we can name the site of being toward end and know that it is also the return.[665] Baudrillard described "'Committed' theory is always a desperate attempt to reconstruct what's on the point of vanishing."[666] We are not committed to the vanishing point, it is already committed to us, not to theory but to being.

228.

> Nature shows us upon an immense scale how the inferior species is sacrificed to the realization of a higher plan. It is the same in humanity. Perhaps, even, we ought to look beyond, this too narrow horizon, and

---

itself....Everydayness forces its way into the urgency of concern, and divests itself of the fetters of a weary 'inactive thinking about death.' Death is deferred to 'sometime later," and this is done by invoking the so-called 'general opinion." Heidegger, Martin. *Being and Time*. Trans. John Macquarrie & Edward Robinson. New York: Harper & Row Publishers, 1962, p. 302.

[664] "As long as this authentic Being-towards-death has not been set forth and ontologically defined," writes Heidegger, "there is something essentially lacking in our existential Interpretation of Being-towards-the-end." Heidegger, Martin. *Sein und Zeit / Being and Time*. Trans. John Macquarrie & Edward Robinson. New York: Harper & Row Publishers, 1962, p. 304.

[665] "The lifespan of man running toward death would inevitably carry everything human to ruin and destruction if it were not for the faculty which is inherent in action like an ever present reminder that men, though they must die, are not born in order to die but in order to begin." Arendt, Hannah. *The Human Condition*. Chicago: The University of Chicago Press, 1958, p 246.

[666] Baudrillard, Jean. *Paroxysm*. Trans. Chris Turner. New York: Verso Books, 1998, p. 20.

only look for justice, the perfect peace, the definite
solution, the complete harmony in a vester whole to
which humanity itself would be subordinated.
- Ernest Renan, *The Future of Science*[667]

The ontological condition is not the basis of our ideological
landscape. That horizon which is used to guide contemporary
thought is no longer contingent on history. In decadence we are
only familiar with the foreground, before us. Gadamer writes:

Everything contained in historical consciousness is in
fact embraced by a single historical horizon. Our own
past and that other past toward which our historical
consciousness is directed help to shape this moving
horizon out of which human life always lives and which
determined heritage and tradition...Are there such
things as closed horizons?...Or is this a romantic
refraction, a kind of Robinson Crusoe dream of
historical enlightenment, the fiction of an unattainable
island, as artificial as Crusoe himself? Just as the
individual is never simply an individual because he is
always in understanding with others, so too the closed
horizon that is supposed to enclose a culture is an
abstraction. The historical movement of human life
consists in the fact that it is never absolutely bound to
any one standpoint, and hence can never have a truly
closed horizon. The horizon is, rather, something into
which we move and that moves with us. Horizons
change for a person who is moving. Thus the horizon of
the past, out of which all human life lives and which
exists in the form of tradition, is always in motion. The
surrounding horizon is not set in motion by historical
consciousness. But in it this motion becomes aware of
itself.... We must always already have a horizon in
order to be able to transpose ourselves into a
situation...But into this other situation we must bring,

---

[667] Renan, Ernest. *The Future of Science*. Boston: Roberts Brothers, 1891, p. 364.

precisely, ourselves...rather, it always involves rising to a higher universality that overcomes not only our own particularity but also that of the other. The concept of "horizon" suggests itself because it expresses the superior breadth of vision that the person who is trying to understand must have. To acquire a horizon means that one learns to look beyond what is close at hand-not in order to look away from it but to see it better, within a larger whole and truer proportion...We are always affected, in hope and fear, by what is nearest to us, and hence we approach the testimony of the past under its influence.[668]

In Gadamer's view, "the horizon of the present is continually in the process of being formed because we are continually having to test all our prejudices...the horizon of the present cannot be formed without the past."[669] Essentially we are in a constant relationship between the past and the future but that view, according to Gadamer is "not absolutely bound to one standpoint." We have ongoing understanding. "Understanding is always the fusion of these horizons supposedly existing by themselves....understanding proves to be an event."[670]

What are we understanding however? How can understand the vanishing point when "the body serves as both a point of departure and as destination."[671] If we consider the model of spectacle, it was the false point of understanding, but represents our need for a shared point. Relativism does not share a point, but we employ it because we no longer believe in the universal

---

[668] Gadamer, Hans-Georg. *Truth and Method.* Translation revised by Joel Weinsheimer and Donald G. Marshall New York: Continuum, 1999, pp. 304-305.
[669] Ibid. p. 306.
[670] Ibid. p. 306 & p. 309.
[671] Lefebvre, Henri. *The Production of Space.* Trans. Donald Nicholson Smith. Cambridge: Blackwell Publishers, 1991, p. 194.

point. Lacan explained that "The Kantian idea that a maxim be put to the test of the universality of its application is only the grimace by which the real manages to save its skin, by being approached only from one side."[672] Even gauging universality is to judge from a particular point of view, rather than orientating ourselves to a vanishing point that escapes our universe. Halbertal and Margalit write:

> A "point of view" is a metaphorical expression whose meaning in the present context includes differences in ontological commitment and differences in emphasis and attention that are reflected in differences in similarity judgments...but there is a more efficient method of preserving the continuity of international identity, and this is the continuous use of a proper name.[673]

Whenever our different points of view share the same horizon, we are effectively communicating but are unable to name it without division. That horizon has been, until this point, historical, ideological and anthropocentric. Whenever we have approached the metaphysical, eternal horizon, we have been occupied by ideological or scientific expectation. We have succeeded in the deconstruction of overdetermining power, but in doing so made the "absolute" point forbidden. The danger is now that we have lost consciousness of an absolute point.

Whether it is the spectacle or the vanishing point, in communication we have understanding only through locating a

[672] Lacan, Jacques. *Television*. Trans. By Denis Hollier, Rosalind Krauss and Annette Michelson. Ed. Joan Copjec. New York: W. W. Norton & Company, 1990, p. 42.
[673] Halbertal, Moshe and Avishai Margalit. *Idolatry*. Trans. Naomi Goldblum. Cambridge, Massachusetts: Harvard University Press. 1992, pp. 147-149.

common point.[674] The real challenge then is in attributing value to the vanishing point, which must always escape value, and essentially be of *less value* than the individuals or collectives involved, otherwise it will by a point of disruption.[675] Halbertal and Margalit write "It is not easy to draw the exact line between attributing value and conferring absolute value."[676] This does not mean there is not an absolute point, but that when we have a common point it must be understood in relation to absolute value. We fear an absolute point because we know the absolute view must not be our own. We fear an absolute truth because we have for centuries believed them to be true, and they have failed us (or have we failed them?).[677]

229.

> As to "what may I hope for?"...do you conceive of hope as without an object?... so that Kant's question may have meaning, I'm going to transform it into: from where do you hope?
> - Jacques Lacan, *Television*[678]

---

[674] "The relation of thought to the current moment in art is one of a localized prescription and not a description. Everything depends upon the point at which one is subjectively situated, and upon the axioms which are used to support judgments. The point at which we choose to situate ourselves is called *L'Art du Cinema*." Badiou, Alain. *Being & Event* Trans. Oliver Feltham Continuum: 2005, p. 109.

[675] "Every radical transformational action *originates in a point*, which inside a situation, is an evental site." Ibid. p. 176.

[676] Halbertal, Moshe and Avishai Margalit. *Idolatry*. Trans. Naomi Goldblum. Cambridge, Massachusetts: Harvard University Press. 1992, p. 246.

[677] "We live in a world of unreality and dreams. To give up our imaginary position as the center, to renounce it, not only intellectually but in the imaginative part of our soul, that means to awaken to what is real and eternal, to see the true light and hear the true silence." Weil, Simone. *Waiting for God*. Trans. Emma Craufurd. New York: G.P. Putnam's Sons, 1951, p. 159.

[678] Lacan, Jacques. *Television*. Trans. By Denis Hollier, Rosalind Krauss and Annette Michelson. Ed. Joan Copjec. New York: W. W. Norton & Company, 1990, p. 43.

So we fix our eyes not on what is seen, but on what is unseen. For what is seen is temporary, but what is unseen is eternal.

- 2 Corinthians 4:18[679]

Locating desire on the absolute is to dislocate desire from all that appears, from all that is manifest before us. This reveals our everyday desire as a dialogue with this reality. We are already centered upon ourselves, or a larger understanding of ourselves as a collective; it is still ourselves, humanity. "To empty ourselves of our false divinity, to deny ourselves, to give up being the center of the world in imagination, to discern that all points in the world are equally centers and that the true center is outside the world, this is to consent to the rule of mechanical necessity in matter and of free choice at the center of each soul. Such consent is love."[680] We have then reached an absolute point that is not our own, a coup de grâce that is then an absolute love. Badiou explains:

> If we can *force* all the bit of knowledge concerned then we end up with the romantic problem of absolute love, the scientific problem of science as integral truth, and the political problem of totalitarianism. This problem can be expressed simply: can we, from the basis of a finite Subject of a truth, *name* and *force into knowledge* all the elements that this truth concerns? How far does the anticipating potency of generic infinity go? My answer is that there is *always*, in any situation, a real point that *resists* this potency. I call this point the *unnameable* of the situation. It is what, within the situation, never has a name in the eyes of truth. The unnameable is what is excluded from having a proper

---

[679] *The Holy Bible.* New International Version. Grand Rapids, Michigan: Zondervan Publishing House, 1996, pp. 969 & 1019.

[680] Weil, Simone. *Waiting for God.* Trans. Emma Craufurd. New York: G.P. Putnam's Sons, 1951, p. 160.

name...the proper of the proper, so singular in its singularity that it does not even tolerate having a proper name. The unnameable is the point where the situation in its most intimate being is submitted to thought; in the pure presence that no knowledge can circumscribe. The unnameable is something like the inexpressible *real* of everything a truth authorizes to be said.[681]

But Badiou continues, "The effect of the event, the subject and the truth, must recognize the unnameable as a *limitation* of its path."[682] We find we always reach a limit to the desire we have or whatever we seek, the end point. Even "once you've gone too far, there's still the limit," writes Lacan.[683] That unnamable limit does not have to be a dark point at which all collapses, it may be an illuminated limit or escape. For each vanishing point is also a point of emergence.

If we allow that we are in dialogue with the vanishing point we are then capable of "be-eternal-ing."[684] One of the essential elements of decadence, to the finite human condition, is to fail to refer to the always already potentiality of being and instead to impatiently wait for the next sensational moment to arrive and if it doesn't then to make it happen, thus the decadent gesture. Being in relation to the vanishing point is not waiting on the vanishing point but continually moving toward the point, revealed in the horizon but immediately unreachable. That is

---

[681] Badiou, Alain. *Infinite Thought.* Trans. Justin Clemens. New York: Continuum, 2003, pp. 65-66.

[682] Ibid. p. 67.

[683] Lacan, Jacques. *Television.* Trans. By Denis Hollier, Rosalind Krauss and Annette Michelson. Ed. Joan Copjec. New York: W. W. Norton & Company, 1990, p. 41.

[684] Lacan, Jacques. *The Seminar of Jacques Lacan: On Feminine Sexuality, The Limits of Love and Knowledge* (Book XX, Encore 1972-1973), Ed. Jacques-Alain Miller, Trans. Bruce Fink, New York: W. W. Norton & Company, 1998, p. 40.

what is offered in the vanishing point–transparency of absolute meaning.

Forgetting

Si me preguntais en donde he estado
debo decir `Sucede.'
Debo de hablar del suelo que oscurecen las piedras,
del rio que durando se destruye:
no se sino las cosas que los pajaros pierden,
el mar dejado atras, o mi hermana llorando.
Por que tantas regiones, por que un dia
se junta con un dia? Por que una negra noche
se acumula en la boca? Por que muertos?

Si me preguntais de donde vengo, tengo que conversar
con cosas rotas,
con utensilios demasiado amargos,
con grandes bestias a menudo podridas
y con mi acongojado corazon.

No son recuerdos los que se han cruzado
ni es la paloma amarillenta que duerme en el olvido,
sino caras con lagrimas,
dedos en la garganta,
y lo que se desploma de las hojas:
la oscuridad de un dia transcurrido,
de un dia alimentado con nuestra triste sangre.

He aqui violetas, golondrinas,
todo cuanto nos gusta y aparece
en las dulces tarjetas de larga cola
por donde se pasean el tiempo y la dulzura.

Pero no penetremos mas alla de esos dientes,
no mordamos las cascaras que el silencio acumula,
porque no se que contestar:

hay tantos muertos,
y tantos malecones que el sol rojo partia
y tantas cabezas que golpean los buques,

y tantas manos que han encerrado besos,
y tantas cosas que quiero olvidar.
- Pablo Neruda, "No Hay Olvido" [685]

230.

Do we forget and so it vanishes or does it vanish and thus we forget?

We take pleasure in forgetting, because it points to our fallibility. With deconstruction, contemporary culture is conscious of the fact that it will be forgotten. We take part in an already overdetermined state of forgetting. We can be as decadent as we want because we will be forgotten anyway.

---

[685] If you ask me where I have been/ and I'll tell you: "Things keep on happening."/ I have to talk about the earth turned dark with stones;/ of the river which ruins itself by staying alive;/ I know only the things that the birds have lost,/ or the ocean behind me, or my sister crying./ Why the distinctions of place? Why should day/ follow day? Why must the blackness/ of nighttime collect in our mouths? Why the dead?/ If you question me: where have you come from, I must talk/ with broken things,/ artifacts tart to the taste,/ with animals quite often rotten,/ and my own inconsolable heart./ What have met and crossed are not memories,/ nor the yellowing pigeon who sleeps in forgetfulness:/ only the face with its tears,/ the hands at our throats,/ whatever the leafage dissevers:/ the dark of an obsolete day,/ a day that has tasted the grief in our blood./ Here are violets, swallows--/ all things that delight us, that we love/ that show in the lengthening train/ through which pleasure and transciency pass./ Here let us halt, in the teeth of a barrier:/ useless to gnaw on the husks that the silence assembles./ For I come without answers: / see: the dying are legion,/ legion, the breakwaters breached by the red of the sun,/ the headpieces knocking the ship's side,/ the hands closing over their kisses,/ and so many things I want to forget. Translation modified with another variation. Bly, Roberts, ed. *Neruda and Vallejo: Selected Poems.* Trans. Robert Bly, et al. Boston: Beacon Press, 1971: pp. 56-57.

231.

What of the past that cannot be forgotten because it has left a scar, a mark that continually recalls of it?

In decadence there is an effort to scar, to decorate and stylize, to make a lasting impression but decadence itself forgets needs, forgets truth and thus forgets survival. "Be careful not to forget." Remembering requires effort, training and reinforcement. Forgetting is an effortless surrender that works backward over our anthropocentric efforts. It erases all the effort, all the work of centuries is surrendered in a moment, without a trace.

232.

The act of writing is rooted in a fear of forgetting. In academic thought, the system of referencing "facts" is rooted in integrity of research but also in preservation. We find however that what is forgotten stays forgotten if it was not interesting or valuable. Some appears again, perhaps not in the original form but in another incarnation (this is principal of fashion). For thought after the dense decadence of ideology, the over production of capitalism and the grand matrix of the internet, we no longer have to recall as much (and much less in Latin). Thought instead operates like a discussion of a car accident, of an aftermath. Our fear of forgetting is now the fear that we will repeat the same mistakes (we will repeat the same mistakes). What has survived deconstruction? Will we remember how to destroy ideology?

233.

Decadence involves a feeling of absence, thus desire for something. Decadence, and all that has been attributed to it, is ultimately a type of hollow shell, emptiness for lost truth. But where is truth? We have forgotten what it looks like and sounds like. We know truth as fact, verification, certainty, but what of truth as unconditional, inevitable, effortless and real?[686] We have forgotten not what is true for a civilization, but true for being. We have forgotten *that it is* being.

234.

"Augustine referred to memory as a permanent doubting," as if what we recall is only what we have not decided upon.[687] The ambivalence of decadence involves the lack of final decision. It is permanent suspense, like Gnosticism that denies that inaction is action. What good is a skeptic who uses a door?[688] Or an existentialist in despair?

235.

We are surrounded by so much obsolescence that we have forgotten original needs. Do we ever forget desire? Desire is often understood as that particular thing that is desired. But the restless craving is like a haunting. We have forgotten what desire is for; it is like an appendix of the spirit. Even in our body, there is something that no longer works (why do we assume it worked?). Is the appendix a memory of a desire that we have forgotten?

---

[686] "The unconditional, representing that highest perfection, cannot possibly be the ground of all that is conditional." Nietzsche, Friedrich. *The Will to Power.* Trans. Walter Kaufmann. New York: Random House, 1968, p. 15.

[687] Kristeva, Julia. *Revolt, She Said.* Trans. Brian O'Keefe. New York: Semiotext(e), 2002, p. 101.

[688] "David Hume once remarked that after a gathering of skeptics...all the members of the gathering nonetheless left by the door rather than the window." Dick, Philip K. *I Hope I Shall Arrive Soon.* New York: Doubleday & Company, 1985, p. 6.

236.

To be mistaken is not the same as to forget. To be mistaken is to believe to know the right answer, condition, point or passage. But often to be mistaken is to re-visit something and not recognize it. Then being mistaken is really to forget, but to forget that we forgot. Misplaced by contrast is to have actively placed something somewhere and then to have forgotten it. We describe it as lost, as if it were not of our own doing. Is forgetting a reminder that we never possess or that we only possess the present?[689] Is remembering only a "doctrine of reminiscence," that we already know everything?[690]

237.

> Let us not pretend to know what it is, this forgetting. And if such is the case, is it for us to question the meaning of forgetting? Or to bring the question of forgetting back to the question of being?
>
> Would the forgetting of a being (an umbrella, for example) be incommensurable with the forgetting of Being?
> - Derrida, *Spurs* [691]

---

[689] "And that which even I must forget *now*, is that necessarily forgotten forever? Happy is it for me that I do forget. The recollection of my former condition would permit me to make only a bad use of the present. How much then should I miss? Is not a whole eternity mine?" Lessing, Gotthold. "The Education of the Human Race," in *Literary and Philosophical Essays*. Ed. Charles Eliot. New York: Collier and Son, 1910, p. 217.

[690] Leibniz discusses Plato's doctrine in relation to recognizing truth. Leibniz, G. W. *Discourse on Metaphysics / Correspondence with Arnaud / Monadology*. Trans. George Montgomery. La Salle, Illinois: Open Court Publishing, 1988, p. 45.

[691] Derrida, Jacques. *Spurs*. Chicago, The University of Chicago Press, 1978, p. 141.

Are we to believe the psychoanalytic model that everything distressing is forgotten? That everything forgotten was distressing? We do not recall the trauma,[692] only the events before and after it, and thus we "elaborate our mourning."[693] And is memory the cure? We often forget things that are useful to survival, as in an umbrella. Can we ever forget Being? Can a parent forget a child? Can we forget nature?[694] Or do we instead forget their tenderness, their majesty, their value? All things surrender to forgetting, including the self. Forgetting is destiny, a vanishing point of all thought.[695]

Uncondition

> Never yet has truth hung on the arm of the unconditional.
> - Friedrich Nietzsche, *Thus Spoke Zarathustra*[696]

238.

The conclusion of decadence is a moment of truth. Most decadents, in time, grow restless from living by self-generated, conditional terms. Or, decadent living results in abundant consequences and depletion of resources. The result, in the span

---

[692] Mitscherlich, Alexander and Margerete. *Inability to Mourn: Principals of Collective Behavior*. New York: Grove Press, 1984.

[693] Lyotard, Jean-François. *The Postmodern Explained to Children: Correspondence 1982-1985*. Trans. Thomas Pefanis. London: Turnaround, 1992, p. 98.

[694] After writing indoors Heidegger states, "I have already forgotten what the 'world' looks like." Arendt, Hannah and Martin Heidegger. *Letters: 1925-1975*. Ed. Ursula Ludz. Trans. Andrew Shields. New York: Harcourt, Inc., 2004, p. 34.

[695] We are "still far from determining the essence of forgetting;" "Forgetting attacks Being" suggests Derrida, and "reigns as the Destiny of its essence." Derrida, Jacques. *Spurs*. Chicago: The University of Chicago Press, 1978, p. 143.

[696] Nietzsche, Friedrich. *Thus Spoke Zarathustra: A Book for All and None*. Trans. Walter Kaufman. New York: The Modern Library. 1992, p. 52.

of moments or generations, is an eventual re-consideration of conditional values.

239.

We have cured many things, but everyday there is another virus. We have reached many destinations, but every day the universe is found to be larger. Other than a change of guard, what has the progress of civilizations done for the human condition, for desire, love, truth or death? As Hegel described in *The Philosophy of History* "through all this restless change no advance has been made."[697]

I am true, like each human being, in my fallibility.[698] In all of my shortcomings, and frailty, I serve as the representation of a myth that humanity is unable to fully understand a concept of ongoing absolute truth. But from where is this story? Is the ongoing truth our only eternal hope? French writer Ernest Renan consistently argued that truth will have no relation to our interference, that we can make no advance of our own; the advance is truth itself.[699]

---

[697] Hegel, Georg Wilhelm Friedrich Hegel. *The Philosophy of History*, in *Half Hours with the Best Thinkers*, Ed. Frank J. Finamore. New York: Gramercy Books, 1999, p. 146.

[698] Derrida discusses Nietzsche: "There is no such thing as the truth of woman, but it is because of that abyssal divergence of the truth, because that untruth is 'truth.' Woman is but one name for that untruth of truth... for him, truth is like a woman." Derrida, Jacques. *Spurs*. Chicago, The University of Chicago Press, 1978, p. 51.

[699] "*The Future of Science* is the title of a book that other priestly named, Ernest Renan, who was also an all-out servant of the truth. He only required one thing of truth–but it was absolutely capital, failing which, he panicked–that it have no consequence whatsoever." *The Seminar of Jacques Lacan: On Feminine Sexuality, The Limits of Love and Knowledge* (Book XX, Encore 1972-1973), Ed. Jacques-Alain Miller, Trans. Bruce Fink, New York: W. W. Norton & Company, 1998, p. 116.

240.

> To accept the universe of language as the absolute
> horizon of philosophical thought in fact amounts to
> accepting the fragmentation and illusion of
> communication.
>
> - Alain Badiou, *Infinite Thought*[700]

After the enlightenment, we exerted our freedom to believe,
including the freedom to reject absolute truth. We allowed
ideology to assume the throne. Badiou writes:

> Vulgar Marxism and vulgar Freudianism have never
> been able to find a way out...the first claimed that truth
> was historically deployed on the basis of the
> revolutionary events by the working
> class....Freudianism...claimed to form a section of
> psychological knowledge, assigning truth to everything
> which was connected to a stable class, the 'adult genital
> complex.'[701]

Deconstruction exposed the illusions of anthropocentric meaning
and languages of knowledge like Marxism and Freudianism. We
also destroyed a metaphysical belief in truth. But we did not
destroy our production of thought.[702] Our decadence has simply

---

[700] Badiou, Alain. *Infinite Thought*. Trans. Justin Clemens. New York:
Continuum, 2003, p. 47.
[701] Badiou, Alain. *Being & Event*. Trans. Oliver Feltham. London: Continuum
International Publishing Group, 2005, p. 334.
[702] "The work of deconstruction only breaks the false logos of
rationalism...Derrida takes apart only the logocentricism of rationalism and
idealism and yet claims to have deconstructed the thought of any presence before
our outside semiological difference... Derrida has deconstructed the metaphysical
belief in a truth proceeding from and present in our own consciousness."
Ingraffia, Brian. *Postmodern Theory and Biblical Theology*. Cambridge:
Cambridge University Press, 1995, p. 224.

fragmented truth. Now there are many types of truths and explanations for all of them.[703]

Now, with everything considered, we have only subjective and conditional terms for understanding. Without absolute truth to unite us, we are individually inclined to make something else the authority. We are now engaged by the meaning we find in identity, but identity is mutable. We know that meaning is validated by action, but action is variable.

In thought, it is language that gives meaning and unites us. Badiou explains that "Language is the crucial site of thought because it is where the question of meaning is at stake...Consequently the question of meaning replaces the classical question of truth."[704]

We have invested in language but are only producing thought as artifice and perversion in which everything is "interesting," remarkable" and "different." We have pursued thought as meaning in itself, but have found that it "withdraws from immediate promises of transparency or meaning," "to the extent that one may no longer be simply guided—by Truth, by light or logos—decisions have to be made."[705] But what decisions? Nothing is urgent. We make decisions to prefer style over absolutes, *a* truth over *the* truth. We are only making decisions about the surface of non-sense, we are only confronting the truth

---

[703] "Representation governs the notion of truth, and thereby every meaning is governed by ontology." Levinas, Emmanuel. *Basic Philosophical Writings*. Ed. Adriann Peperzak et al, Indianapolis: Indiana University Press, 1996, p. 99.
[704] Ibid. 47.
[705] First quotes are from various descriptions of the work of Avital Ronell, followed by her own quote. Ronell, Avital. *Crack Wars: Literature, Addiction, Mania*. Lincoln: Univ. of Nebraska Press, 1992, p. 58.

of our desires.[706] The only "accepted" shared truth for contemporary thought is death and the proposition of the eternal return. The absolute truth abides in our physical reality and is not contingent on our efforts or justification; death does not need our defense. It is a truth resilient enough to withstand our efforts to control it, a truth that survives us all.

241.

> Through such a declaration *being*-true ends up in the position of stand-in for the *act* of Truth.
> - Alain Badiou, *Infinite Thought*.[707]

Even in academia, "philosophy wrongfully declares itself productive of truths," writes Badiou. The truth we have in the present is never good enough, is never right enough. It does not satisfy. Scholarship still hunts for the truth like a seeking archeologist, approaching everything with wonder ("perhaps this could be the truth?"). We expect truth to be found at the very bottom of the coldest, darkest place, where all things subtle retire and are re-discovered. We value "scientific" observations of hidden truths as if they are supernatural revelations.[708]

---

[706] "What discourse must fight against is not so much the unconscious secret as the superficial abyss of its own appearance; and if discourse must triumph over something, it is not over fantasies and hallucinations heavy with meaning and misinterpretation, but the shiny surface of non-sense and all the games that the latter renders possible." Baudrillard, Jean. *Seduction*. Trans. Brain Singer. New York: St. Martin's Press, 1990, p. 54.

[707] Badiou, Alain. *Infinite Thought*. Trans. Justin Clemens. New York: Continuum, 2003, p. 167.

[708] "The world of the Bible is a literally real but veiled landscape, never changing, hidden from our sight, but available to us by revelation," Dick, Philip K. *I Hope I Shall Arrive Soon*. New York: Doubleday & Company, 1985, p. 22.

Uncovering prior errors and misconceptions however, is not the same as knowing the truth.[709]

242.

We can say something *was* true, meaning that evidence of it is not in the present reality. We say something *will be* true, that the evidence will be procured later. Something is true only if it corresponds to reality, and shows "fidelity to an event."[710] "Reality is that which, when you stop believing in it, doesn't go away," explained Philip K. Dick.[711] Yet have we lost the essential means of believing un-validated truth? We have fought for the freedom of speech in order to speak truth by declaration.[712] But witness testimony is considered unreliable.[713] And having many witnesses who concur is not evidence of an infallible truth.[714]

---

[709] We have argued like Xenophanes "that even if a man should chance to speak the most complete truth, yet he himself does not know it; all things are wrapped in appearances." Xenophanes. *Fragmente der Vorsokratiker, Vol. 1.* Ed. Hermann Diels and Walther Kranz. Wiedmann: Berlin, 1951, Fragment 34.

[710] Badiou, Alain. *Infinite Thought.* Trans. Justin Clemens. New York: Continuum, 2003, p. 58.

[711] Dick, Philip K.. *I Hope I Shall Arrive Soon.* New York: Doubleday & Company, 1985, p. 4.

[712] "The necessary turning-point of history is therefore the open confession, that the consciousness of God is nothing else than the consciousness of the species." Feuerbach, Ludwig. *The Essence of Christianity.* Trans. George Eliot. New York: Harper & Brothers Publishers, 1957, p. 270.

[713] "Testimony, as Freud knew, revert to the privilege of testicles, engendering truth within the seminal flow of testimonial utterance...Standing as witness, in step with Freudian logic, and bearing testimony, swearing in the truth of one's testimony upon one's testicles, implies that the subject before the law some under the threat of castration. The truth is related to this threat." Ronell, Avital. *Finitude's Score.* Lincoln: University of Nebraska Press, 1994, p. 325.

[714] Ludwig Feuerbach wrote, "The human is the true and real; for the human alone is the rational; man is the measure of reason...Do not wish to be a philosopher in contrast to being a Man; but nothing more than a thinking Man...Think as a real living being, as one exposed to the vivifying and refreshing surge of the sea of worldly experience; think in existence, in the world as part of it, not in the vacuum of abstraction...Truth is only the sum of human life and being...only in community." Feuerbach, Ludwig. *The Essence of*

Prophecy is an almost outdated form of truth that is conferred in what follows.[715] What of other ancient means of truth?[716] Revelation, truth without reason, is now considered questionable, though Lessing found it essential.[717] We have also made the claim that "truth is what is not said," or "truth is what not revealed."[718] Badiou describes that truth is in many ways incommunicable, "the schema of connection of the four subtractive figures (undecidable, indiscernible, generic, and unnameable) specifies a philosophical doctrine of the truth."[719] We have approach the mysterious vanishing point again. Badiou describes:

> We find ourselves here at the threshold of a decisive advance, in which the concept of the 'generic' – which I hold to be crucial... will be defined and articulated in

Christianity. Trans. George Eliot. New York: Harper & Brothers Publishers, 1957, p. xiii.

[715] "One can call prophecy this reversal whereby the perception of the order coincides with the meaning of this order, made up by the one who obeys it...all of man's spirituality would thereby be prophetic." Levinas, Emmanuel. *Basic Philosophical Writings.* Ed. Adriann Peperzak et al, Indianapolis: Indiana University Press, 1996, p. 105.

[716] "Both the ancient myths and the modern poetry, so false as history, may be very near truth as prophecy." Lewis, C.S. "The Weight of Glory," Preached originally as a sermon in the Church of St Mary the Virgin, Oxford, on June 8, 1942. *The Essential C.S. Lewis.* Ed. Lyle W. Dorsett. New York: Simon & Schuster, 1988, p. 368.

[717] Lessing explained that "education is revelation coming to the individual man; and revelation is education which has come, and yet is coming, to the human race." Revelation then is essential to the communication of knowledge "gives nothing which the human left to reason might not attain...and still gives to it, the most important of these things earlier." Lessing, Gotthold. "The Education of the Human Race," in *Literary and Philosophical Essays.* Ed. Charles Eliot. New York: Collier and Son, 1910, p. 195.

[718] "We do not believe the truth remains true once the veil has been lifted," wrote Nietzsche which inspired the modernist and post-modernist view that there was an uncovering of the truth. Baudrillard provides no source for this quote attributed to Nietzsche. Baudrillard, Jean. *Seduction.* Trans. Brain Singer. New York: St. Martin's Press, 1990, p. 59.

[719] Badiou, Alain. *Infinite Thought.* Trans. Justin Clemens. New York: Continuum, 2003, p. 167.

such a manner that it will found the very being of any truth. 'Generic' and 'indiscernible' are concepts which are almost equivalent... Because 'indiscernible' conserves a negative connotation, which indicates uniquely, via non-discernibility, that what is at stake is subtracted from knowledge or from exact nomination. The term 'generic' positively designates that what does not allow itself to be discerned is in reality the general truth of a situation, the truth of its being, as considered as the foundation of all knowledge to come. 'Indiscernible' implies a negation, which nevertheless retains this essential point: a truth is always that which makes a hole in a knowledge. What this means is that everything is at stake in the thought of the truth/knowledge couple.[720]

Badiou implies that truth makes a hole in knowledge. What we observe in the truth/knowledge couple, whether it be philosophy, science or ideology, is that knowledge cannot sustain the already subtractive aspect of truth. This is the reason that we must free ourselves of subjectivity: "It is absolutely necessary to abandon any definition of the subject which supposes that it knows the truth, or that it is adjusted to the truth. Being the local moment of the truth, the subject falls short of supporting the latter's global sum. Every truth is transcendent to the subject, precisely because the latter's entire being resides in supporting the realization of truth."[721] But how can we release subjectivity when we each have a different center of the universe, a different truth?[722] We currently occupy a world of relativity in which each individual

[720] Badiou, Alain. *Being & Event.* Trans. Oliver Feltham. London: Continuum International Publishing Group, 2005, p. 327.
[721] Ibid. p. 397.
[722] "We live in a world of unreality and dreams. To give up our imaginary position as the center, to renounce it, not only intellectually but in the imaginative part of our soul, that means to awaken to what is real and eternal, to see the true light and hear the true silence." Weil, Simone. *Waiting for God.* Trans. Emma Craufurd. New York: G.P. Putnam's Sons, 1951, p. 159.

point of view is respected as valid.[723] What Badiou proposes is only possible by basis of a force of truth that is consistent from one subject to the next.

243.

> Do I believe myself to speak truth, seeing Thou art the Truth, and every man a liar?... Let truth spring out of the earth.
> - St. Augustine, *Confessions*[724]

Whatever we know and hold to be true, convicts us. Renan expressed that "The wise man does not feel anger against any one, for he knows that human nature only has its passions moved for the incomplete truth."[725] Yet, even if we know only incomplete truth, it does not limit us from desire for complete truth. Badiou continues:

> It is absolutely necessary to abandon any definition of the subject which supposes that it knows the truth, or that it is adjusted to the truth. Being the local moment of the truth, the subject falls short of supporting the latter's global sum. Every truth is transcendent to the subject, precisely because the latter's entire being resides in supporting the realization of truth.[726]

---

[723] "Because the subject is a *local* configuration of the procedure, it is clear that the truth is equally indiscernible 'for him'–the truth is global. 'For him' means the following precisely: a subject, which realizes a truth, is nevertheless incommensurable with the latter, because the subject is finite, and the truth is infinite." Badiou, Alain. *Being & Event*. Trans. Oliver Feltham. London: Continuum International Publishing Group, 2005, p. 396.

[724] Augustine of Hippo, Confessions, 13.18.22 & 13.25.38, University of Pennsylvania, http://ccat.sas.upenn.edu/jod/augustine.html

[725] Renan, Ernest. *The Future of Science*. Boston: Roberts Brothers, 1891, p. 351.

[726] Badiou, Alain. *Being & Event*. Trans. Oliver Feltham. London: Continuum International Publishing Group, 2005, p. 397.

We tolerate partial truth, in abundance.[727] We do not achieve truth through subjectivity and diplomacy of point of view. Whatever solution we may devise for negotiating ontological truth, we occupy it as a present destiny. All of our truths, the stories of our lives are connected, as Badiou explains, "a truth groups together all the terms of the situation which are positively connected to the event."[728] We are unified by a point, a vanishing point to which all meaning converges.

244.

> Thus the ethic of truths, relation or un-relation, between the construction of a truth and its potency, is that by which we take the measure of what our times are capable of, as well as what our times are worth. Such is, in a word, the very task of philosophy.
> - Alain Badiou, *Infinite Thought*[729]

How do we ask a question of truth without a question of time and one of ethics?[730] In our time, we have the International Criminal Court or the United Nations to represent the ethical

---

[727] Walter Benjamin described as early as 1933, "the oppressive new abundance of ideas which, the revival of astrology and yoga, Christian Science and palmistry, vegetarianism and Gnosticism, Scholasticism and Spiritualism, has spread among–or rather, over–people is merely the reverse side of wretchedness." Benjamin, Walter. "Experience and Poverty," *Walter Benjamin: Selected Writings, Vol. 2 1927-1934.* Cambridge: Harvard University Press, 1999, p. 732.

[728] Badiou, Alain. *Being & Event.* Trans. Oliver Feltham. London: Continuum International Publishing Group, 2005, p. 335.

[729] Badiou, Alain. *Infinite Thought.* Trans. Justin Clemens. New York: Continuum, 2003, p. 68.

[730] "The Nietzschean ethic can be accepted only if we are ready to scrap traditional morals as a mere error and then to put ourselves in a position where we can find no ground for any value judgments at all." Lewis, C.S. *The Essential C.S. Lewis.* Ed. Lyle W. Dorsett. New York: Simon & Schuster, 1988, p. 446.

truth of universal peace.[731] This is our absolute "ethics of mortality," that whatever is life preserving is good, thus whatever is destructive to life is bad. This is a life ethics rooted in a defense of survival and lack of faith in being. It is the best we have to offer but also the result of human reason.[732] We employ a metaphysics of fear.[733] We allow for reason and protection to give us an assurance we should have from truth. The idea that diplomats or philosophers are around to decipher between many truths is problematic because it puts the diplomat or philosopher on a throne of judgment above the truth. What is above truth, when truth is beyond all of us? What are we capable of when even Badiou finds in the words of Samuel Beckett "the naked existence of a generic humanity"?[734]

245.

Where does the truth end?
- *The Omen*[735]

Can we ever shed individual desires or forget the proposition of absolute truth. We surrender to our desires for momentary

---

[731] "If God is that which fixes human meaning, as ontotheology claims, then the absence of a God means that human meaning is unfounded and plays on an abyss." Ingraffia, Brian. *Postmodern Theory and Biblical Theology*. Cambridge: Cambridge University Press, 1995, p. 6.

[732] "We should therefore, vanquish god's shadow, the shadow god created by human reason and imagination that we might seek revelation." Ingraffia, Brian. *Postmodern Theory and Biblical Theology*. Cambridge: Cambridge University Press, 1995, p. 241. While we must vanquish the shadow of religion that involves "seeking" revelation. We do not seek it.

[733] "We never replace God; with nothing but another God, like man," Blanchot quoted in Jean-Luc Nancy lecture, European Graduate School, Saas-fee, Switzerland, June 15, 2004.

[734] Badiou, Alain. *Infinite Thought*. Trans. Justin Clemens. New York: Continuum, 2003, p. 68.

[735] Commentary in advertising for the Academy Award winning film *The Omen*, 1976.

solutions, and we allow for an eternal return. But have we sufficiently explained the world away as an absolute claim to nothing?[736] Badiou explains:

> It is quite impossible to anticipate or represent a truth, because it manifests itself solely through the course of the enquiries, and the enquiries are incalculable...a subject uses names to make hypotheses about the truth...That such as the status of names of the type 'faith,' 'salvation,' 'communism,' 'transfinite,' serialism,' or those names used in a declaration of life, can easily be verified. These names are evidently capable of supporting the future anterior of a truth...they *displace* established significations and leave the referent void: this void will have been filled if truth comes to pass as a new situation (the kingdom of God, an emancipated society...)[737]

All of the truth claims—communism or salvation—are united by faith. Faith is not a separate category but there is faith in *the* truth. We may have faith in a mutable system like the economy. When we lose faith, the system fails. But when we regard a truth not by faith but by consistency, as in the laws of science such as gravity, our faith does not sustain it. Rather, it is the truth sustains our faith.

In the realm of thought, we have the capacity to consider all that exists and all that does not exist, a total territory, including

---

[736] "You cannot go on 'explaining away' forever: you will find that you have explained explanation itself away. You cannot go on 'seeing through' things forever. The whole point of seeing through something is to see something through it...If you see through everything, then everything is transparent. But a wholly transparent world is an invisible world." Lewis, C.S. *The Essential C.S. Lewis.* Ed. Lyle W. Dorsett. New York: Simon & Schuster, 1988, p. 458.

[737] Badiou, Alain. *Being & Event.* Trans. Oliver Feltham. London: Continuum International Publishing Group, 2005, p. 399.

truth.[738] Badiou writes, "nothing of the truth, in its authentic sense, remains accessible if we allow that the phenomenon of truth occurs in the proposition."[739] If the proposition is of infinity or of absolute value we have already prepared an answer. Yet how can we generate a proposition of truth when truth is already ingrained in the structure of language. There is no longer any original proposition. Rather we are recipients of the original invitation of truth, of which we did not generate. This then means that truth is not a name or type that is then easily verified, nor a proposition, but rather a pre-condition.

246.

> There is but one victory, and it is eternal. That is the
> one I shall never have. That is where I stumble and
> cling... It is man's demands made against his fate.
> - Albert Camus[740]

In the most simple terms, we call truth unchangeable facts. But in complex thought we call truth unknowable. Why is there a shift from truth as given and fixed to sought and mutable? The great uncondition of truth is that is endures our subjectivity in every generation. The truth never forces us to believe, it simply survives our disbelief.[741]

---

[738] "The world has no supplement." Nancy, Jean-Luc. *Being Singular Plural.* Trans. Robert D. Richardson and Anne E. O'Byrne. Stanford: Stanford Univ. Press, 2000, p. 11.

[739] "My entire argument will be to acknowledge that truth remains unthinkable if we attempt to contain it within the form of a proposition." Badiou, Alain. *Infinite Thought.* Trans. Justin Clemens. New York: Continuum, 2003, p. 59 & 60.

[740] Camus, Albert. *The Myth of Sisyphus.* Trans. Justin O'Brien. New York: Vintage International, 1955, p. 87.

[741] "The mind is not forced to believe in the existence of anything." Weil, Simone. *Gravity and Grace.* Trans. Arthur Wills New York: G.P. Putnam's Sons, 1952, p. 113.

247.

"People do not fight for what is dead; whatever stirs the pulse
the most is that which is fullest of life and truth."[742] We never
think at the beginning of anything that what we are saying,
choosing, writing or doing could all be done for nothing in the
end. Something is always left, for the next generation. What is
nothing? It does not exist. What survives however is not of our
effort but rather the preceding truth.

---

[742] Renan, Ernest. *The Future of Science*. Boston: Roberts Brothers, 1891, p. 323.

Revelation

Les vices les vertus tellement imparfaits
La ressemblance des regards de permission avec les yeux
   Que tu conquis
La confusion des corps des lassitudes des ardeurs
L'imitation des mots des attitudes des idées
Les vices les vertus tellement imparfaits

L'amour c'est l'homme inachevé
- Samuel Beckett, "A perte de vue dans le sens de mon corps"[743]

---

[743] The vices the virtues that are so imperfect / The eyes consenting resembling the eyes thou didst / vanquish / The confusion of the bodies the lassitudes the ardours / The imitation of the words the attitudes the ideas / The vices the virtues that are so imperfect / Love is man unfinished / -Samuel Beckett, "Out of sight in the direction of my body," 1977. Beckett, Samuel. *Collected Poems*. Trans. Paul Eluard. London: John Calder Publishers, 1984, p. 100-101.

Being alive means before the end.[744] Who has been witness to absolute end? The "apocalypse" was originally used to describe a revelation of truth and now the word is associated with the end of time, as if when truth is unveiled we reach the end. The "end times" is a socially shared concept built of cinematic form, an apocalypse of global destruction. But the only end that we can know is circumstantial. Here in this circumstance of this text about decadence the end is as you choose it. It began as a consideration and has ended as a consideration that continues in the considerations of writer and reader. And of decadence what is the concluding thought? What is the final word? We have at last, the freedom we had at first—everything is permitted. We can see through decadence, that not everything is beneficial.[745] What see in decadence is desire as end, of living all for nothing. It is a love of the world without the question of truth.

This text has not attempted to be *about* decadence but rather to take the form of decadence to illustrate the force. We are temporal as are our desires and anything we produce. We are unfinished, with a blood of desire that intoxicates us so that we long to rest. But we rise again and again indulging in decadence each generation.

So like every other generation we have the same assignment: overcome the last. Yet this time through deconstruction, the efforts of prior eras have already been broken down. Ideology was a performance for a future that will not exist. Naming of the

---

[744] "We always begin in the middle," Lyotard, Jean-François. *The Postmodern Explained to Children: Correspondence 1982-1985.* Trans. Thomas Pefanis. London: Turnaround, 1992, p. 116.

[745] "Hold firmly to the end the confidence we had at first." Hebrews 3:14 and "'Everything is permissible'-but not everything is beneficial"1 Corinthians 10:3. *The Holy Bible.* New International Version. Grand Rapids, Michigan: Zondervan Publishing House, 1996, pp. 969 & 1010.

eternal return has only verified continuing life indifferent to philosophies. We need truth because it alone survives our particular efforts and unifies human experience. If we are not open to absolute truth then we are not open to absolute love, or to all meaning or to all being. Thus our generation, and specifically this text, can do nothing that has not been already done–meaning it can acknowledge truth. Badiou writes:

> There is a moment where it [philosophy] falls on the radical underside of all sense, the void of all possible presentation, the hollowing of truth as a hole *without borders*. This moment is that in which the void, absense–such as philosophy ineluctably encounters them at them at the point of truth's proving itself–must be themselves presented and transmitted.[746]

The borderless void of truth is not a time or place but the only sustenance, the uncondition that survives the flux of the human condition. It is not that through our postmodern relativity we have legitimized many truths (which is the common argument) but that we have revealed that truth survives subjectivity.

I always look at the final conclusion of a writer, to see the lasting significance of the text. Is the reader left with a memory, a new hope, breathless for the next love letter?: "Yes, I am coming soon."[747] In Husymans' conclusion of *A Rebours*, Des Esseintes has surrendered his inheritance to his every desire and concludes: Seigneur, prenez pitié du chrétien qui doute, de l'incrédule qui voudrait croire, du forçat de la vie qui

---

[746] Badiou, Alain. *Infinite Thought*. Trans. Justin Clemens. New York: Continuum, 2003, p. 104.
[747] Concluding words of the Bible, Revelation 22:20. *The Holy Bible*. New International Version. Grand Rapids, Michigan: Zondervan Publishing House, 1996, p. 1048.

s'embarque seul, dans la nuit, sous un firmament que n'éclairent plus les consolants fanaux du vieil espoir.[748] Pity the man who has no hope. Pity the reader who needs to be given hope. In this text I found that by privileging hope and possibility, we become entrenched with desire toward decadence. Too much is never enough. May we not hold to hope so that it prevents its best fulfillment in reality.

But what of concluding in truth? Because in our era we allow only "facts" to be truth, I thought of ending with a fact from a reference source–a dictionary. We normally do not consider the last page of a dictionary any more conclusive than the first. So I consulted a printed dictionary given to me by the prior generation and the last page reads: "Miscellaneous Symbols: X– a mark made by someone unable to write; the name is added by someone else."[749] This is the truth, a mark made by someone else, and I add my name. Five centuries earlier Teresa of Avila wrote:

> I mention neither my own name, nor that of any person whatever. I have written it in the best way I could, in order not to be known; ...Persons so learned and grave as they are have the authority enough to approve of whatever right things I may say, should the Lord give me the grace to do so; and if I should say anything of the kind, it will be His, and not mine... The Truth of which I am speaking, and which I was given to see, is Truth Itself, in Itself. It has neither beginning nor end.

---

[748] Lord, take pity on the Christian who doubts, on the skeptic who would fain believe, on the slave of life who puts out to sea alone, in the darkness of night, beneath a firmament illumined no longer by the consoling beacon-fires of the ancient hope. Huysmans, J.K. *A Rebours*. French Edition. France: Fasquelle Éditeurs, 1972, p. 269. *A Rebours*. Trans. Havelock Ellis. New York: Dover, 1969, p. 206.

[749] *Webster's New World Dictionary of the American Language*, New York: The World Publishing Company, 1960, p. 1724.

All other truths depend on this Truth, as all other loves depend on this Love, and all other grandeurs on this Grandeur.[750]

The truth needs no author and no defense. This text has been given to you and what does not vanish is not ours.

---

[750] Teresa of Avila, *The Life of St. Teresa*, Trans. David Lewis, Ed. Benedict Zimmerman, London: Thomas Baker, 1924, p. 75 & 408.

BIBLIOGRAPHY

Adorno, Theodor. Minima Moralia. Trans. E.N. Jephcott. New York: Verso Books, 1997.

Agamben, Giorgio. Homo Sacer: Sovereign Power and Bare Life. Trans. Daniel Heller-Roazen. Stanford: Stanford University Press, 1998.

_. State of Exception. Trans. Kevin Attell. Chicago: The University of Chicago Press, 2005.

Aquinas, Thomas. Summa Teologica, in Half Hours with the Best Thinkers, Ed. Frank J. Finamore. New York: Gramercy Books, 1999, pp. 60-67.

Arendt, Hannah. The Human Condition. Chicago: The University of Chicago Press, 1958.

_. Love and Saint Augustine. Chicago: University of Chicago Press, 1998.

Arendt, Hannah and Martin Heidegger. Letters: 1925-1975. Ed. Ursula Ludz. Trans. Andrew Shields. New York: Harcourt, Inc., 2004.

Auge, Marc. Non-Places. Trans. John Howe. New York: Verso, 1995.

Badiou, Alain. Being & Event. Trans. Oliver Feltham. London: Continuum International Publishing Group, 2005.

_. Infinite Thought. Trans. Justin Clemens. New York: Continuum, 2003.

Barth, Karl. The Humanity of God. Richmond, Virginia. John Knox Press, 1970.

Barthes, Roland. The Fashion System. Trans. Matthew Ward & Richard Howard. Berkeley: University of California Press, 1983.

_. A Lover's Discourse. Trans. Richard Howard. New York: Vintage Classics, 1977.

__. Mythologies. Trans. Annette Lavers. New York: Noonday
    Press, 1972.

Barnard, Malcolm. Fashion as Communication. New York:
    Routledge, 1996.

Barzun, Jacques. From Dawn to Decadence. New York: Harper
    Collins, 2000.

Bataille, Georges. The Accursed Share. Trans. Robert Hurley.
    New York: Zone Books, 1988.

__. Visions of Excess: Selected Writings 1927-1939.
    Minneapolis: University of Minnesota Press, 1985.

Baudelaire, Charles. The Flowers of Evil. Trans. William
    Aggeler. Fresno, CA: Academy Library Guild, 1954.

__. Oeuvres, Vol. 2. Ed. Yves-Gerard Le Dante. Paris:
    Bibliothèque de la Pléïade, 1931-2.

Baudrillard, Jean. America. Trans. Chris Turner. New York:
    Verso Books, 1998.

__. Impossible Exchange. Trans. Chris Turner. New York: Verso
    Books, 2001.

__. Paroxysm. Trans. Chris Turner. New York: Verso Books,
    1998.

__. Passwords. Trans. Chris Turner. New York: Verso Books,
    2003.

__. Screened Out. Trans. Chris Turner. New York: Verso Books,
    2002.

__. Seduction. Trans. Brain Singer. New York: St. Martin's
    Press, 1990.

Beckett, Samuel. Endgame. New York: Grove Press, 1958.

__. Collected Poems 1930-1978. London: John Calder Limited,
    1999.

Benjamin, Walter, Charles Baudelaire: A Lyric Poet in the Era
    of High Capitalism. Trans. Harry Zohn. London: NLB,
    1969.

__. One-Way Street and Other Writings. Trans Edmund Jephcott and Kingsley Shorter. New York: Verso, 1997.

__. Illuminations. Ed. Hannah Arendt and Trans. Harry Zohn. New York: Schocken Books, 1985and version Illuminations. Ed. Hannah Arendt and Trans. Harry Zohn. London: Pimlico, 1999.

__. Walter Benjamin: Selected Writings, Vol. 2 1927-1934. Cambridge: Harvard University Press, 1999.

Bernbaum, Ernest, Ed. Anthology of Romanticism. New York: The Ronald Press Company, 1933.

Bernheimer, Charles. Decadent Subjects. Baltimore: The Johns Hopkins University Press, 2002.

Bly, Robert, Ed. Neruda and Vallejo: Selected Poems. Trans. Robert Bly, et al. Boston: Beacon Press, 1971.

Bois, Yve-Alain and Rosalind Krauss, Formless: A User's Guide. New York: Zone Books, 1997.

Borges, Jorge Luis. Selected Poems. Ed. Alexander Coleman. New York: Viking Penguin Group, 1999.

Bourriaud, Nicholas. Relational Aesthetics. Trans. Simon Pleasance & Fronza Woods. Paris: Les Presses du Reel, 2002.

Brecht, Bertol. Leben Des Galilei. Ed. H. F. Brookes and C. E. Fraenkel. London: Heinemann Educational Books, 1955.

Breton, André. Communicating Vessels. Trans Mary Ann Caws et al. Lincoln: University of Nebraska Press, 1990.

Butler, Judith. The Psychic Life of Power. Stanford: Stanford University Press, 1997.

Byron, Lord. Selected Poems. New York: Gramercy Books, 1994.

Camus, Albert. The Myth of Sisyphus. Trans. Justin O'Brien. New York: Vintage International, 1955.

_. The Rebel. Trans. Anthony Bower. New York: Vintage International. 1956

Conrad, Ulrich. Programs and Manifestoes on 20th-century Architecture. Cambridge: MIT Press, 1997.

Constable, Liz and Dennis Denisoff and Matthew Potolosky, Eds. Perennial Decay: One the aesthetics and politics of decadence. Philadelphia: University of Pennsylvania Press, 1998.

Danto, Arthur C. The Transfiguration of the Commonplace. Cambridge: Harvard University Press, 1981.

Danzinger, Pamela. Let Them Eat Cake: Marketing Luxury to the Masses and the Classes. New York: Kaplan Business, 2004.

De Beauvoir, Simone. The Ethics of Ambiguity. Trans. Bernard Frechtman. New York: Citadel Press, 1996.

Debord, Guy. In Girum Imus Nocte Et Consummimur Igni. London: Pelagian Press, 1990.

_. The Society of the Spectacle. Trans. Donald Nicholson-Smith. New York: Zone Books, 1994.

De Montaigne, Michel. "What is a Classic," in Literary and Philosophical Essays. Ed. Charles Eliot. New York: Collier and Son, 1910, p. 126-139.

Descartes, Rene. Meditations on First Philosophy. Trans. Donald A. Cress. Cambridge: Hackett Publishing Company, 1979.

Derrida, Jacques. "A Number of Yes," Deconstruction, A Reader. Ed. Martin McQuillan. New York: Routledge, 2000, pp. 97-106.

_. "Before the Law," In Acts of Literature. Ed. Derek Attridge, New York: Routledge. 1992, p. 180–220.

_. Dissemination. Chicago: The University of Chicago Press, 1981.

_. Given Time: I. Counterfeit Money. Chicago: The University of Chicago Press, 1991.

__. Spurs. Chicago: The University of Chicago Press, 1978.

__. Politics of Friendship. Trans. George Collins. New York and London: Verso, 1997.

__. Voyous. Paris: Galilée, 2003.

__. Writing and Difference. Chicago: University of Chicago Press, 1978.

De Tocqueville, Alexis. Democracy in America. Trans. G. Lawrence. New York: Penguin Classics, 1969.

Dick, Philip K. I Hope I Shall Arrive Soon. New York: Doubleday & Company, 1985.

Dickens, Charles. Great Expectations. Oxford: Oxford University Press, 1998.

Dostoevsky, Fyodor. Notes from Underground. New York: Vintage Books Random House, 1993.

Edwards, The Rev. Jonathan. Freedom of the Will. Morgan, Pennsylvania: Soli Deo Gloria Publications, 1996.

Eliot., T.S. The Cocktail Party. New York: Harcourt, Brace and Company, 1950.

__. The Complete Poems and Plays 1909-1950. New York: Harcourt, Brace and Company, 1980.

Eugenides, Jeffery. The Virgin Suicides. New York: Warner Books, 1993.

Feuerbach, Ludwig. The Essence of Christianity. Trans. George Eliot. New York: Harper & Brothers Publishers, 1957.

Fitzgerald, F. Scott. The Beautiful and Damned. New York: The Modern Library, 2002.

Flaubert. Gustave. Madame Bovary. Trans. Francis Steegmuller. New York: The Modern Library, 1982.

Fourier, Charles. The Theory of Four Movements. Ed. Gareth Jones, et al. Cambridge: Cambridge University Press, 1996.

Freud, Sigmund. The Freud Reader. Ed. Peter Gay. New York:
     Norton & Company, 1989.

___. The Interpretation of Dreams. New York: Gramercy Books,
     p. 1996.

Furbank, P.N. and A. M. Cain. Mallarmé on Fashion. New York:
     Berg. 2004.

Gadamer, Hans-Georg. Truth and Method. Translation revised
     by Joel Weinsheimer and Donald G. Marshall. New York:
     Continuum, 1999.

Genet, Jean. Elle. Paris: L'Arbalète, 1989.

Gibbon, Edward. The Decline and Fall of the Roman Empire.
     New York: Random House, 2003.

Gilman, Richard. Decadence: The strange life of an epithet. New
     York: Farrar, Straus and Giroux, 1979.

Habermas, Jürgen. The Structural Transformation of the Public
     Sphere. Cambridge, Massachusetts: The MIT Press, 1989.

Halbertal, Moshe and Avishai Margalit. Idolatry. Trans. Naomi
     Goldblum. Cambridge, Massachusetts: Harvard University
     Press, 1992.

Harris, Sam. The End of Faith: Religion, Terror, and the Future
     of Reason. New York: Norton & Co., 2005.

Hebdige, Dick. Subculture: The Meaning of Style. New York:
     Routledge, 1979.

Hegel, G.W.F. Lectures on Aesthetics. Trans. T.M. Knox.
     Oxford: Oxford University Press, 1998.

___. Philosophy of Mind: Part III of the Encyclopedia of
     Philosophical Sciences (1830). Trans. William Wallace.
     London: Oxford University Press, 1971.

___. The Philosophy of History, in Half Hours with the Best
     Thinkers, Ed. Frank J. Finamore. New York: Gramercy
     Books, 1999, p. 145-153.

Heidegger, Martin. Basic Writings. Ed. David Farrell Krell. London: Harper Collins, 1993.

__. Being and Time. Trans. John Macquarrie & Edward Robinson. New York: Harper & Row Publishers, 1962.

---. The Concept of Time. Trans. William McNeill. Oxford: Blackwell, 1992.

__. Existence and Being. Washington D.C.: Regnary Gateway, 1949.

__. An Introduction to Metaphysics. Trans. Gregory Fried. New Haven: Yale University Press, 2000.

__. The Question Concerning Technology. Trans. William Lovitt. New York: HarperCollins, 1982.

Hölderlin, Friedrich. Essays and Letters on Theory. Trans. Thomas Pfau. New York: State University of New York Press, 1988.

The Holy Bible. New International Version. Grand Rapids, Michigan: Zondervan Publishing House, 1996.

Houellebecq, Michel. Atomized. Vintage: New York, 2001.

Huysmans, J.K. A Rebours. Trans. Havelock Ellis. New York: Dover, 1969.

__. A Rebours. French Edition. France: Fasquelle Éditeurs, 1972.

Ibsen, Henrik. A Doll's House. New York: Dover Publications, 1992.

Ingraffia, Brian. Postmodern Theory and Biblical Theology. Cambridge: Cambridge University Press, 1995.

Jencks, Charles. Le Corbusier and the Continual Revolution in Architecture. New York: The Montacelli Press, 2000.

James, Henry. The Aspern Papers. New York: The Book of a Month Club, 1996.

Kafka, Franz. The Complete Stories. Trans. Nahum Glatzer and Willa and Edwin Muir. New York: Schocken Books, 1971.

Kant, Immanuel. Anthropology from a Pragmatic Point of View. Trans. by Victor Lyle Dowdel. Carbondale, IL: Southern Illinois University Press, 1978.

__. "Perpetual Peace", in Kant: Political Writings, Ed. H. Reiss. Cambridge: Cambridge University Press, 1991, pp. 93-130.

__. Critique of Judgment. Trans. J.H. Bernard. Amherst: Prometheus Books, 2000.

__. "Zum ewigen Frieden", in Kants Werke. Trans. by H. Nisbet. Berlin: Prussische Akademie Ausgabe, vol. VIII, 341-386.

Kierkegaard, Søren. Attack Upon "Christendom." Trans. Walter Lowrie. Princeton: Princeton University press, 1944.

__. Concluding Unscientific Postscript to the Philosophical Fragments Trans. Howard Hong and Edna Hong. Princeton: Princeton University Press, 1992.

__. A Kierkegaard Anthology. Ed. Robert Bretall. New York: The Modern Library, 1946.

__. The Point of View. Trans. Walter Lowrie. London: Oxford University Press, 1939.

__. Provocations: The spiritual writings of Søren Kierkegaard, Ed. Charles E Moore, Farmington: The Plough Publishing House, 1999.

__. The Sickness unto Death. Trans. Howard Hong and Edna Hong. Princeton: Princeton University Press, 1980.

__. The Concept of Anxiety. Trans. by R. Thomte and A. Anderson. Princeton: Princeton University Press, 1980.

__. The Point of View. London: Oxford University Press, 1950.

Kearney, Richard. Dialogues with Contemporary Continental Thinkers: The Phenomenological Heritage. Manchester: Manchester University Press, 1984.

Kristeva, Julia. Revolt, She Said. Trans. Brian O'Keefe. New York: Semiotext(e), 2002.

Kunstler, James Howard. The Geography of Nowhere. New York: Simon & Schuster, 1993.

Lacan, Jacques. The Seminar of Jacques Lacan: On Feminine Sexuality, The Limits of Love and Knowledge (Book XX, Encore 1972-1973), Ed. Jacques-Alain Miller, Trans. Bruce Fink, New York: W. W. Norton & Company, 1998.

__. Television. Trans. Denis Hollier, Rosalind Krauss and Annette Michelson. Ed. Joan Copjec. New York: W. W. Norton & Company, 1990.

Lang, Peter and William Menking. Superstudio: Life without Objects. New York: Rizzoli, 2003.

Leibniz, G. W. Discourse on Metaphysics / Correspondence with Arnaud / Monadology. Trans. George Montgomery. La Salle, Illinois: Open Court Publishing, 1988.

Lefebvre, Henri. Everyday Life in the Modern World. Trans. Sacha Rabinovitch. New York: Harper & Row, 1968.

__. The Production of Space. Trans. Donald Nicholson Smith. Cambridge: Blackwell Publishers, 1991.

Lehmann, Ulrich. Tigersprung: Fashion in Modernity. Cambridge: Massachusetts, 2000.

Lessing, Gotthold. "The Education of the Human Race," in Literary and Philosophical Essays. Ed. Charles Eliot. New York: Collier and Son, 1910, p. 194-217.

Levinas, Emmanuel. Basic Philosophical Writings. Ed. Adriann Peperzak et al, Indianapolis: Indiana University Press, 1996.

Lewis, C.S. The Essential C.S. Lewis. Ed. Lyle W. Dorsett. New York: Simon & Schuster, 1988.

Liberia Editrice Vaticana. Catechism of the Catholic Church for the United States of America. New York: Doubleday, 1995.

Livius, Titus. The History of Rome, Vol. 5. Ed. Ernest Rhys. Trans. Canon Roberts. London: Dent & Sons, 1905.

Lipovetsky, Gilles. The Empire of Fashion. Tans. Catherine Porter. Princeton: Princeton University Press, 1994.

Luther, Martin. De Servo Arbitrio / The Bondage of Will. Trans. James L. Packer. Grand Rapids, Michigan: Baker Book House Company, 1957.

Lyotard, Jean-Francois. The Inhuman: Reflections on Time. Trans. Rachel Bowlby. Stanford: Stanford Univ. Press, 1992.

___. The Postmodern Explained to Children: Correspondence 1982-1985. Trans. Thomas Pefanis. London: Turnaround, 1992.

Maritain, Jacques. The Person and the Common Good. Trans. John Fitzgerald. Baltimore: University of Notre Dame Press, 1966.

Marx, Karl, Early Writings. Trans. T. B. Bottomore. New York: McGraw-Hill, 1964.

___. The Marx-Engels Reader. New York: Norton, 1963.

Marx, Karl and Friedrich Engels. Collected Works, vol. 11. London: Lawrence & Wishart, 1979.

Maslow, Abraham. Toward a Psychology of Being. New York: Van Nostrand Reinhold, 1968.

Mast, Gerald, et al. Film Theory and Criticism. Oxford: Oxford University Press, 1992.

Milbank, John. Being Reconciled: Ontology and Pardon. New York: Routledge, 2003.

Mitscherlich, Alexander and Margerete. Inability to Mourn: Principals of Collective Behavior. New York: Grove Press, 1984.

Momin, Shamim. Banks Violette. New York: Whitney Museum of American Art, 2005.

Nancy, Jean-Luc. Being Singular Plural. Trans. Robert D. Richardson and Anne E. O'Byrne. Stanford: Stanford Univ. Press, 2000.

___. The Experience of Freedom. Trans. Bridget McDonald. Stanford: Stanford University Press, 1993.

_. Hegel: The Restless of the Negative. Trans. Jason Smith and Steven Miller. Minneapolis: University of Minnesota Press, 2002

Nancy, Jean-Luc and Philippe Lacoue-Labarthe. Retreating the Political. Ed. Simon Sparks. London: Routledge, 1997.

Niemeyer, Oscar. The Curves of Time: The Memoirs of Oscar Niemeyer. London: Phaidon, 2000.

Nietzsche, Friedrich. Beyond Good and Evil. Trans. Walter Kaufman. New York: Vintage Books Random House, 1966.

_. The Birth of Tragedy and The Case for Wagner. New York: Vintage, 1967.

_. The Gay Science. New York: Vintage Books, 1974.

_. Twilight of the Idols / The Anti Christ. New York: Penguin Books, 1990.

_. Thus Spoke Zarathustra: A Book for All and None. Trans. Walter Kaufman. New York: The Modern Library. 1992.

_. The Will to Power. Trans. Walter Kaufmann. New York: Random House, 1968.

Obrist, Hans Ulrich. Interviews, Volume 1. Milan: Charta, 2003.

Ortega Y Gasset, Jose. The Revolt of the Masses. Trans. Anonymous. New York: Norton, 1957.

Owens, Craig. Beyond Recognition: Representation, Power and Culture. Berkley: University of California Press, 1992.

Packard, Vance. The Status Seekers. New York: Simon and Schuster, 1959.

Plato. Phaedrus. Trans. Alexander Nehamas and Paul Woodward. Cambridge: Hackett Publishing Company, 1995.

Poiret, Paul. King of Fashion: The Autobiography of Paul Poiret. Trans. Stephen Haden Guest. Philadelphia: Lippincott, 1931.

Proust, Marcel. Remembrance of Things Past. Trans. C. K. Scott Moncrieff. New York: Random House, 1932.

Renan, Ernest. The Future of Science. Boston: Roberts Brothers, 1891.

Riley, Robert and Walter Vecchio. The Fashion Makers. New York: Crown Publishers, 1968.

Rilke, Rainer Maria. Stories of God. Trans. M. D. Herter Norton. New York: Norton and Company, 1963.

Ronell, Avital. Crack Wars: Literature, Addiction, Mania. Lincoln: Univ. of Nebraska Press, 1992.

__. Finitude's Score: Essays for the End of the Millennium (Texts and Contexts). Lincoln: University of Nebraska Press, 1998.

Rothschild, Lord. The Shadow of a Great Man. London: Hand Press Limited, 1991.

Rutenborn, Guenter. The Sign of Jonah. Trans. Bernhard Ohse and Gerhard Elston. Chicago: The Lutheran Student Association of America, 1954.

Saint Nikodimos and Saint Makarios. The Philokalia. Trans. G. E. H. Palmer, et al. London: Faber and Faber, 1995.

Salinger, J.D. Franny and Zooey. New York: Little, Brown and Company, 1955.

Santner, Eric. Friedrich Hölderlin: Narrative Vigilance and the Poetic Imagination. New York: Rutgers University Press, 1986.

Sartre, Jean Paul. Existentialism and Human Emotions. Trans. Bernard Fretchman and Hazel E. Barnes. New York: Citadel Press, 1995.

__. Huis Clos. New York: Appleton-Century-Crofts, 1962.

Scheerbart, Paul. Gray Cloth and Ten Percent White. Cambridge, Massachusetts: MIT Press, 2001.

Schirmacher, Wolfgang. "Art(ificial) Perception: Nietzsche and Culture after Nihilism." Poiesis Vol. 1. Toronto: EGS Press, 1999.

__. "From the Phenomenon to the Event of Technology," in Philosophy and Technology. Ed. F. Rapp, Reidel: Dordrecht, 1983.

__. "Media as Lifeworld." in Technology and Lifeworld. Ed. Lester Embree. Lanham: University Press of America, 1989.

__. "Homo Generator: Media and Postmodern Technology," in Culture on the Brink: Ideologies of Technology. Ed. G. Bender, T. Duckrey. New York: The New Press, 1994/1999.

Schmidt, Carl. Die Diktatur: von den Anfängen des modernen Souverätsgedankens bis zum proletarischen Klassenkampf. Berlin: Duncker and Humblot, 1994.

Schopenhauer, Arthur. Philosophical Writings. Ed. Wolfgang Schirmacher. New York: The Continuum Publishing Company, 2002.

Serra, Richard. Writings / Interviews. Chicago: University of Chicago Press, 1994.

Shakespeare, William. The Complete Works. Ed. G. B. Harrison. New York: Harcourt Brace, 1952.

Smithson, Robert. Robert Smithson: The Collected Writings. Ed. Jack Flam. Berkeley: University of California Press, 1996.

Snell, Bruno. The Discovery of the Mind: In Greek Philosophy and Literature. Trans. T. G. Rosenmeyer. New York: Dover, 1982

Sokal, Alan and Jean Bricmont. Intellectual Imposters. New York: Economist Books, 2003.

Speyer, Ariana, ed. The Real Thing: Fashion Interviews. New York: Index Books, 2003.

Spinoza, Benedictus. Spinoza: Complete Works. Trans. Samuel Shirley. Ed. Michael Morgan. Cambridge: Hackett Publishing Company, 1998.

Springer, Oswald. The Decline of the West. New York: Knopf, 1947.

Stone, Allcquère Rosanne. The War of Desire and Technology at the Close of the Mechanical Age. Cambridge, Massachusetts: MIT Press, 1995.

Susann, Jacqueline. Valley of the Dolls. New York: Grove Press, 1966.

Tillich, Paul. The Courage to Be. New Haven: Yale University Press, 1952.

Vanderbilt, Gloria. It Seemed Important at the Time. New York: Simon & Schuster, 2004.

Veblen, Thorstein. The Theory of the Leisure Class. New York: Dover Publications, 1994.

Venturi, Robert, et al. Learning from Las Vegas. Cambridge: MIT Press, 1971.

Virilio, Paul. Strategy of Deception. Trans. Chris Turner. New York: Verso Books, 2000.

Voltaire. Candide. Trans. John Butt. New York: Penguin, 1947.

Von Goethe, Johann Wolfgang. Faust. New York: Anchor, 1962

Von Schiller, J. C. Friedrich. "Letters Upon the Aesthetic Education of Man," in Literary and Philosophical Essays. Ed. Charles Eliot. New York: Collier and Son, 1910, p. 220-313.

Vreeland, Diana. D.V. New York: De Capo Press, 1984.

Ward, Rachel K. Scenic Drive: Edward Ruscha and the cartography of social space. Masters Thesis, University of Florida, 2001.

_. Terminal 5. Ed. Andrew Lee Walker. New York: Lukas and Sternberg, 2004.

Warhol, Andy. The Philosophy of Andy Warhol. New York: Harcourt Brace & Company, 1975.

Waugh, Evelyn. Decline and Fall. Boston: Little, Brown and
    Company, 1956.

__. Vile Bodies. New York: Little, Brown and Company, 1958.

Weil, Simone. Gravity and Grace. Trans. Arthur Wills New
    York: G.P. Putnam's Sons, 1952.

__. Waiting for God. Trans. Emma Craufurd. New York: G.P.
    Putnam's Sons, 1951.

Xenophanes. Fragmente der Vorsokratiker, Vol. 1. Ed. Hermann
    Diels and Walther Kranz. Wiedmann: Berlin, 1951.

Yeats, W. B. The Yeats Reader. Ed. Richard Finneran. New
    York: Scribner, 1997.

Žižek, Slavoj. The Abyss of Freedom / Ages of the World.
    Trans. Judith Norman and cont. F.W.J. Schelling. Detroit:
    University of Michigan Press, 1997.

__. The Parallax View. Cambridge, Massachusetts: MIT Press,
    2006.

__. The Sublime Object of Ideology. London: Verso Books,
    December 1989.

__. Tarrying With the Negative: Kant, Hegel, and the Critique of
    Ideology. Durham: Duke University Press, 1993.

__. The Žižek Reader. Ed. Elizabeth and Edmund Wright.
    Oxford: Blackwell Publishers, 1999.

Think Media: EGS Media Philosophy Series

Wolfgang Schirmacher, editor

The Ethics of Uncertainty: Aporetic Openings. Michael Anker

Trans/actions: Art, Film and Death. Bruce Alistair Barber

Trauma, Hysteria, Philosophy. Hannes Charen and Sarah Kamens

Literature as Pure Mediality: Kafka and the Scene of Writing.
Paul DeNicola

Deleuze and the Sign. Christopher M. Drohan

The Suicide Bomber and Her Gift of Death. Jeremy Fernando

Hospitality in the age of media representation. Christian Hänggi

Transience: a poiesis, of dis/appearance. Julia Hölzl

**The Organic Organisation: freedom, creativity and
the search for fulfilment.** Nicholas Ind

Media Courage: impossible pedagogy in an artificial community.
Fred Isseks

Mirrors triptych technology: Remediation and Translation Figures.
Diana Silberman Keller

Sonic Soma: Sound, Body and the Origins of the Alphabet. Elise Kermani

The Art of the Transpersonal Self: Transformation as Aesthetic and Energetic Practice.
Norbert Koppensteiner

Can Computers Create Art? James Morris

Propaganda of the Dead: Terrorism and Revolution. Mark Reilly.

The Novel Imagery: Aesthetic Response as Feral Laboratory. Dawan Stanford.

Community without Identity: The Ontology and Politics of Heidegger. Tony See

other books available from Atropos Press

Teletheory. Gregory L. Ulmer

Philosophy of Culture-Kulturphilosophie: Schopenhauer and Tradition. Edited by Wolfgang
Schirmacher.

Grey Ecology. Paul Virilio
Edited with introduction by Hubertus von Amelunxen. Translated by Drew Burk

Laughter. Henri Bergson. Translated by Drew Burk

Talking Cheddo: Liberating PanAfrikanism. Menkowra Manga Clem Marshall

The Tupperware Blitzkrieg. Anthony Metivier

Che Guevara and the Economic Debate in Cuba. Luiz Bernardo Pericás

Follow Us or Die. Vincent W.J. van Gerven Oei and Jonas Staal

Just Living: Philosophy in Artificial Life. Collected Works Volume 1.
Wolfgang Schirmacher

CPSIA information can be obtained at www.ICGtesting.com
Printed in the USA
LVOW12s0835020813

345771LV00001B/301/P